INFORMATION
PLEASE

Mark Poster

INFORMATION
PLEASE

CULTURE AND
POLITICS IN THE AGE OF
DIGITAL MACHINES

Duke University Press
Durham and London 2006

© 2006 Duke University Press

All rights reserved

Printed in the United States of America on acid-free paper ∞

Designed by Heather Hensley

Typeset in Quadraat and Linotype Trade Gothic by Tseng Information Systems, Inc.

Library of Congress Cataloging-in-Publication Data and republication
acknowledgments appear on the last printed pages of this book.

FOR ZACHARY KAROL, IN MEMORIAM

CONTENTS

ACKNOWLEDGMENTS

I have been fortunate in being invited to present my work to many groups around the world, especially in North America, Europe, and Australia. My method has been to subject these groups to germinating ideas. Their suggestions and objections have pointed to directions for rethinking my formulations and revising my ideas. I have learned a great deal on these occasions from often spirited conversations, and this book is much improved as a consequence. My students and colleagues at the University of California, Irvine, in particular receive my thanks. I have benefited greatly from discussions of my work with Jon Wiener, John Carlos Rowe, Vinayak Chaturvedi, Victoria Johnson, Sean Hill, and the Critical Theory Institute members at UCI, members of the Multi-Campus Research Group on Digital Culture, Tama Leaver and David Savat in Perth, Bernhard Debatin in Berlin, Gary Hall in London, Mick Dillon in Lancaster, and my coeditors of the Electronic Mediations series at the University of Minnesota Press, Kate Hayles and Sam Weber, as well as Doug Armato, the press editor. Doug Kellner read the entire manuscript and provided me with invaluable suggestions. Winifred Poster and Jamie Poster have provided much support and many ideas, and I thank them for it. Annette Schlichter has been a careful reader of my work and a truly sympathetic companion.

Special thanks are due to Ken Wissoker and Courtney Berger of Duke University Press and to the readers whose advice they sought, who provided me with excellent feedback.

INTRODUCTION

In days of yore, before digital mobile phones, the Internet, automatic switchboards, and telephones with dialing abilities, one picked up the telephone receiver and spoke to an operator. If one did not know the telephone number of the person one wished to call, one said, "Information please," and the switchboard operator looked up the number. My memory of this procedure was dim, so naturally I Googled the phrase "information please" and found the following anonymous Web site:

Information Please

When I was quite young, my father had one of the first telephones in our neighborhood. I remember well the polished old case fastened to the wall. The shiny receiver hung on the side of the box. I was too little to reach the telephone but used to listen with fascination when my mother used to talk to it.

I discovered that somewhere inside the wonderful device lived an amazing person; her name was "Information Please," and there was nothing she did not know. "Information Please" could supply anybody's number and the correct time.

My first personal experience with this genie-in-the-bottle came one day while my mother was visiting a neighbor. Amusing myself at the tool bench in the basement, I whacked my finger with a hammer.

The pain was terrible, but there didn't seem to be any point in crying because there was no one home to give sympathy. I walked around the house sucking my throbbing finger, finally arriving at the stairway.

The telephone!

Quickly, I ran for the footstool in the parlor and dragged it to the land-ing. Climbing up, I unhooked the receiver in the parlor and held it to my ear. "Information Please," I said into the mouthpiece just above my head.

There followed a click or two, and a small clear voice spoke into my ear. "Information."

"I hurt my finger . . ." I wailed into the phone. The tears came readily enough now that I had an audience.

"Isn't your mother home?" came the question.

"Nobody's home but me," I blubbered.

"Are you bleeding?"

"No," I replied. "I hit my finger with the hammer and it hurts."

"Can you open your icebox?" she asked. I said I could. "Then chip off a little piece of ice and hold it to your finger," said the voice.

After that, I called "Information Please" for everything. I asked her for help with my geography and she told me where Philadelphia was. She helped me with my math. She told me my pet chipmunk that I had caught in the park just the day before would eat fruits and nuts. . . .

Another day I was on the telephone. "Information Please."

"Information," said the now familiar voice.

"How do you spell fix?" I asked.

All this took place in a small town in the Pacific Northwest. When I was nine years old, we moved across the country to Boston. I missed my friend very much. "Information Please" belonged in that old wooden box back home, and I somehow never thought of trying the tall, shiny new phone that sat on the table in the hall.

As I grew into my teens, the memories of those childhood conversations never really left me. Often, in moments of doubt and perplexity I would recall the serene sense of security I'd had then. I appreciated now how patient, understanding, and kind she was to have spent her time on a little boy.

A few years later, on my way west to college, my plane put down in Seattle. I had about half an hour or so between planes. I spent 15 minutes or so on the phone with my sister, who lived there now. Then without thinking what I was doing, I dialed my hometown operator and said, "Information Please."

Miraculously, I heard the small, clear voice I knew so well, "Information." I hadn't planned this but I heard myself saying, "Could you please tell me how to spell fix?"

There was a long pause. Then came the soft-spoken answer, "I guess your finger must have healed by now."

I laughed. "So it's really still you," I said. "I wonder if you have any idea how much you meant to me during that time."

"I wonder," she said, "if you know how much your calls meant to me. I never had any children, and I used to look forward to your calls."

I told her how often I had thought of her over the years and I asked if I could call her again when I came back to visit my sister.

"Please do," she said, "Just ask for Sally."

Three months later I was back in Seattle. A different voice answered "Information." I asked for Sally.

"Are you a friend?" she asked.

"Yes, a very old friend," I answered.

"I'm sorry to have to tell you this," she said. "Sally had been working part-time the last few years because she was sick. She died five weeks ago."

Before I could hang up she said, "Wait a minute. Did you say your name was Paul?"

"Yes."

"Well, Sally left a message for you. She wrote it down in case you called. Let me read it to you." The note said, "Tell him I still say there are other worlds to sing in. He'll know what I mean."

I thanked her and hung up. I knew what Sally meant.[1]

We may leave aside the nostalgic tone and charm of this post and still remark at the changes the past century has brought. Increasingly one retrieves information not from a person, such as a telephone switchboard operator, but from an information machine, especially from networked computers. And thus we are ever more normally brought into contact not with other humans directly but with information machines. "Information Please," as the post reminds us, was once a person; now it is a machine.

The anonymous poster as a boy, interestingly enough, misinterpreted the role of the information operator, thinking she could answer any question, such as "How do you spell 'fix'?" I find it most curious that the boy, Paul, anticipated the advent of the Internet, where indeed one can "ask" any question and most likely receive the answer (although in order to ask the question about spelling the word "fix," one must already know how to spell when using a search engine like Google). From the hindsight of today, Paul's "mistake" was remarkable. Search engines on the Internet, to be sure, will not be as friendly as Sally, the telephone operator in the posting, but will likely remember the user's queries and do so with more accuracy than Sally.

This book is an attempt to contribute to the comprehension of these changes in our everyday lives. I am interested in particular in the cultural significance of the migration of information from humans to machines, the change in the nature of information, the way it mediates relationships and creates bonds between humans and machines, as well as the political implications that ensue.[2] I wish to inquire how texts, images, and sounds —the various forms that information takes—are different when they are mediated by information machines, how this difference changes us, and what possibilities they open for reducing the burdens of domination.

My procedure is, in the first instance, to examine the concepts that enable us to grasp our culture and enact a confrontation between them and the current conditions of the media. In most cases I argue that cultural theory has not considered in depth the implications of the new media for the constitution of the self and for culture in general. I look especially at the work (in alphabetical order) of Homi Bhabha, Judith Butler, Michel de Certeau, Gilles Deleuze, Michel Foucault, Félix Guattari, Michael Hardt, Henri Lefebvre, Jean-François Lyotard, Karl Marx, Antonio Negri, and Gayatri Spivak, culling their works for insights about new media and asking, when relevant, about the consequence of gaps and lacunae regarding the question of the relation of humans and information machines. I do so not to condemn them to theoretical irrelevance, for I greatly admire their discursive accomplishments, but to pinpoint the places where cultural theory would benefit from revision and alteration by attention to new relations of humans and information machines.

The second method I employ is to select a few aspects from the recent past of media in which the question of cultural change appears particularly exigent. I look at peer-to-peer file sharing, identity theft, the television series *Teletubbies*, and a certain confusion that occurred in October 2003 in a protest in Bangladesh against the bombing of Afghanistan by the United States. In each case, the media phenomena did not fit into the culture and politics of the established order, and in each case, though certainly in varying degrees, confusion and conflict resulted and indeed persist. I could just as easily have explored innumerable other incidents and media content, and I make no excuses for the appropriateness of my selections here.

I have resorted to this combination of theoretical inquiry and media content analysis since I published *The Mode of Information* in 1990. In fact, *Information Please* may be regarded as version 4.0 of that earlier book, with *The Second Media Age* (1995) and *What's the Matter with the Internet?* (2001) taken as the intervening releases. But the metaphor of software publishing only goes so far. It indicates a close connection between the works but fails to express perfectly the relationship between the several issues. I have no illusion of a clear line of progress from 1.0 to 4.0. Some aspects of the earlier work clearly require reprogramming, but others are arguably superior to the revisions, unlike the situation with most computer software. Surely there are "bugs" in all four books. What impresses me most about the question of media and culture is the enormity of the task before the human sciences in making so much as a dent in articulating the important questions. And that—defining and clarifying the significant questions to ask—has been, and continues to be, my chief concern.

PART I.
GLOBAL POLITICS AND NEW MEDIA

1

PERFECT TRANSMISSIONS: EVIL BERT LADEN

My contention is that information increasingly appears in complex couplings of humans and machines.[1] Culture can thus no longer be understood as separate from technology. If this is so, many assumptions long held in modern society require revision. One such assumption is that cultures are in essence national. Yet the emerging mode of information, tethering humans and machines, is recognizably global. In this context, I begin with an analysis of how cultures interact in planetary human-machine relations by examining one case of Internet-mediated communications.

In the globally networked world, strange, unexpected, and sometimes amusing events occur. I will analyze one such happening with the purpose of understanding how the global communication system affects national cultures. It is my hypothesis that the condition of globalization, of which the Internet is a major component, imposes a new and heightened level of interaction between cultures. This interactivity changes each culture in many ways, one of which I highlight: the degree of autonomy of each culture is significantly reduced as a consequence of the global information network, and at the same time, the task of constructing a planetary culture is posed. On the one hand, all attempts to sustain such autonomy tend to become retrograde and dangerous. Local beliefs, values, and practices can no longer be held as absolute or as exclusive, at the expense of others. On the other hand, a new opportunity arises for a practical definition and articulation of global, human, or better posthuman culture. In short, more and more, the local becomes relative, and the global may become universal. This universal, unlike earlier attempts to define it or impose it, will be differential; it will consist of heterogeneous glocal fragments.

Although there are significant economic and demographic components of the new level of global interactivity, I limit my discussion to the issue of the flow of cultural objects within cyberspace. New media contribute greatly to the quantity and quality of the planetary transmission of cultural objects. Cultural objects—texts, sounds, and images—posted to the Internet exist in a digital domain that is everywhere at once. These objects are disembodied from their point of origin or production, entering immediately into a space that has no particular territorial inscription. As a result, the Internet constitutes distributed culture, a heteroglossia that covers the (virtual) earth. Cultural objects in new media are thus disjunctive from their societies. They are intelligible only through the medium in which they subsist—cyberspace. Cultural objects embedded in cyberspace raise the question of a new hermeneutic, one that underscores the agency of the media, rendering defunct figures of the subject from all societies in which it persists and has persisted in a position understood to be separate from objects.

The Internet enables planetary transmissions of cultural objects (texts, images, and sounds) to cross cultural boundaries with little "noise." Communications now transpire with digital accuracy. The dream of the communications engineer is realized as information flows without interference from any point on the earth to any other point or points. As Claude Shannon and Warren Weaver theorize: "The fundamental problem of communication is that of reproducing at one point either exactly or approximately a message selected at another point" (Shannon and Weaver 1949, 3). Cybernetic theory is seemingly fulfilled by the Internet: both machines and the human body act on the environment through "the accurate reproduction" of information or signals, in an endless feedback loop that adjusts for changes and unexpected events (Wiener 1950). The physicist's theory of communication is apparently realized as messages circulate around the globe in radio frequency channels, fiber-optic cables, or copper cables with each element of text, image, or sound being reproduced, transmitted, and stored in a single, instantaneous operation.[2]

And yet, as Derrida (1987) argues in *The Post Card*, things are not so simple. All the bits and bytes are there all right, but the message does not always come across or get decoded. Misunderstandings abound in our new global culture, sometimes in quite pointed ways. This chapter is about one such miscommunication. It concerns a perfect transmission of an image halfway around the globe that somehow went awry. Indeed, one may argue that the global network, with its instantaneous, exact communications, systematically produces the effect of misrecognition as cultural objects are transported across cultural boundaries. Global communications, one might say, signifies transcultural confusion. At the same time, the network creates conditions of intercultural exchange that render politically noxious any culture which cannot decode the messages of others, which insists that only its transmissions have meaning or are significant. As never before, we must begin to interpret culture as multiple cacophonies of inscribed meanings as each cultural object moves across cultural differences. Let us look at one instance of the issue that I have in mind.

The second week of October 2001 was eventful with the onset of U.S. and British bombing in Afghanistan. Like many Americans, I attempted to get my bearings on the events by listening intently to reports of the war and to analyses by informed commentators and academics. On Friday of that week, a few days after the start of the bombing, I heard, on a National Public Radio broadcast, one expert on Middle Eastern cultures explain to the interviewer and audience that among the many aspects of American society that antagonize Islamic fundamentalists, the greatest irritant is American popular culture. Even more than American support for Israel or the American-led embargo of Iraq, the enemy, in the eyes of these Muslims, is, of all things, American popular culture. Samir Amin has argued to this effect for some time, pointing out that "the prodigious intensification of communication by the media, now global in scope, has both quantitatively and qualitatively modified the contradiction generated by the unequal expansion of capitalism. Yearning for access to Western models of consumption has come to penetrate large numbers of the popular masses" (Amin 1989, 140). In the context of the Middle East, the fundamentalist Muslims are threatened by this "yearning" by other Middle Easterners for Western styles and commodities. With some surprise, I filed this bit of knowledge somewhere in my brain's database and continued my ride home.

Much could be said about American popular culture in the age of what Michael Hardt and Antonio Negri call "Empire" (Hardt and Negri 2000). Here I need only note that a peculiarity of many Americans is an emotional fixation they often develop for figures in popular culture, not simply for acknowledged celebrities but for all manner of objects: clothing, food products, animated figures, music styles, television shows, and so forth. Americans obsess about selected aspects of popular culture. One such American is Dino Ignacio, who had an intense dislike for Bert, a muppet on public television's long-standing children's show *Sesame Street*. For Mr. Ignacio, Bert was evil. To satisfy his obsession, Ignacio created a Web page entitled "Bert Is Evil." There, with the aid of a Web browser, one finds Ignacio's "evidence" of the muppet's alleged misdeeds. Among this evidence is a series of images that Ignacio thinks prove the point: Bert is pictured with Hitler, with the KKK, with Osama bin Laden, and with a long list of other evildoers (see figures 1–3).

Bert's crimes are thus detailed with fastidious and unrelenting hostile energy.[3] Perhaps Ignacio has too much time on his hands, but in any case, his Web design is characteristic of the commitment of many Americans to their peculiar, fetishistic attachments to popular culture figures. An understanding of this aspect of popular culture in the United States is essential to appreciating what follows. It must be noted, however, that Ignacio is an immigrant, a native of the Philippines who, as a child, viewed *Sesame Street* from the distance, by means of satellite television transmissions, and created the "Evil Bert" Web site in Manila. This site won Ignacio a prize— "the Webby prize for best weird site in 1998," according to the media historian Roy Rosenzweig[4]—and brought him to San Francisco to study art. American popular culture is thus far advanced in its global reach.

On Sunday, October 14, a friend and colleague, Jon Wiener, e-mailed me with an urgent message to look at the *New York Times* for an incredible story concerning a protest in Bangladesh begun on October 8 against American bombing in Afghanistan. The story he referred to by Amy Harmon, one of the most astute journalists writing on new media, included a picture of the protesters in Bangladesh carrying a poster of Osama bin Laden that was an attractive collage composed of several images of him along with a tiny picture of Bert, the *Sesame Street* muppet, sitting on his left shoulder and staring smugly (figure 4).

Another photograph that I found on the Web reveals more clearly the face of Evil Bert (figure 5). Bert is in the highlighted circle, grimacing at the viewer more fiercely than Osama. How was it possible for Bert to get

FIGURE 1. Bert and Hitler
(http://carcino.gen.nz/images)

FIGURE 2. Bert with the KKK
(http://carcino.gen.nz/images)

FIGURE 3. Bert and Osama
from the Evil Bert Web site
(http://carcino.gen.nz/
images)

FIGURE 4. Image from the Web that appeared in the *New York Times*, October 8, 2001 (AP/World Wide Photos. Reprinted with permission.)

into the heavily charged political scene in Bangladesh? Amy Harmon could not explain the inclusion of Bert in the poster, but there he was for all the world, and especially protesting Islamic militants, to see. Perhaps he truly was evil, living up to Ignacio's image of him, siding with the al-Qaeda terrorists.

I was fascinated by Harmon's story and the accompanying photograph. Out of curiosity, I searched the Web for more information about Bert's remarkable presence in Bangladesh. A simple image search for "Evil Bert" in Google yielded a number of photographs that confirmed the one reproduced in the *New York Times* article (see figures 6–9). They are also significant to understanding more of the story.

The photograph in figure 9 yields the best information about how Evil Bert managed to appear in the poster. It shows that the image of Bert in the poster is taken from Ignacio's Web page. The image on the Evil Bert page has simply been set into a collage of images of bin Laden. There are eight images of bin Laden in the poster, including one from the Evil Bert

FIGURE 5. Bert is highlighted (www.papillonsartpalace.com)

page. In fact, the image of bin Laden that Ignacio combined with one of Bert is the same one that is positioned centrally in the poster. Aside from noting the pleasing arrangement of the images and noticing the visage of *Sesame Street*'s Bert, I, as a Westerner with little knowledge of Muslim culture, was able to decode the image no further.

When I presented one version of this chapter in a paper at a conference at the University of Wisconsin, Milwaukee, in April 2002, Brian Larkin, a participant who is knowledgeable about the cultures of Islam, pointed out that the composition of the poster contains several Islamic and Hindi references. The pattern of a central image surrounded by several smaller images all depicting bin Laden is characteristic of posters for recent Bollywood films in which the star's face in the center is complemented by smaller images that depict him or her in various roles: action figure, comedian, singer, and so forth. Similarly the smaller images in the Bangladesh protest banner portray bin Laden in his many roles: religious leader, warrior, orator, and so forth. Moreover, these roles closely match the roles of Muhammad, likening the al-Qaeda leader to the founder of Islam. The images in the poster thus construct a narrative of bin Laden, visually representing him as a great Arab leader comparable to the prophet Muhammad.

A colleague at the University of California, Irvine, Dina Al-Kassim, a scholar of Middle Eastern culture, offered a different reading. To understand this reading, we need to locate each image. If we begin with the

FIGURE 6. Photo from protest in Bangladesh (electronicintifada.net)

FIGURE 7. Photo from protest in Bangladesh (www.mlcsmith.com)

FIGURE 8. A longer shot showing an English banner (www.stopviolence.com)

FIGURE 9. A poster that indicates Evil Bert's image in the collage (www.heise.de)

large image of bin Laden in the center of the poster as number 1, we can number the smaller images, beginning in the lower left corner and moving clockwise around the perimeter of image number 1. In figure 2 the eight images are all visible, and this poster serves as a good reference for what follows. Al-Kassim reads image 5, at the top left of the poster, not as a warrior but as a judge. Image 6, in which bin Laden gestures by holding up a finger, is typical of the religious scholar giving a lecture. Continuing clockwise, bin Laden in figure 7 is holding a utility dagger with the handle visible. In image 3, bin Laden speaks into a microphone, wearing a scarf that is common to the region of the Saudi peninsula, perhaps addressing a large audience concerning political matters. Images 1, 2, and 4 are simply portraits without specific social context. Although many of the images contain contextual references, it is difficult to construct, on their basis, a clear narrative.

But what is Bert's visual function? Brian Larkin suggested that Bert, as a cuddly muppet, perhaps represents bin Laden as a family man. This interpretation assumes that the designers of the banner recognized Bert, were willing to code him as cuddly, and included him in the main visual narrative. Each of these claims is highly dubious. As we shall see, the graphics company that produced the poster admitted they did not recognize Bert. Further, cute as he may be, Bert is hardly cuddly in this image as he stares at the viewer more fiercely than bin Laden or even the protesters captured by the photographers. However one interprets Bert's inclusion in the poster, I find significant my own inability to read the visual iconography of the banner, placing me in a position of symmetrical ignorance with the banner's designers and the protesters, none of whom could decode the image of Bert.

When I began to relate the story of Bert's appearance in a pro-Taliban demonstration to colleagues and students at UCI, I encountered another strange twist: about half the people to whom I showed the *New York Times* story and photo concluded that it indicated a sophisticated knowledge of American pop culture by the Bangladesh militants. They had appropriated, as cultural studies scholars would say, the nasty image of Bert and shoved it in the face of Westerners as if to say, if you think Osama is evil, we'll take Evil Bert on our side and use him against you. Another 25 percent of my respondents simply did not believe the photo at all. In the age of digital images, they surmised that the photo was doctored: someone in the West had added the figure of Bert to the photo that appeared in the *New York Times*. Evil Bert, they concluded, never appeared in the protest in Bangladesh. The rest of my respondents accepted the image at face value and were utterly perplexed by it.

I went online again to pursue the Web discussion. I found a flurry of comments about the photo. Some Scandinavian newspapers were convinced it was a hoax.[5] Others assumed that the protesters in Bangladesh, unlike their Taliban compatriots, watched American television and were avid *Sesame Street* fans. The photo produced a variety of misunderstandings by Westerners of Bangladesh culture. The Babel-like confusion of cultural tongues only heightened with the transmission of more and more information from across the globe.

Meanwhile Mr. Ignacio must not be left out of the picture, so to speak. He also became a victim of information overload attributed to the Internet. His reaction to the *New York Times* story was guilt. He quickly took down the Evil Bert Web page and posted in its place an apology. He concluded that somehow his Web page abetted terrorism. On his "apology" Web site, he confessed his remorse, admitting that "reality" had intruded into his fantasy. In his words, "This has gotten too close to reality" (Ignacio 2001) Suddenly his obsession with Bert decathected and left him. Thus brutally shorn of his libidinal outlets, we may surmise, he was left staring fixedly at his own superego-induced guilt. With a global audience presumably shocked and angered at his Web design, Ignacio now suffered from the burst bubble of his fetish.

But that was not the end of his woes. The Internet does not so easily forget the "crimes" of its producers. What Ignacio wanted to hide simply would not disappear. Other Web authors, admiring his work, created mirror sites of the Evil Bert page. Indeed, at least nine of them were up and running at one point shortly after October 14, all boldly displaying the full variety of Evil Bert's deeds and photographic evidence for them, including the controversial image of Bert with Osama bin Laden. The emergence of the mirror sites complicates the cultural confusion. It demonstrates how networked computing, in new and unforeseen ways, subverts the power of authors to control their work. Not only did the anti-American militants of Bangladesh unknowingly and without authorization appropriate Evil Bert, but other Americans, admiring the handicraft of Ignacio, perpetuated his work for their own ends.[6] The mingling of cultures through planetary communications systems creates new kinds of translation problems.

For their part, the producers of Sesame Street were also not amused by the perfect transmission of the image of Bert. Like most American entertainment companies, they seem to believe that they alone control the cultural figures they create. And they too learned how impossible this quest is in the context of the Internet. They are quoted in a CNN report with the following response to the event: "Sesame Street has always stood for mutual respect and understanding. We're outraged that our characters would be used in this unfortunate and distasteful manner. This is not humorous" (CNN 2001). Language has a way of imposing the opposite conclusion to assertions like this. One is reminded of Richard Nixon's claim "I am not a thief." If Sesame Street did not see any humor in the appropriation of their image of Bert, others surely did.

How did the image get on that poster in Bangladesh? The answer is simpler in one sense, and more complex in another, than the views and imaginings of my UC Irvine respondents. After a few days, a journalist discovered who had made the poster, telephoned the company, and unraveled at least part of the mystery. A local graphics company in Bangladesh had been hired by the militants to produce a poster for the demonstration.

It had to be done quickly because the protest was planned for the day after the bombing commenced in Afghanistan. In these circumstances, the company did what anyone today would do. It went on the Web, performed an image search for Osama bin Laden, and presto, downloaded a number of pictures, including the image from the Evil Bert Web page. Employees also put out a request to friends who e-mailed images to them as attachments. The representative of the graphics company admitted outright that the employees did not notice Bert when they put together several images of bin Laden for the poster. Here, incredible as it might seem to some, is the report on the Urban Legends Web site: "Mostafa Kamal, the production manager of Azad Products, the Dhaka shop that made the posters, told the AP he had gotten the images off the Internet. 'We did not give the pictures a second look or realize what they signified until you pointed it out to us,' he said" (Mikkelson and Mikkelson 2001). It was as simple as that: the transmission of Bert's image went completely unnoticed in the culture of Bangladesh. As the bits of the image crossed cultural boundaries, it arrived at its destination and, at the same time, disappeared from view. Invisible to the militants of Bangladesh, Bert sneaked into the poster, where he was indeed noticed by Western journalists covering the story of the protest.

Skeptics might object that the poster company's representative lied to the Western journalist, perhaps not wanting to take responsibility for the inclusion of Bert in the poster. Or it might have been the case that the representative did not have accurate information about what happened to the image of Bert in the production process. Another possibility is that the company intentionally put Bert in the poster as a joke or as an ironic comment either to the West or to the protesters. Even if any of these hypotheses were true, the fact remains that the protesters themselves appear not to have noticed the image of Bert and were certainly not likely to recognize his image from the *Sesame Street* program.

But it is true that the photos of the demonstration indeed show some banners in English. Even the notorious photo in the *New York Times* has a caption with bin Laden's name in the Roman alphabet. At least some of the demonstrators were aware of Western media coverage of the event and were interested in getting a message to the West about whom they supported and what they wanted to happen.[7]

Nonetheless, with the use of the banners in the protest, the circuit of transmission was provisionally closed. We may conclude that in all likelihood the protesters in Bangladesh did not see the image of Bert. From Ignacio's anticult Web site to the anti-American pop culture protest halfway around the world, and back again to the West in the medium of print journalism, Evil Bert's digital bytes circumnavigated the globe in a series of misrecognitions, perfect transmissions, confusions, and blends of politics and culture that surely speaks much of our current global culture.

The conditions of global cultural transmissions in the case of Bert Laden initiate many changes in communications practices in all societies. The Internet imposes everywhere new challenges and offers new opportunities.[8] The political consequences of the response to the Internet are serious indeed. Just as the mixing of peoples within a nation renders especially noxious parochial ethnic and racial attitudes, so the mixing of cultural objects in the Internet compels each culture to acknowledge the validity, if not the moral value, of such objects that may be alien and other. With Bert Laden, the stakes are especially high in the context of the war between al-Qaeda and the American-led coalition.

Scholars of mass communications tell us that the Bangladesh protesters' failure to recognize Bert is a case of "aberrant decoding" (Fiske and Hartley 1978). The protesters failed to interpret correctly the image of Bert and Osama. This omission was, however, highly motivated. The protesters cherished a preexisting hostility toward American popular culture, even though they inadvertently displayed one of its minor icons in their demonstration. Their hostility to U.S. popular culture, like that of other fundamentalist Islamic groups, derives, as the Middle Eastern scholar I heard on NPR shortly before the appearance of the photo in the New York Times contended, from a wish to maintain the autochthony of their own beliefs and values. They wish to insulate themselves against American popular culture, viewing it as a potent threat to their own way of life, perhaps in good part because of its popularity with other Muslims or Middle Easterners. Yet exactly this effort at insulation proved impossible in the instance at hand.

In another example of parochial attitudes, a highly respected Middle Eastern journalist, Ali Asadullah, reported in an Islamic online newspaper about the problem with American and, in this case, Western culture. In an article entitled "Spice Girls: Exactly the Reason Why Bin Laden Hates the West" (Asadullah 2001), he reported that a former Spice Girl, Geri Halliwell, on October 6, one day before the bombing began in Afghanistan, entertained British Troops in Oman. For this esteemed Muslim journalist, that was all the proof needed to explain, and indeed to justify, disdain by some people of Islamic faith for U.S. and British society. "The core causes for terrorist rage and aggression against the United States," he wrote, were "the Spice Girls," not "hatred of freedom, liberty and democracy." Muslims, he continued, "want their cultures, traditions and religious and societal standards to be respected." We can assume that "freedom, liberty and democracy," surely not hallmarks of Asadullah's Muslim cultures, are not all offensive to their faith. If that is the case, one wonders why "freedom, liberty and democracy" are not more widely practiced in the Middle East, indeed, why they are completely absent from that part of the world.

I argue that Asadullah's position is exactly the logic that no longer works. With globally networked digital communications, one must be especially careful in taking as an offense the legitimate cultural practices of another even if they are on one's own soil. I will not make any invidious comparisons between the practices of the Taliban with regard to women to those of the British, but here the cultural differences are sharp, and it is quite painful for either side to acknowledge the value of the position of the other. Yet this becomes the task and the dilemma in the global context. Since cultural objects circulate everywhere, there is no longer any *local* soil on the earth. Moral outrage directed at the cultural practices of others, especially in regard to those that do no physical harm, today becomes particularly obnoxious.[9] Journalists and intellectuals such as Asadullah, with his smug air of moral repugnance at Western popular culture, do much harm in justifying the sentiments from which arose the hideous murders of September 11, 2001.

What is more, the luxury of such a moral claim, inspired in this and many other cases not by any means limited to the world of Islam, is today often grounded in versions of monotheism. It may be that, in the present context, the collective human intelligence embodied in the Internet is set in a deep cultural opposition to parochialism in general and to versions of monotheism in particular that refuse the condition of cultural pluralism. The one and only God will have to make way for many one and only Gods. As Jean-Luc Nancy writes, "What is coming upon us is an exhaustion of the thought defined by the One and by a unique destination for the world" (Nancy 2003a, 23). He notes astutely that global conditions, however much they may have been and are continually imposed by the West, cannot be countered by insularity, even as insularity becomes one response to them. Nancy argues, "In times past, communities were able to think of themselves as distinct and autonomous without seeking their assumption in a generic humanity" (24). Hybridity of cultural objects and their continual transformation in planetary exchanges now form the matrix of human experience.

In characteristic deconstructionist discursive moves, Nancy rescues Christianity from theism. He first posits the undoing of monotheism, and Christianity in particular: "I will give the name, 'deconstruction of monotheism,' to the research project consisting in the dismantling and analysis of the constitutive elements of monotheism, and more directly of Christianity, thus of the West, in order to go back to (or proceed toward) the resources that might form simultaneously the buried origin and the imperceptible future of the world that calls itself 'modern' " (Nancy 2003b, 41). This Westerner rightly and critically reflects on his own cultural formation in pointing to the Christian version of monotheism as a difficulty. But quickly the limits of monotheism, in his hands, become a source of strength, pointing to a new, a-theistic future: "Christianity, in other words, points out, in the most active way . . . how monotheism accommodates within itself . . . the principle of a world without god . . . monotheism is in truth atheism" (ibid.). Christianity, he maintains, contains within itself the seeds of both a universal and atheistic world. In the transcendence of the Christian God, Nancy locates the deconstructivist's critique of presence. The path to a new universal culture of globalism is thus hidden in the margins of Christianity: "This truth [of Christian monotheism] is nothing other than the following: the universal cannot be given in a presence" (Nancy 2003c, 52).

And yet, despite Nancy, the commitment of millions to versions of monotheism, as a cultural belief that stands in the way of planetary culture and is a resort of great resistance to it, exhibits itself as full presence in countless domains, not least the actions of al-Qaeda on September 11,

2001. If any of the major monotheist religions can point in its history to the building of a multimonotheist social regime, it is certainly not Christianity but ironically perhaps Islam in the great Mediterranean civilization of the thirteenth century that included groups from all three monotheisms. The distinguished scholar of Islam Janet Abu-Lughod is worth quoting: "What is noteworthy in the world system of the thirteenth century is that a wide variety of cultural systems coexisted and cooperated, and that societies organized very differently from those in the west dominated the system. Christianity, Buddhism, Confucianism, Islam, Zoroastrianism, and numerous other smaller sects often dismissed as 'pagan' all seem to have permitted and indeed facilitated lively commerce, production, exchange, risk taking, and the like. And among these, Christianity played a relatively insignificant role" (Abu-Lughod 1989, 354–55). This period of peace and mutual tolerance, if not appreciation, stands as a unique exception to the bloody history that befouls the relations of monotheist polities. The task of building a planetary culture that admits of differences rules out the comfort, if that is what it is, of a single deity, all-powerful, omniscient, reigning with love or with anger over the universe. If that is the case, then the Bert Laden incident is more than an amusing series of cross-cultural confusions but an allegory of changes in contemporary culture, pointing to conditions rife with profound political implications.

The main interest of my intervention is not, however, to engage in a theological dispute. Rather, my purpose is to raise the questions of the general role of media in culture and the particular role of new media, to point to the importance of the linkage of humans with machines as the cornerstone of possible new planetary cultures. Transmissions of images, texts, and sounds may now, in the digital domain, be both noiseless *and* incoherent. Interpretive practices must accordingly recalibrate themselves to the conditions of planetary culture. Since cultural objects undergo continuous, unlimited alterations, appropriations and reappropriations enabled and encouraged by networked computing, research about any cultural object in cyberspace entails an infinite series of interpretive acts. Translation is now a central dimension of any cultural study. Texts, images, and sounds now travel at the speed of electrons and may be altered at any point along their course. They are as fluid as water and simultaneously present everywhere. They mock the presuppositions of all previous hermeneutics and the subject positions associated with them. They require a discipline of study unlike any that has subsisted in academic institutions. From this vantage point, Evil Bert, the emblem I have selected to designate cyberculture, is indeed a troublemaker.

In the next chapter, I examine postcolonial theory of the 1980s to see if it affords the resources for a critical understanding of global communications systems. I argue that the accomplishments of postcolonial theory, however important to a comprehension of the contemporary world situation, have not advanced far enough regarding questions of media and especially the role of human and machine links in the process of forming a global culture.

2

POSTCOLONIAL THEORY AND GLOBAL MEDIA

To the vast new techniques of power correlated with multinational economies and bureaucratic States, one must oppose a politicization which will take new forms.
—Michel Foucault, *Power/Knowledge*

I turn now to postcolonial theory and assess the degree of its recognition of information machines.

PROBLEMS OF POSTCOLONIALITY AND ITS DISCOURSE IN A GLOBAL AGE

Is the epoch of postcolonial studies over? Is the present era still one best characterized in terms of resistance to Western hegemony by states that were formerly administered by the imperial branches of European and American governments? Or are we now in a post-postcolonial epoch? Put differently, I offer the hypothesis that as globalizing processes continue to disseminate and to multiply, postcoloniality appears more and more as a moment in a declining phase, continuing or shifting to be sure, of the larger phenomenon of globalization. To put the matter somewhat differently, one might ask the following: from the standpoint of the former colonies of Europe, the United States, and Japan, also known as the postcolonial nations, can it be said that the chief hegemonic power limiting their freedom is the heritage of colonialism, or is it rather the spreading and deepening tentacles of globalization? For the purposes of this chapter, I will explore the hypothesis that postcoloniality is now folding into globalizing movements and trends. I do so for the reason that, since the 1970s, emergent forms of domination now present themselves as the exigent difficulty.

Certainly there is a continuing heritage of Western imperialism in many parts of the world. This heritage can be seen in the institutional forms that persist from the imperialist era, along with the elites that emerged under the condition of colonial rule. It is also the case that many, if not most, of the colonized nations of the Western imperial epoch from 1500 to 1950 continue to suffer from subordinate relations with the United States and Europe. Even granting these continuities with the past, the current situation of globalization, spearheaded by transnational corporations, might best be comprehended not from a standpoint of postcolonialism but from one that takes its point of departure from emergent forms of domination. After the Western nations established a so-called free market system in the 1980s with the NAFTA and GATT treaties on international trade, the initiative of global relations has shifted to the processes of economics, migration, and communication. The theoretical implications for a critique of the current situation of these alterations in planetary power relations can be approached first by reviewing some of the presuppositions about postcoloniality of the 1980s and 1990s. To what extent, one might ask, does the tradition of postcolonial theory prepare the way for a critique of trends that now subsist under the sign of globalization?

The leading theorists of postcoloniality, from Frantz Fanon and Albert Memmi to Edward Said, Gayatri Spivak, and Homi Bhabha, give priority to the binary of colonizer and colonized.[1] The starting point for the critique of colonial reason is thus a reformulation of the couple colonizer-colonized. It might be noted that Aijaz Ahmad's critique of the postcolonial theory of the 1980s and 1990s misses this aspect of the work of Said, Spivak, and Bhabha, complaining instead that such postcolonial theory is merely "literary" and "culturalist." Ahmad contends that the more important moment of postcolonial theory from the 1970s took up the problem of the state, a "real" political question (Ahmad 1992, 1995a). Certainly the problem of state formation in postcolonial nations is important. It may also be admitted that Said, Spivak, and Bhabha do not contribute much to the analysis of the state. Ahmad, however, displays the weakness of the tendency toward totalization in Marxist versions of postcolonial theory by refusing to accord any value to the "culturalist" position. In this respect, a Foucauldian acceptance of a plurality of critiques is much preferred to the monotheistic purity of Ahmad's Marxism.[2] A better strategy than the somewhat rigid theorizing of Ahmad would be to recognize contributions to the critique of postcoloniality from diverse, even incompatible, perspectives.[3]

The opposition colonizer-colonized was configured during the phase of globalization from the fifteenth century through the mid-twentieth century, during which Europe, and then the United States and Japan, extended their influence and power throughout the world, not covering every acre of land with colonial forces, to be sure, but undermining to a large extent most preexisting local political systems. As Stuart Hall suggests, we must understand "that the rise of the West is also a *global* story" (Hall 1996, 187). The conflict of colonizer and colonized characterizes the entire trajectory of Western globalization, but in each phase of that history, the figure of the colonizer and the figure of the colonized take on different dimensions and are fraught with different patterns of strife.[4] The early theorists of postcoloniality open a discourse about the agency of the colonized as a counterweight to the hegemonic narratives of "progress" from within the colonizing nations.[5] More recent theorists of postcoloniality complicate the picture by exploring the interaction of colonizer and colonized in particular at the cultural level.

For our purposes, we need only focus on the recent history of the past fifty years and investigate, however briefly, the ways this opposition has changed. The theorization of the opposition colonizer-colonized has focused on the political, psychological, and cultural dimensions of the binary. In the theories of Fanon, Bhabha, and the other writers mentioned earlier, the presence of the Westerner in Asia, Latin America, Africa, the Middle East, Polynesia, and Australia is the origin of a relationship of complexity and strife. One might well say that the planet Earth during the period 1500 to 1950 was characterized by the encounter of peoples that up to that time had had little contact with one another; that it was primarily Europeans who entered the zones of others;[6] and that all parties were ill equipped, mentally and emotionally, to comprehend or to appreciate the "other." Mary Louise Pratt terms this territory a "contact zone." She writes: "What I like to call 'contact zones' [are] social spaces where disparate cultures meet, clash, and grapple with each other, often in highly asymmetrical relations of domination and subordination" (Pratt 1992, 4). In a study of the role of technology in the confrontation of the West and the rest, Michael Adas (1998) relates an incident, illustrative of Pratt's "contact zone," in which, in the 1740s, William Smith, traveling on the Gambia River, regarded the people he met as "ignorant savages" and they, in turn, were filled with confusion and anxiety not only by the appearance of Europeans but by their technical instruments. During the entire period in question, humans were, from the perspective of today, exceedingly parochial, regarding their own group as the only true members of the species. Territorial ethnicity and religion were the referents of rigid identity structures for all participants.

The West incited these relations and came to dominate them almost everywhere they engaged non-Westerners. But all parties to the encounter were challenged by it to account for the other and to reflect back on the implications of the discovery of others for their own cultural identity. Sadly, they enjoyed sparse cultural resources for these tasks. Even if the relations of the West and the rest had been more symmetrical, one could not be optimistic about the level of mutual understanding in their outcome. One might say that the culture of each party at the meeting operated as an unconscious system—linguistic, emotional, and cognitive—that ensured a deep level of misrecognition for everyone. Certainly there were numerous examples of genuine interest in the difference of the peoples as they discovered one another, but these were insignificant compared to the general hostility and strife that characterized this great encounter. In this context, it should come as no surprise that postcolonial theorists of the past two decades give priority to the "hybridity" of identities of the colonized (Bhabha 1994), or to the rebound effect of colonization on the colonizer (Stoler 1995), or to the impossibility of the subaltern to speak in the colonial relation (Spivak 1988).[7]

Homi Bhabha's concept of the hybrid postcolonial subject opens the question of the cultural translation between colonizer and colonized but also forecloses the relation of the media to intercultural encounters. He initiates his intervention by framing the question of culture in terms of misunderstandings that occur when different peoples interact: "Culture only emerges as a problem, or a problematic, at the point at which there is a loss of meaning in the contestation and articulation of everyday life, between classes, genders, races, nations" (Bhabha 1994, 34). Bhabha proceeds to account for the "mistakes" each participant makes concerning the meaning of the other's statement by introducing the term "Third

Space." He argues that the cultural encounter between the colonizer and colonized happens in an "indeterminate space of the subject(s) of enunciation" (37). This Third Space, neither the colonizer's homeland nor the territory of the colonized, invokes the general logic of language as the condition for the interaction and dialogue: "The production of meaning requires that [the subject of a proposition (*énoncé*) and the subject of enunciation] . . . be mobilized in the passage through a Third Space, which represents both the general conditions of language and the specific implication of the utterance in a performative and institutional strategy of which it cannot 'in itself' be conscious" (36). Every act of "cultural enunciation" points to an outside, a beyond that "is crossed by the *différance* of writing" (ibid.). Bhabha thus complicates the analysis of the postcolonial contact zone by introducing an element—a general logic of language as *différance*—that pervades the contact zone of cultures and leads to the constitution of subjects in hybridity.

He goes on to argue that the consequence of the Third Space is to undermine any effort to render univocal a cultural enunciation by linking it to a particular context: "There is no way that the content of the proposition will reveal the structure of its positionality; no way that context can be mimetically read off from the content" (ibid.). By disengaging the encounter of cultures from any specificity of context, Bhabha thwarts all attempts to account for differences in the media of enunciation: speech, writing, television, film, Internet. In a revealing citation from Frantz Fanon, Bhabha, however, underscores the necessity of just such an analysis. In the following passage cited by Bhabha, Fanon criticizes native intellectuals for neglecting the question of context and media: "[Native intellectuals] forget that the forms of thought and what [they] feed . . . on, together with modern techniques of information, language, and dress have dialectically reorganized the people's intelligences" (Fanon 1963, 35; Bhabha 1994). Fanon berates these intellectuals for failing to update their critical skills in line with innovations in areas such as "modern techniques of information." Fanon, unlike Bhabha, apparently does not hesitate to contextualize the basis of the native intellectuals' inability to critique the postcolonial condition. With the introduction of satellite television, international circuits of film, and globally networked computing, a quite determinate context intrudes on the Third Space, opening new questions for the enunciations between postcolonial subjects and the continuing presence of colonizing processes. These remain decidedly cultural questions with deeply political implications. Bhabha's notion of hybridity remains pertinent to conceptualizing the media context of the contact zone. His emphasis on the "general conditions of language" must be acknowledged as an effective critique of positivist approaches and as putting foundationalist arguments into question. But the concept of hybridity must not be fashioned as an ontology of transculture, one that precludes the investigation of particular contexts, such as that of the media.

What I want to underscore as I interrogate the circumstances of contemporary globalization is that the horizon of postcolonial theory has been the face-to-face encounter of the West and the rest, its resonance for those not directly engaged in it, and the theoretical articulations derivative thereof. Into this theoretical and practical scenario, I introduce the deus ex machina of recent globalizing trends, specifically the planetary communications systems that today enable and promote new kinds of relations across cultures.[8] I argue that postcolonial theory of the 1980s presumes a proximate relation of colonizer and colonized that obscures the transculture of new media, communications that inscribe types of hybridity in electronic spaces very different from that envisaged by Bhabha and other theorists. As Emily Apter contends, networked computing "conjures forth an identity no longer split between First and Third World, between metropole and native home, but rather, a body so fragmented that its morphology is a diaspora."[9] Although Western media, especially film, have long crossed the divide of First and Third Worlds, in what follows I will focus primarily on networked computing.

After the intense globalization of the past thirty years, the post-postcolonial situation is altered and more complex still. For one thing, the peoples of the non-Western world are now, in large numbers, in the Western World, an outcome that has led to theories of multiculturalism and diaspora. To some extent, this is not new: Jews and Muslims inhabited Europe before Western globalization. The Chinese immigrated throughout Asia (Ong 1999). Africans have been (unwillingly) placed in the West since the early days of globalization. Postcolonial theories of colonizer and colonized do not lend themselves to illuminating this sort of mixing. Second, the tremendous impact of the economic aspect of globalization has brought Western commodities to the rest of the world and has incorporated non-Western labor into the design and manufacture of Western goods, and even increasingly for services, for markets all over the world. Postcolonial nations are now suffused with Western commodities, including the labor skills learned in Western universities and exported back home. Third, and what is the subject I address in this chapter, cultural objects now extend back and forth between the West and the rest through global communications systems.

Before moving on to consider such media and their relation to the unconscious, I summarize by saying that the migration of non-Westerners to the West, the massive penetration of Western commodities into the non-West, and the exchange of cultural objects between the West and the non-West all introduce relations between peoples around the globe that do not fit easily into the categories of colonizer and colonized.

THEORIZING GLOBAL MEDIA

Some cultural critics have recognized the role of media in the situation of postcoloniality and globalization. Among the most influential of these is Arjun Appadurai.[10] An anthropologist and cultural theorist, Appadurai urges us to attend especially to the interplay and entwinement of migration and media in the context of globalization. In no uncertain terms, he states his thesis that migration and media must be understood together:

> Implicit in this book is a theory of rupture that takes media and migration as its two major, and interconnected, diacritics and explores their joint effect on the *work of the imagination* as a constitutive feature of modern subjectivity. The first step in this argument is that electronic media decisively change the wider field of mass media and other traditional media. . . . Electronic media give a new twist to the environment within which the modern and the global often appear as flip sides of the same coin. (Appadurai 1996, 3)

Unlike Bhabha and Spivak, who focus on the proximate relation of colonizer and colonized in the colony,[11] Appadurai points out that the colonized are on the move. They are the ones, in the age of globalization, who disperse themselves around the planet, even entering the bastions of the colonizer. He also insists that such diasporas introduce media into the relations of the colonized among themselves and between them and the colonizers. Appadurai's insights constitute a major shift in the understanding of the postcolonial situation, but equally they disrupt the narratives of globalization, pointing to the centrality of migration from the former colonies and their attachment to media as constituent of their emerging cultural formation. Appadurai continues: "Those who wish to move, those who have moved, those who wish to return, and those who choose to stay rarely formulate their plans outside the sphere of radio and television, cassettes and videos, newsprint and telephone. For migrants, both the politics of adaptation to new environments and the stimulus to move or return are deeply affected by a mass-mediated imaginary that frequently transcends national space" (Appadurai 1996, 6). Media are thus central to the story of diaspora.

As the migrants circulate through the space of nations, affected by mass media and armed with their own media, the condition of postcoloniality is altered. Postcoloniality depended on a stable geography of nations, each one harboring its people or better peoples with the asymmetry of the West and the rest shaping the cartography of interaction and strife. In the age of postcoloniality, in other words, the nation remained the matrix of the political. And some postcolonial critics insist on the beneficial aspects of the nation-state for the former colonies. Pheng Cheah, for example, proclaims: "The decolonizing nation is not an archaic throwback to traditional forms of community based on the blind ties of blood and kinship but a new form of political community engendered by the spectrality of modern knowledge, techno-mediation, and modern organization" (Cheah 1999, 250). And Aihwa Ong's criticism is equally sharp: "Appadurai's formulation begs the question of whether imagination as social practice can be so independent of national, transnational, and political-economic structures that enable, channel, and control the flows of people, things, and ideas" (Ong 1999, 11). Appadurai, to the contrary, stresses the disruptive and novel aspects of the play of media and migration in the global context: "Diasporic public spheres, diverse among themselves, are the crucibles of a postnational political order. The engines of their discourse are mass media (both interactive and expressive) and the movement of refugees, activists, students, and laborers" (Appadurai 1996, 22). Migrants for him constitute emerging political arenas that infest the nation with difference, from the point of view of some, but open spaces of a new, postnational order that might be the germinating point for a democratizing politics of the global, a counter to the oppressive, neoliberal celebration of greed at any price. Appadurai, against Cheah and others, locates the dialectic of liberation not within the reproduction of the West's nation-state but directly within the monster of globalization.

Appadurai's search for possible democratizing tendencies within the post-postcolonial order of globalization is not limited to what he characterizes as new public spheres among the migrants. He sees also a general tendency of multiplying possibilities of life choices and styles, one that derives not only from migrations and the mixing of peoples but from the media themselves: "There is a peculiar new force to the imagination in social life today. More persons in more parts of the world consider a wider set of possible lives than they ever did before. One important source of this change is the mass media, which present a rich, ever-changing store of possible lives, some of which enter the lived imaginations of ordinary people more successfully than others" (Appadurai 1996, 53). More efficiently and relentlessly than the migrants, media represent and transport figures of culture and ways of life across national boundaries. Celebrities from Hollywood are known around the world and in the least likely places. The media produce distributed culture, inciting mixtures of all sorts. No doubt many resist and resent this intrusion on their happy, complacent localism. Some applaud the resistance of national cultures to the imposition of American culture (Jameson 1998). Others explain the ferocious fundamentalisms like that of al-Qaeda as a response to the appeal of Western popular culture, as we have seen in chapter 1 (Asadullah 2001). Others still find in the dissemination of cultures an emerging global culture, as in global music or global English, practices that cannot be traced to one source or attributed to the influence of one center (Yúdice 1992). And finally some scholars from within the postcolonial nations contest the imperialist inflection given by others to the spread of cultures and detect the emergence of multicultural formations in the adaptation of popular culture in everyday life (Garcia Canclini 2001). No doubt the nerve that Appadurai has exposed elicits diverse responses. Yet the importance of the phenomenon of cultural mixing through migration and media cannot be gainsaid.[12]

Appadurai's thesis of globalization as migration and media, productive as it is, does not adequately explore the specificity of different media or appear to reflect a sensitivity to this question. The subtlety of his analysis does not extend to an appreciation of the particular material and cultural forms of media. In the passage quoted earlier, for instance, he attributes the "rupture" introduced by media in the constitution of the contemporary imaginary to "electronic media." This is far too general a term. He seems to be referring to networked computing. But "electronic" refers as well to radio, television, and film, not to mention satellite communications systems and mobile phones. In other passages, he refers to mass media in a way that does not exclude the Internet but probably should, since networked computing is a many-to-many communications system, not a few-to-many technology like television or film. The murkiness of Appadurai's understanding of media inhibits the analytic power of his argument. It does not account for the difference between media controlled by transnational capital and media that afford individuals new positions of speech, between media that enforce and reproduce the opposition of producer and consumer to media that challenge that separation.

THE MEDIA UNCONSCIOUS

The media constitute a complex, vast apparatus of forms and contents — Appadurai (1990) terms it a "mediascape" — that increasingly characterize cultural exchanges and do so in an increasingly global expanse. In their form, technologies of the media are more and more deterritorialized. As we move from print to telegraph and telephone, then to radio, film, and television, and finally to digital networks with fiber-optic conduits and satellite transmissions, cultural objects (words, texts, sounds, and images) are progressively removed from territorial space into physical realms of electrons, sound waves, and light pulses that are less palpable to the human senses and less subject to control by established institutions, especially the nation-state and the corporation. In their content, cultural objects, flowing within the newer media, increasingly cross national, linguistic, geographic, and cultural boundaries. Films, television episodes, e-mails, Web pages, even phone calls today travel across the continents, proliferating and disseminating like viruses. In both respects, regarding form and content, cultural objects are restructured in such ways that local contexts lose their powers of familiarization. Individuals no longer form identities exclusively through local practices. In the context of global media, new types of unconsciousness emerge for both the recipients and the transmitters of culture.

In this media context, one must perforce rethink the question of the unconscious. Initiated by Freud, the concept of the unconscious was developed in relation to the psyche, specifically in relation to the region of emotional life. It indicated that the individual did not have conscious access to his or her own feelings, desires, and fantasies. Jacques Lacan translated the Freudian unconscious into linguistic terms. Others have fruitfully extended its reach into other domains such as Fredric Jameson's notion of the political unconscious (Jameson 1981) or the cultural unconscious (MacCannell 1986). What is different about the media unconscious from these other positions is that media are technologies, or information machines. The psychic, the political, and the cultural unconscious are all registered in a field of human relations; by contrast, the media unconscious includes the dimension of the thing. The media unconscious estranges the human from itself, introducing a symbiosis of human and machine that destabilizes the figures of the subject and object. Hitherto machines were objects par excellence, tools, in the Western ontology that Heidegger (1977) deconstructed, that stood at a distance from the human and functioned as its other, or, as one might say, a pure object. In the media unconscious, the tool of the information machine insinuates itself within the processes of culture, reconfiguring what had been the subject and the object into a new construct that I call the humachine.

Implicated in a media culture, the individual and group find themselves nodes in a network, a condition or state of being that is reminiscent of the way Foucault represented the individual in his theory of power.[13] In particular, Foucault's notion of productive power is especially germane in the understanding of media. For Foucault, power produces relations and subject positions within those relations. Power for him is an apparatus (*dispositif*) or mechanism, combining architectural spaces, practices, rules, and discourses. In Foucault's writings, the confessional, the prison, the workshop, and the school are prime examples of the operations of productive power. In each case, individuals are positioned in such a manner that they construct themselves in relations with others and with themselves. These relations are always asymmetrical, including some degree of domination. Individuals in these subject positions, however, are to a large extent unconscious of all the mechanisms that structure the situation in which they find themselves. The child becomes a "student" without entirely grasping how the classroom is arranged, how the teacher is credentialed, how the rules of the school are developed, what limitations and possibilities are entailed in his or her position. Resistance is part of the student's situation, but such an oppositional stance is contained within the subject position, not outside it. This concept of power is particularly useful in understanding media effects, and in fact some of Foucault's depictions of power sound as if he were speaking about computer networks. For example, he writes:

> Power must . . . be analyzed as something that circulates. . . . It is never localized here or there. . . . Power is exercised through networks, and individuals do not simply circulate in those networks; they are in a position to both submit to and exercise this power. They are never the inert or consenting targets of power; they are always its relays. . . . Power passes through individuals. It is not applied to them. (Foucault 2002, 29)

Individuals are thus "relays" (today we might say "nodes") in a network.

The media unconscious is, like Foucault's depictions of power, ubiquitous, not centered in an institution like the state, but not absent from that place either. A node in a network, the subordinate individual in a power relation has his or her attention drawn to the constraints indicated and performed by the superior individual. But what is outside consciousness is the relationship through which the superior individual is able to establish those constraints and make them applicable to the subordinate individual. Directly confronting the psychoanalytic notion of the unconscious, Foucault gives the example of the child in the Oedipal situation.[14] The psychoanalytic paradigm depicts the parent denying libidinal gratification to the child. The parental "law" invokes the "no" as the castrating or inhibiting gesture, producing a gap within the child between consciousness and desire. Foucault's important intervention in the play of psychoanalytic discourse is to point out that the therapist and the parent first implant in the child the libidinal desire for the parent of the opposite sex. That is the productive moment of familial or therapeutic power. Subsequently this desire is denied, a denial that the child recognizes consciously. Attention is drawn to the denial of desire, but the implantation of desire is the more crucial step in the play of power of the discourse of psychoanalysis. In Foucault's words, psychoanalysis "had the consequence of sexually exciting the bodies of children while at the same time fixing the parental gaze and vigilance on the peril of infantile sexuality."[15] What escapes the child is the implantation of desire. This is the unconscious aspect of power relations that Foucault adds to and substitutes for the psychoanalytic unconscious.

Wherever individuals deploy media, they are in the midst of a system of power relations that remains out of phase with their conscious mind. Media structure the self much as language does, not from the outside but in the communication practice itself. This seems obvious, but it is worth pointing out that when watching TV or cinema, speaking on a telephone (wired or wireless), listening to the radio, or engaged in some aspect of the computer network, one's attention is focused on the content of the technology, not on its machinic or formal qualities. McLuhan captured this feature of the media when he reminded us that the medium is the message. The significant aspect of television for McLuhan is not its program but its action on what he called "the sense ratio." Television changes us into creatures with visual dominance not by what it says but by its (technical) mode of communication. And so it is with all media, although I would argue that the pertinent object of change is not the sense ratio but rather the human-machine interface, the general construction of the self, indeed the basic features of culture.

GLOBAL DISSEMINATION OF MEDIA

How, then, does the globally networked communication system of digitized computing implicate users unconsciously in new configurations of subjectivation? This apparently innocent question is complicated by three areas of concern: first is the question of the multiple nature of the Internet; second, and related to the first, is the relation of preexisting social and cultural forms that influence digital culture; third is the relation of non-Western cultures with the Internet mode of information that was originally developed in the West. I will briefly address these issues before turning to the question of digital selves.

The Internet consists both of functions developed directly in relation to it and of functions that have been added to it either from older media or from institutions outside the Internet that have adapted to it since 1993, when the World Wide Web was initiated. Some of the functions that origi-nated with the Internet are file transfer protocol, e-mail, Listservs, Usenet, Internet Relay Chat, massively multiuser games, MUDs and MOOs, and more recently blogs. Other media such as newspapers and print media in general, fax, telephone, radio, and television have been added to the Internet, as have economic activities (business-to-business networks, fi-nancial markets and services, retail services), government activities (data-bases of services to citizens, surveillance at all levels, income tax filing, electoral campaign activities, protest organizing, political mobilization), entertainment and cultural offerings (sports information, movie listings, museum exhibitions, library catalogs, distance learning), and military logistics. Indeed, one would be hard pressed to find any social practice that has not been adapted to the Internet. The answer to the question of the Internet as a technology of power that (unconsciously) constructs sub-jects depends very much on the aspect of global communications one has in mind and the area of social and cultural practice one studies, especially the degree to which the communication function and the social practice are inherent in the Internet or imported from outside it. The media effect of global networks is likely very different for a fifty-year-old selling a stock and a twelve-year-old enjoying an online massively multiplayer game such as *EverQuest*.

The other important consideration in understanding the media con-struction of the self in global networks is non-Western online practices. There are enormous variations in the way different societies have appropri-ated the Internet, so much so that one may not be able to pose the question at a general level in relation to this broad category. Early studies of Inter-net use across cultures have indicated a continuum that goes from almost complete disinterest in the medium (Afghanistan), to deep suspicion (the government of China), to ambivalent tolerance (Singapore's enthusiasm for high technology but resistance to social and cultural experimentation, for example), to open acceptance (Trinidad's recognition of the Internet as a direct extension of their culture of "liming") (Miller and Slater 2000), to complete celebration (Kenya and computers).[16] In addition to understanding the way the Internet has received varying degrees and different forms of acceptance in different cultures and nations, one also needs a separate discussion of the use of global networks by migrants (those who are at a distance from their birthplace), as well as by ethnic, social, and cultural minorities (those who cannot expect recognition by the majority group). In each case there are special uses of the Internet: foreign workers use e-mail as an inexpensive and convenient way to contact distant family and friends; immigrants use Web pages to maintain ethnic identities (Dewitte 2002); minorities such as gays go online to find community. Migrants and minorities in general use networked computing in exceedingly diverse and continuously changing practices.

One characteristic, then, of the new media landscape is that positions of enunciation now extend throughout the globe (of course, not equally), bringing into contact multiple and heterogeneous cultures (of course, many of the bits and bytes flow between friends or acquaintances, within preexisting groups like nations, and are within the same language). Transculture is emerging as a major aspect of media exchanges. Cultural objects increasingly find their way across their territorial point of origin (Poster 2003). At the same time, networked computing promotes interactions among the like-minded, within subcultures of all kinds, groups that do not wish to open themselves to a larger world.[17] In globally networked computer media, both tendencies proliferate simultaneously. Everyone now appropriates and changes the culture of everyone else, while the like-minded of every stripe find it easier to locate members of their group. A practice or belief that was once a stable part of one culture may now be repurposed by another and redefined in the process of reception. As Maria Fernandez (1999) points out, "the history of the Habsburgs is no longer only European." In such a mediascape, my concern is primarily with the spread of a global public sphere that is differential in its cultural and linguistic character.

DIGITAL SUBJECTS GLOBALLY

The material specificity of the global computer network constitutes subject positions in an unprecedented planetary public sphere.[18] The digital nature of subject positions in the Internet and the digital character of the texts, images, and sounds that they generate, store, transmit, and receive are the chief conditions that determine the configuration of this public sphere. Because this public sphere is digital, it is different from the agora, the town hall, the coffee shop, the salon, and other territorial locations that are associated with the emergence of public spheres in modern society. The public sphere on the Internet is heavily mediated by information technologies, so that copresence of participants is possible under very strict limitations. In the digital world there are no face-to-face, proximate meetings, and this is so even if visual and aural information is present such as through the use of Webcams and Internet telephony. The self that participates in planetary discussions on the Internet is configured by computer and network technologies, so that communications are transformed by digital mediations. There can be no illusion of full presence in the digital public sphere. As we have learned from poststructuralist theory, however, full presence is an interpretation of encounters that disavows the spacing and temporal displacements that are more easily recognized in writing (Derrida 1978). My argument is not that the digital public sphere destabilizes the full presence of face-to-face meetings but that it constructs the subject through the specificity of its medium in a way different from oral or written or broadcast models of self constitution. Postcolonial subjectivity, as Emily Apter contends, "often project[s] a redemptive longing for transparent meaning, oral and narrative tradition, wholeness, homeliness, civil equality, collective agency, and focused political anger" (Apter 1999, 214). These sentiments may easily obscure the imbrication of the local in the global. Global networks militate precisely against such forgetting.[19]

The digital self that participates in Internet public spheres is different from the individual speaking in the agora or the coffee shop, as well as from the representative of individuals speaking in democratic institutions like parliaments. Digital information machines construct subjects who are present only through their textual, aural, and visual uploads. The requirement of networked computing constructs subjects as producers of cultural objects, like the speeches uttered in coffee shops or the essays published in newspapers, journals, and books. Networked computing also enables subjects to distribute their own work to countless numbers of recipients, by means of blogs, Listservs, multiple e-mail distributions, Web pages, peer-to-peer file-sharing networks, and file transfer protocol programs. In this respect, the digital self is more like a broadcaster than like an individual speaker at a meeting. Like some other media, a degree of anonymity is enabled by networked computing, so that the assurances one has about identity in face-to-face situations or in publications that have strong gatekeeper functions such as newspapers and in print in general are much less certain.

Given the media specificity of the digitally constructed self, territorial conditions that characterize the performance of the subject in historic public spheres are minimized, if not entirely eliminated. As a consequence, the self that appears in the digital public sphere is a new construct, one that does not conform nicely to earlier incarnations of individuality. We cannot yet be confident in giving shape to this emergent identity, but we must acknowledge its novelty. Since the digital self also absorbs the affordances and constraints of the Internet, we can say that the positions of speech that are made possible in this medium are greatly expanded from what we have known before. To obtain such a speaking position in the digital world is easier and more affordable than any comparable participation in the past. To speak in the agora, one had to be a member of the elite of free citizens of Athens; to speak in the coffeehouse of early modern London, one had to be an adult, Christian (probably Protestant), and male at least of the bourgeoisie; to speak in a salon in eighteenth-century Paris, one had to be an invited aristocrat or bourgeois. To speak on the Internet, there are no age limits, no gender limits, and no religious, ethnic, or national requirements. Indeed, there is no way to discern these traits in most Internet discussion forums, from Usenet to chat rooms, from Listservs to blogs.

The digital subject, then, is located automatically in the *global space* of the network. Colonizer and colonized subject positions are far less exigent here than in other media frameworks. Admittedly the Internet is not deployed completely in this manner. Many if not most online users pursue with unambiguous assurance their territorial identities, seeking to find and to engage those of similar characteristics, those with the same identity, the same political position, the same religious persuasion, the same nationality, the same gender, and the same sexual orientation. It should not come as a surprise that the entire history of the human race, defined as it is by these sorts of group identities, is reproduced all too faithfully in the network. Yet the digital subject continues the trend of other media, starting from print and continuing with the telephone, film, radio, and television, and geometrically expanding it in the sense of abstracting from territorial identities and constructing the self in the virtual space of the Net. In this regard, digital subjects are solicited not to stabilize, centralize, and unify the territorial identity that they were given by birth or social position, but to invent and construct themselves in relations with others. In the digital medium, subject formation becomes a task inherent in cultural exchange. And it does so at a planetary level.

CONCLUSION: GLOBAL MEDIA
AND POSTCOLONIAL THEORY

The media change the relations of Westerner and non-Westerner enormously and therefore have serious implications for postcolonial theory. Perhaps the best location to examine in relation to my argument is India, the place that has arguably been most central to the development of postcolonial theory, with Homi Bhabha, Gayatri Spivak, the Subaltern Studies Group, Dipesh Chakrabarty, Inderpal Grewal, and so many other important scholars contributing to the understanding of Western imperialism and its wake. If we look at the role of media in India at the start of the new millennium, we may gain a foothold on the question of postcoloniality in the age of globalization.

India has played a central role in the development and extension of various media. Its film industry is among the largest in the world and has for some years been exporting films to the West. India's workforce has also contributed for many years to the computer software industry, giving a new meaning to the term *homework* by writing and exporting code through the Internet to the United States. Recently such "commuting" has been extended to telephony, as thousands of Indians work in call centers that communicate primarily with the United States. These workers are trained to assume American identities to give callers the impression of speaking to fellow countrymen (Poster 2005). Migration patterns also affect Indian participation in media. India's technical universities, among the leading institutions of their kind in the world, export workers around the world to build high-tech and media industries. In all these ways, Indians have adapted Western technologies and practices to their own cultural and social habits, complicating any understanding of this nation as "postcolonial."

More pertinent than the participation of Indians in the computer software industry and the great success of their film production is the formation in India of transnational culture through media. As Ravi Sundaram (2000) has argued, Indian national identity has been greatly transformed or, in his word, "remapped" through the spread of "virtual spaces" in global media. While still modest in number compared to the United States, western Europe, and several nations of Asia, Internet use in India is growing rapidly and has a disproportionate importance owing to users' demographic traits as relatively wealthy, style-setting males. The discourse elicited by cyberspace in India has been a central ingredient in the Indian redefinition of the nation and its future, or so Sundaram argues. A shift has occurred from the understanding of Indian nationalism under Nehru as dependent on "development," understood as building industrial infrastructure such as dams (very much indebted to Western ideas of modernity), to one that defines the problem in terms of communications systems.[20] In Sundaram's words, "The way forward was computerization, networking, and a new visual regime based on a national television network" (276). In the 1980s and 1990s, a new generation of Indians thus defined their (post)modernity not as an imitation of the Western industrial revolution but as participation in a globally networked world of media and consumption. True enough, the new path was not specifically anti-Western or even non-Western. Yet by its means, Sundaram writes, "the Third World is allowed entry into hitherto prohibited spaces," and India is no longer defined by its colonially generated borders (280). By means of the global media, diasporic Indians are included in the nation, and at the same time, national identity ironically becomes transnational as "new cultural landscapes" inspire the adaptation of lifestyles from around the world, albeit primarily from the West. Sundaram calls the phenomenon of globally mixed culture "an entirely new geography of desire" (283). In this manner, India escapes from the postcolonial ideology of development and enters the "postmodern" transculture of global media. Certainly other responses to India's adaptation of new media have occurred, such as reactionary nationalism. Intensified nationalism is perhaps even more characteristic of the current situation than Sundaram's "new geography of desire."[21] But reactions such as these are likely eventually to fade as globalization continues to become characteristic of the contemporary political situation.

To be sure, these tendencies are in their infancy, and their dissemination might produce results that do not resemble the somewhat exaggerated hopes that Sundaram discerns in Indian discourse.[22] Yet the lines of emergence of a differential digital transculture are clearly enough visible on the horizon. They point to a new constellation of planetary culture that, under the right political circumstances, might yield an instantiation of globalization that was neither foreseen nor desired by its neoliberal proponents.[23]

In the next chapter, I will examine a leading formulation of the political side of globalization, the prospect of a regime of Empire. I will again test the extent to which the conceptualization of Empire accounts for the role of the media, especially global networking.

3

THE INFORMATION EMPIRE

I have argued that postcolonial theory has been overtaken by globalization and that it has disregarded at great cost the place of media in the current planetary situation. Both of these contentions are clarified and furthered by turning to the question of new political formations in the global expanse, again with particular attention to the question of networked computing.

INTRODUCTION

Since the collapse of the Soviet Union in 1989, the United States has found itself in a position of unchallenged power. It accedes to the hegemonic position established by the past five centuries of imperialism in which Europe extended its control over most of the world and, after World War II, lost that control. The question of defining a strategy of resistance to U.S. power must first acknowledge that power. Debates in U.S. media have sadly ignored that issue, leaving open disastrous policies of "preemptive" aggression in the name of democracy, farcical as such a claim is. In response to U.S. bullying, various forms of resistance have emerged, many of which serve only to fuel the engine of American bellicosity. Some of these tactics produce counterproductive results that only increase the resolve and support of neoconservative hawks and render more remote any tendency toward planetary democracy. The best recent example of counterproductive tactics is al-Qaeda's murderous acts of September 11, 2001, playing as they did right into the hands of George W. Bush and his crew in their warmongering, hypernationalist designs.

One aspect of the challenge for critical thought today is to redefine globalization outside its "free market" capitalist model in favor of one that recognizes the multiple cultures that must build a new planetary polity. To that end, the cultures of the past must give up their claims to autonomy, recognizing their mutual dependence in a world community. All must abandon positions that dismiss others as barbarian, infidel, pagan. These terms must be politically discredited, and those who preach them must be seen as an ally, not an enemy, of American hegemony. One of the features of globalization that potentially works against U.S. hegemony is the increasing incidence of planetary communications. Thanks to the planetary flows of people, goods, and information, we are cheek to jowl with others, confined to a relatively small territory in which cultural crossing is not exceptional but ordinary. We must ask, then, what are the resources of this crossing, and how can we deploy them to construct a planetary democracy?

Critical social theorists and comparative theorists of culture have begun to recognize the imposing fact of global formations. Fantasies of spiritual unification in monotheist religions, aspirations toward universality in Enlightenment thought, and urges toward international resistance to capitalism in Marx—all may now be seen as imaginary and discursive anticipations of a planetary human ecology. Recent works by Manuel Castells (Castells 1996, 2001) and Michael Hardt and Antonio Negri (Hardt and Negri 2000, 2004) proceed from a standpoint of emergent global integration. At every point of human life, old lines of division—systems of order, relations of signification, hierarchies of value and power—are palpably beginning to crumble. While local groupings are by no means extinct and in fact in some ways are more prominent than ever, there is no question that a new mapping, a new, planetary distribution of things, is emerging.[1] Everyone and everything is affected by the disruption. Many humans are irritated, to say the least, by the trend, if the horrific events of September 11, 2001, are any indication. Others are hopeful that globalization is not simply an extension of capitalist markets but the beginning point of a new form of collective human life.

These musings about a new global landscape are hardly revelatory and should come as no surprise. The difficulty, however, is to get one's bearings amid the novel circumstances, to find a way to achieve some feeble purchase on the enormous drift in which we are all being tossed about seemingly without choice of direction. It is probably futile, and may even be counterproductive, to respond to the changes by adopting a stance of outside observer or attempting to occupy the position of truth that marked critical thought in the period of modernity. Characteristics of discursive subject positions today are contingency and paradox, heterogeneity and multiplicity, the frank recognition that we are within something that is huge and perplexing, something that engulfs all cultures and standpoints, providing perches of epistemological privilege to no one. It is then wisest, perhaps, to adopt the mode of the hypothetical.

If I am granted such a modest epistemological posture, I propose here to discuss the assemblage of networked digital information and humans in relation to globalization. I intend by this combination of humans and machines to designate not prosthesis, not a machinic addition to an already complete human being, but an intimate mixing of human and machine that constitutes an interface outside the subject-object binary.[2] I address the relation of this interface or assemblage to globalization because I continue to sense that those most widely read writers about digital media (John Perry Barlow, Nicholas Negroponte, and even Pierre Lévy, for example) do not give one confidence of a critical adroitness regarding globalization. By the same token, those most impressive thinkers who write about the economic and political aspects of globalization (I have mentioned Hardt and Negri already) sometimes appear shaky and uncertain about the technological side of the assemblage of digital information and humans.[3] In pursuit of the double objective of new media and globalization, I hope to sustain three arguments about the assemblage of networked digital information and humans:

1. They are an evolving, unavoidable, and central aspect of globalization.
2. They contain countless challenges and at the same time afford considerable resources for highly dangerous prevailing agglomerations of power.
3. They offer serious points of resistance to those powers and may serve as a base for developing auspicious, decentralized, multicultural global networks.

These theses are mutually related, sustainable only together.

One problem facing the would-be analyst of globalization and new media must be indicated from the outset: the assemblage of networked digital information and humans is neither one of subjects nor one of objects. The global economy, by contrast, may be understood as the sum of countless human practices in which machines are used as tools, as a myriad of rules, institutions, and habits that to some extent change over time. But if we look at the planetary media as partially distinct from the global economy, a different picture emerges. The assemblage of networked digital information and humans is a concept that presumes the intertwining of humans and machines to such an extent that properly speaking one cannot locate in it a position that resembles that of a subject or that of an object. Language theory of the past century has been important in conceptualizing this relation because it is one of the few models that capture the mutual construction of speaker and cultural system at the point of enunciation without resort to the freedom-determinism binary of ontologies that inscribe subjects and objects. Neither determinism nor transcendentalism is helpful in articulating the practices of networked digital information and human assemblages. There is no determinism and no freedom, properly speaking, in this cultural and practical world. Instead, in addition to the linguistic theories of structuralism and poststructuralism, one would do best to turn to concepts such as autopoiesis in Humberto Maturana and Francisco Varela (Maturana and Varela 1980) and the idea of emergence in Steve Johnson's sense (Johnson 2001), however much these categories might differ from each other. The phrase "assemblages of networked digital information and humans" presupposes the presence of humans and machines, subject to certain constraints, to be sure, but impervious at important levels to critiques from vantage points that presume a stable field of subjects that act on the world and objects that are manipulated by that action, in short, to many modernist perspectives. There are numerous complex difficulties and discrepancies at play in the positions I have alluded to, but I cannot do justice to them here.[4] I indicate them at this juncture only to signal the recognition of a point of rupture from certain habits of mind that might be invoked in response to what I have to say.

One more caveat is in order before I begin. I use the terms *global* and *planetary* without apology. Many scholars today prefer the term *transnational* to refer to the processes I invoke with the term *global* (Grewal and Kaplan 2001). They favor the transnational because it stresses the asymmetries of globalization and suggests the emergence of a new form of neocolonialism. Others point out, however, that the term *transnationalism* may underplay the utopian horizon of current planetary processes in an overly cautious resonance that is better expressed by terms such as *postcolonial* and *postnational* (Rowe 2003). I stick, perhaps perversely, with *globalization* precisely for its troubled and troubling association with economic activities that routinely cross national frontiers. I aspire to take back the term *global* from the free marketeers and new-millennium imperialists. The term *global* suggests both a crossing and mixing of cultures and the installation of a new level of politics and culture somewhat outside preexisting instances and in problematic relation to them.

THE VIRTUAL AND THE MATERIAL

The global network treats information differently from the manner with which we are familiar from the experience of earlier media. Instead of flows of information from a discrete number of fixed points that are produced by known economic entities, regulated by established nation-states, and announced by published schedules of programming, the Net is an amorphous, myriad constellation of ever-changing locations and facilities that are subject to fundamental alteration by anonymous, undesignated, unsalaried, and unauthorized users. The defeat of copy protection on DVDs by a program posted to the Net by a fifteen-year-old in Norway (Jon Johansen) and the creation of a program to exchange files by an eighteen-year-old American (Shawn Fanning) sent the film industry and the music industry reeling into hysterical disorder. The Davids in this case are small and young; the Goliaths are huge, powerful, and rich, having at their disposal resources that habitually undermine democracy with payoffs, bribes, and influence peddling. These examples of defeating copy protection and proliferating file transfers between peers are well known and could be multiplied many times in the relatively short history of the global network. Their implications need to be examined seriously because they are both unprecedented and point to unique properties of the Net. Here I want only to mention them as a reminder of the truly novel circumstance of networked computing.

Digital machines, however much they have been supported by military institutions around the world and however much they have been appropriated for pecuniary purposes by economic organizations, have been developed in the university and have been designed, as the dictates of cybernetic theory and academic computer science culture prescribe, to transfer information as quickly and efficiently as possible and with minimal interference or noise from *any* source. The culture of computer programming developed consequently with no attention at all to such basic questions as who is authorized to speak, when, to whom, and what may be said on these occasions. Such rules, we can reasonably speculate, have accompanied every instance of human communications since its inception with the emergence of the human species. But these restraints are not aspects of the design of digital machines. Certainly there was an oversight here, and it is a fateful one indeed. These machines have not been engineered to kill people, and they have not been built with the intention to generate income, although under certain conditions they can do both. To accomplish their purposes of speed and efficiency, digital machines departed from the comparatively slow regions of spoken voice and writing by translating numbers, then text, then images and sound, into an electronic region governed by physical rules that are far different from those of voice and writing. When one participates in the Net, in whatever capacity and regardless of the apparent normality of the practice, one cannot avoid communicating by means of a highly novel underlying material structure. Online the user may not care about this or may not be conscious of it, but using a networked computer means deploying zeros and ones moving, in principle, near the speed of light, a very different physical world from that of the spoken voice or the printed page.

The consequence of culture transformed into electronic digits is that the world has turned upside down, with many of our assumptions put into question about time and space, body and mind, human and machine, subject and object, gender, race, and class. When an unknown high school student from a remote part of the world e-mails you with questions about a term paper, or when you receive a virus that destroys weeks of work, or when a long forgotten relative communicates with you out of the blue to renew the ties of kinship, or when hundreds of spam messages appear in your in-boxes, in these and countless other instances you are at the tip of the iceberg, for better or for worse, of new conditions of culture. You are as close, in time and space, to a high school student in Taiwan as you are to a long lost relative in Des Moines and to a neighbor next door. When these events occur, we are as helpless in defining the communicative action as a hammer is when being deployed to bang a nail into wood. When a word-processing program automatically corrects our spelling errors or indicates a grammatical flaw in our writing, we are as ignorant as a second grader and as well informed in language use as the dictionary and the grammar book. So consequential is the bundling of culture with digital machines that many observers refuse to apply to it the term *reality* and instead favor the vague adjective "virtual."[5] Nothing has really changed in all of this, but everything is somehow different or virtual.

Digital conditions of culture mean that the creation of works, their unlimited reproduction, and infinite distribution are functions at the disposal of everyone who has access to networked computers. Digital culture enables the transformation of any text, image, or sound, so that fixed objects like books and films—a fixity that has been taken for granted in modernity—are no longer default features of art. Digital conditions of cultural life also bypass physically determined identities, including disabilities (even paraplegics can communicate on computers), bodily characteristics, ethnic origins, national citizenship. And all of this in principle occurs with no external authority or censor. Networked digital information and human assemblages thus vastly transform the fundamental conditions of culture and vastly expand the characteristics of the population of those who participate in it. Complaints that the Net inundates everyone with information overload should be understood as the statement of those who are comfortable with earlier restrictions on who speaks, to whom, when, as well as with the content of what may be said. These guardians of culture, as we know, have been predominantly, though by no means exclusively, middle-aged, middle-class, white males. For this grouping in particular, perhaps, the cultural conditions are challenging, but nonetheless even they become inured to them. And, let us recall, all of this change depends on the condition of the digital—the shift to the electronic format of zeros and ones or the on-off switch. It is pointless to bemoan or to celebrate the new conditions; one must instead work to comprehend critically their limits and affordances.

VIRTUAL EMPIRE

To translate these cultural conditions into an understanding of their implications for planetary politics and to relate the spread of networked digital information and human assemblages to other globalizing trends and to do so from a critical perspective is a daunting task. If the job is intimidating, it is also essential. Jean-Luc Nancy explicates well the enormity of the task:

> Create the world means: immediately, without delay, to reopen each possible struggle for a world, that is to say, for what must constitute the opposition to the unjust globalization that has its basis in the general equivalent. But this struggle must be led precisely in the name of what this world is not, that it is without precedent and without model, without principle and without pre-given purposes, and it is exactly this that constitutes justice and the meaning of the world. (Nancy 2002, 63)

The word world must be given a new sense, and this in critical relation to globalization.

We must then express our gratitude to Michael Hardt and Antonio Negri for their effort to begin this discussion with their works simply entitled Empire and Multitude.[6] While others such as Castells have presented critical overviews of the economic and social aspects of globalization, Hardt and Negri stand out in theorizing the political dimension of that phenomenon, although they are certainly not alone in addressing it.[7] Hardt and Negri's work has deservedly excited widespread interest and, as might be expected, much criticism.[8] In what follows, I attempt to revise their thesis in light of my understanding of networked digital information and human assemblages.[9] But my critical remarks ought not to be taken as in any way diminishing my appreciation of the fundamental advance of Hardt and Negri in conceptualizing the new situation of globalization.[10]

Hardt and Negri define Empire as "a new form of sovereignty . . . that effectively regulates . . . global exchanges" (xi). Certainly global exchanges have increased dramatically in the late twentieth century, and certainly some new forms of power that will attempt to control those exchanges are in process of formation. How developed these new forms of power have become is surely a debatable issue. For some, it is too soon to begin to define such types of power. To Hardt and Negri's credit, they persevere nonetheless. Like Marx, who theorized industrial capitalism in the mid-nineteenth century when it barely existed as a form of economic organization and activity, Hardt and Negri investigate empire as an emergent phenomenon. Only the most hidebound positivist—one who insists on examining only those realities that are numerically extensive—would deny the world-historical significance of what Hardt and Negri study. Even if little actual power exists outside the clutch of nation-states in the post-national configurations that Hardt and Negri term "Empire," what happens in this germinating realm is far more portentous than the ongoing party politics of Tweedledum and Tweedledee as they are breathlessly and scrupulously reported in every major media in every nation-state, and this 24/7. But even if we acknowledge the emergence of Empire there remains a problem with the way Hardt and Negri conceptualize it: they regard Empire as a "political subject," indicating to me that already there is a theoretical difficulty in their formulation, since, as I have argued, the information component of global exchanges does not fit well into the subject-object dichotomy. But let us first explore further their understanding of Empire.

Hardt and Negri's Empire is different from earlier large political groupings of power, since it is truly global and thereby "deterritorializes" older political forms such as the nation-state. Also unlike the nation-state, Empire is "decentered" or not specifiable by markers of land. Instead of being rooted in earthly territory, Empire is instituted as communication networks. "Empire," they contend, "manages hybrid identities, flexible hierarchies, and plural exchanges through modulating networks of command" (xiii). Empire is thus postmodern, but it is also, as they argue, virtual. For Hardt and Negri, Empire "appears in the form of a very high tech machine: it is virtual" (39). Hardt and Negri metaphorically transfer the attributes of "a very high tech machine" to their concept of Empire. But the term "high tech" or even "very high tech" is too vague. They undoubtedly do not mean very high tech machines such as a nuclear reactor or a linear accelerator. One senses in their use of this term a basic unfamiliarity with "high tech." There is nothing necessarily "virtual" about "high tech." If they mean that Empire is not territorial in the sense that the nation-state was territorial, then they may be referring to the organizational quality of Empire that is like some high-tech corporations (not machines) because these firms structure themselves nonhierarchically and are not centered in territorial space. Such companies consist of networks in multiple locations that are flexible and easily alterable. Hardt and Negri might intend therefore to characterize Empire as a virtual corporation.[11]

If, on the contrary, "high tech machine" refers to the Internet, then its material structure is not at all virtual, consisting as it does of a quite material myriad of wires, cables, and communication satellites connected to millions of computers, each of which is indeed locatable in space. The Internet is virtual not in its lack of territoriality but in its departure from space-time configurations associated with earlier forms of communication, its migration from the Newtonian registers of time and space to the microelectronic level of on-off switches. It affords virtual presence in the sense that it reduces distance and time factors in communication almost to zero. The vagueness and near total lack of examples [12] about information technology in *Empire* and *Multitude* seriously obscure the efficacy of Hardt and Negri's argument. [13]

The conceptual sloppiness of Hardt and Negri in using the term *virtual* is more than a minor oversight. Networked digital information and human assemblages are central to their thesis concerning Empire, and their deficient understanding of digital technology seriously detracts from their work. They argue in *Empire* that the crucial aspect of Empire is the formation of new subjectivities, which, in turn, might be the basis for a new counter-Empire. These subjectivities, they assert, are at least in part a direct consequence of networked digital information and human assemblages: "In this new world of communicative media and networks, the mechanisms of modern sovereignty were no longer sufficient to rule the new subjectivities" (251). Or in another formulation, they write: "Today we participate in a more radical and profound commonality than has ever been experienced in the history of capitalism. The fact is that we participate in a productive world made up of communication and social networks, interactive services, and common languages. Our economic and social reality is defined less by the material objects that are made and consumed than by co-produced services and relationships. Producing increasingly means constructing cooperation and communicative commonalities" (302). Instead of specifying the precise mechanisms by which "new subjectivities" are formed through "media and networks," Hardt and Negri, predisposed as neo-Marxists to a production-based model, discover a postmodern economy centered on new media: "In postmodernity the social wealth accumulated is increasingly immaterial; it involves social relations, communication systems, information, and affective networks"

(258). Here again one must object to the characterization of postmodern social wealth as "immaterial."

There is nothing immaterial about networked digital information systems. In fact, as I have argued, it is precisely the new *form* of materiality, its electronic and machine-level language, that enables these systems to work the way they do. Only ignorance about new media allows one to characterize them as "immaterial." One cannot develop a critical theory of new media if one begins from the assumption that they are somehow immaterial. Only by recognizing the *specificity* of the materiality of new media can one assess the potentials for critique and the risks of appropriation by established orders of domination that might be developed around them. Instead, Hardt and Negri, beholden to a Marxist opposition of labor power and information technologies, attempt to attribute to labor the qualities at play in new communication systems. They write: "The only configurations of capital able to thrive in the new world will be those that adapt to and govern the new immaterial, cooperative, communicative, and affective composition of labor power" (276). In such a scenario, the critique of capital in the "new world" of Empire is comfortably returned to the labor process and confined therein, however much this labor process is expanded and redefined. This analysis misses precisely what is new about networked digital information systems: the (laboring) human is connected with the information machine in a manner that disrupts the subject-object binary and calls for new categories of thought. These must be developed before critique may be elaborated.[14]

The critical theory of Empire does, it must be acknowledged, heed in some ways the integration of humans with machines in the condition of postmodernity. Hardt and Negri are well aware of the theory of the cyborg, at least in Donna Haraway's version, which they cite (Haraway 1985). Their exposition of cyborg theory pretends to account for altered conditions but remains rooted in a subject theory of the human. They write: "Interactive and cybernetic machines become a new prosthesis integrated into our bodies and minds and a lens through which to redefine our bodies and minds themselves. The anthropology of cyberspace is really a recognition of the new human condition" (291). However, if cyborg theory is correct, it follows that there can be no "anthropology of cyberspace" as they claim but rather a post-anthropology of the human-machine interface.[15] If, as Hardt and Negri contend, "in the passage to the informational economy, the assembly line has been replaced by *the network* as the organizational model of production" (295), then one must contrast the relation of humans to machines in the industrial period of the Fordist assembly line, where dead labor is alienated from living labor, with that of the network, where humans monitor and work in conjunction with computers (Zuboff 1988). And one must ask if there is not a fundamental shift, in the age of Empire, to a realm beyond production, as it appears in the age of industry, to one that might more appropriately be characterized as a realm of culture. Production may be understood as the use of tools to transform natural materials into commodities. Contemporary work increasingly takes the contrasting form of designing objects, inventing sales pitches, monitoring computers that regulate production, and deploying programs that administer the movement of the objects from the factory to the consumer. These symbol-manipulating practices might well be termed "culture."[16]

The understanding of networked digital information and human assemblages must not become the basis for a new totalization or metanarrative. However compelling the new media may be, they do not constitute the only basis for understanding contemporary conditions, and they are not the only component of the larger process of globalization. While networked digital information and human assemblages are implicated in other aspects of globalization such as the demographic and the economic, they must not be confused with them. Finance capital, for instance, may have changed a great deal by going online, but there remain fundamental features of it which are not affected by digitalization. Hardt and Negri too easily and too much expand the reach of new media, and they do so with language derived from the analysis of an earlier social world. In this respect, they write in *Empire*: "Empire takes form when language and communication, or really when *immaterial labor* and cooperation, become the dominant productive force. The *superstructure* is put to work, and the universe we live in is a universe of *productive linguistic networks*" (385; italics mine). Statements of this kind do as much to obscure the processes they refer to as to point to new avenues of investigation. "Superstructure," "immaterial labor," "productive linguistic networks"—these terms conceal more than they reveal about the mechanisms of power at play in networked digital information and human assemblages. The planetary system that is rapidly emerging is enabled by discourses and practices that are coupled with specific technologies, as well as by complex movements of populations and economic reorganizations.

At the heart of Empire rests an analysis that derives not from Marx but from Foucault and Deleuze. Hardt and Negri narrate the emergence of Empire as a change in mechanisms of power from societies of discipline to societies of control. The thesis that a new mode of political power is coming into being—Empire—replacing the nation-state, requires a new mode of social regulation. Just as Foucault succeeded in defining the technology of power commensurate with the nation-state, Hardt and Negri contend, so Deleuze accomplished the same task for Empire. Networked digital information and human assemblages again play a central role in this process. Hardt and Negri's ability to theorize these media is crucial to the success of their effort.

Foucault, especially in Discipline and Punish and to a somewhat lesser extent in The History of Sexuality, Volume 1, outlined the combination of discourses and practices that effectively constructed the modern subject. The prison, the workshop, the school, the hospital, and the military all relied on confining architectures to operate on the individual, in varying ways, so as to instill a form of discipline by which the subjects, acting independently and regarding themselves as free, conformed to the utilitarian calculus of the culture of modern industrial, democratic society. Discipline imposed on the body and mind of each subject a "rational" regime of possible action in which identity was fixed, stable, and unified. Here we have Freud's description of the self-understanding of the ego in Victorian morality as allegedly "the captain of the soul" and the proud individualist of Western society, thinking himself autonomous. This individual, to some the glowing achievement of Western civilization, might participate in law, democracy, private-enterprise economics, and nuclear families, but only on the cultural premise of discipline, of having been constructed as a subject in specific architectural spaces. Foucault, quoting Samuel Beckett, dreamed of an escape from such disciplined identity formations into another language system, in which the basic premise would be "What does it matter who speaks?" [17]

A decade later, Deleuze opined that discipline no longer required spaces of confinement. Borrowing a term from William Burroughs, Deleuze dubbed the new system of power "control societies." Deleuze writes: "*Control societies* are taking over from disciplinary societies. 'Control' is the name proposed by Burroughs to characterize the new monster" (Deleuze 1995, 178). In *Naked Lunch*, a meditation on drug addiction, Burroughs obsesses about control both by addicts and by the U.S. government (Burroughs 1993). Deleuze's use of the term does not seem to harmonize nicely with that of Burroughs, especially because Deleuze relates "control" to the widespread deployment of computers by government and corporations, a technology that was at best nascent in 1959 when *Naked Lunch* appeared. Burroughs, in his introduction to the novel, asserts that drug addiction and especially the "hysterical" response it evokes by the government are leading social concerns: "The junk virus is public health problem number one of the world today" (11). Virus as metaphor might equally claim adjectival place with control in the sense that Deleuze indicates. He writes, for example, "Control societies function . . . with information technology and computers, where the passive danger is noise and the active, piracy and viral contamination" (Deleuze 1995, 180). The metaphor of the virus has the advantage of suggesting the networked quality of new types of domination, whereas *control* is a less-precise term and might equally apply to other, precomputerized social systems.[18]

Nor does Deleuze advance very far in characterizing the control aspect of the control society. In his brief piece from 1990, the much-discussed essay "Postscript on Societies of Control," Deleuze emphasizes, rather, the absence of confining spatial arrangements in the exercise of domination afforded by the use of computer technology. "What has changed," in the formulation of Deleuze's argument by Hardt and Negri, "is that, along with the collapse of the institutions, the disciplinary dispositifs have become less limited and bounded spatially in the social field. Carceral discipline, school discipline, factory discipline, and so forth interweave in a hybrid production of subjectivity" (Hardt and Negri 2000, 330). From the individuality constructed by disciplinary technologies of power, we have moved to the "dividuality" or multiplicity of subject formation in the societies of control (Colwell 1996). Beyond the different results of subject formation and the negative trait of the absence of "major organizing sites of confinement" (Deleuze 1995, 177), control societies are, in this text, maddeningly undefined. Deleuze discusses the control society again in "Having an Idea in Cinema" (Deleuze 1998), but he is once more both brief and vague, only adding to his previous discussion that since "information is precisely the system of control" (17), "counter-information" becomes a form of resistance (18). All of which suggests to me that Deleuze's understanding of networked digital information and human assemblages remains rudimentary. It is hard to imagine what "counter-information" might be, for example. Does he mean that critical content is resistance? Or does the form of the critical content constitute resistance?

It might seem logical to conclude from the binary terms "societies of discipline" and "societies of control" that Deleuze places himself in opposition to Foucault, or at least that he sees himself going beyond Foucault by discerning forms of domination not recognized by the historian of the Panopticon. Yet such is not at all the case. Instead Deleuze proclaims his agreement with Foucault, citing Burroughs again as the fulcrum of the matter. Deleuze writes: "Foucault agrees with Burroughs who claims that our future will be controlled rather than disciplined" (Deleuze 1992b, 164). But Deleuze gives no evidence that Foucault anticipated a transformation to societies of control, relegating discipline to the garbage can of history. It would appear that Deleuze was unwilling to position himself as the thinker who went beyond Foucault, even as, in the same paragraph just cited, Deleuze compellingly characterizes the break between the two orders of domination. In the following passage, Deleuze insists that Foucault adopts the notion of societies of control: "The disciplines which Foucault describes are the history of what we gradually cease to be, and our present-day reality takes on the form of dispositions of overt and continuous *control* in a way which is very different from recent closed disciplines" (ibid.).

Deleuze's stadial theory, moving from discipline to control, also suffers from being far too linear in character. Elements of "control" existed in Europe in the early modern period as the state hired spies to keep track of suspected miscreants. Equally forms of "discipline" proliferate in the twenty-first century as the United States, for example, erects more and more prisons under the so-called "get tough" policies of recent and current administrations. The shift from discipline to control also is Eurocentric, overlooking the very different disposition of these state strategies in the southern hemisphere. Françoise Vergès points out, for example, that "in postcolonial Reunion, these two strategies have concurrently occurred. New types of sanction, education, and care have constructed a web of control around the Creoles, and along with the creation of a vast social network of control, there has been a multiplication of prisons, a criminalization and psychologization of politics" (Vergès 1999, 219). Deleuze's model of control as the next stage after discipline thus overlooks different deployments of technologies of power, betraying problems at numerous levels.

In an essay from 1998, Michael Hardt attempts to explicate the concept of societies of control beyond what Deleuze has given us. He asserts that, as the chief new form of power, "The metaphorical space of the societies of control is perhaps best characterized by the shifting desert sands, where positions are continually swept away; or better, the smooth surfaces of cyberspace, with its infinitely programmable flows of codes and information" (Hardt 1998, 32). Smooth surfaces are opposed to striated planes, categories one recalls from A Thousand Plateaus that designate respectively homogeneous and heterogeneous spaces (Deleuze and Guattari 1987). But Hardt overlooks the side of cyberspace that resists the power formation of control society, all kinds of spaces in which copyright law, fixed identities, censorship, and so forth are continuously evaded and challenged. Cyberspace is hardly Hardt's smooth surface of transparency and control, but rather a highly differentiated field of resistance, conflict, and uncertainty.

For Hardt, control societies are "smooth" because civil society has collapsed, rendering the social lacking in mediations. Hardt analyzes the dialectic of civil society from Hegel to Foucault, concluding that "what has come to an end, or more accurately declined in importance in post-civil society, then, are precisely these functions of mediation or education and the institutions that gave them form" (Hardt 1998, 36). Foucault's disciplinary institutions have lost their ability to position and give identity to individuals. Replacing the spaces of confinement, according to Hardt, are the media. But again one must object: the media are also mediating, albeit in a different form from the older establishments like education and the family. What is lacking in Hardt's understanding of the move from discipline to control is precisely an analysis of the media as technologies of power. Surely media are different from prisons, schools, and so forth, but one must understand the specificity of the media as structuring systems, as well as pay attention to the difference of media from one another. Television, print, and the Internet are each a disciplinary institution, in this sense, different from each other but also similar to prisons in that they construct subjects, define identities, position individuals, and configure cultural objects. True enough, media do not require spatial arrangements in the manner of workshops and prisons, but humans remain fixed in space and time, at the computer, in front of the television set, walking or bicycling through city streets or riding on a subway with headphones and an MP3 player or a cell phone. I refer to this configuration of the construction of the subject as a "superpanopticon" to indicate its difference from modern institutions (Poster 1990). The term "control society" suffers from the disadvantage of only a limited ability to capture the new technologies of power.

In the more recent work *Multitude*, Hardt and Negri alter somewhat their earlier reliance on Deleuze's notion of societies of control by claiming that a third form of power has emerged in relation to Empire, biopower. Biopower is of course a concept developed by Foucault, most notably perhaps in *The History of Sexuality, Volume 1* and also in *Society Must Be Defended*. Hardt and Negri then return to Foucault, bypassing Deleuze, to present a new characterization of the type of power found in Empire. Here they resort to Foucault's argument that alongside but separate from the development of discipline in modern society went another form of power that he first called "governmentality" but later biopower, a form of power that emanates from nation-states to control populations. Hardt and Negri expand this type of power to argue that Empire produces social relations: "What is produced . . . is not just material goods but actual social relations and forms of life. We will call this kind of production '*biopolitical*'" (94). According to Hardt and Negri, Foucault's concept of biopower disposed of life and decided who will die, whereas in Empire, biopower "rules over life, producing and reproducing all aspects of society" (ibid.). Regardless of the validity of this distinction between Foucault's version of biopower and Hardt and Negri's, *Multitude* makes much of biopower as a critical basis for the multitude to transform Empire into democracy. The relation of biopower to networked computing, however, remains largely unexplored by Hardt and Negri.

Hardt ignores versions of civil society different from Hegel's where institutions are viewed mainly as supporting the state. Jürgen Habermas (1989), for example, argues that places such as coffeehouses and salons constitute an aspect of civil society by promoting the formation of critical reason, thereby suspending some of the inequalities that militate against free speech and other democratic rights. In this case, a public sphere is formed within civil society that fosters resistance to formal institutions of the state. One might well argue that some media promote such a public sphere. If television detracts from critical reason by short-circuiting dialogue in its broadcast model of transmission, the Internet in part at least provides interactive spaces where critical reason might flourish, most notably perhaps in blogs. Usenet, chat rooms, e-mail, Listservs, instant messaging, and other functions of cyberspace arguably also promote interactive dialogue that might contribute to a new civil society, a new public sphere. I argue that Habermas's position overlooks important differences between proximate speech and life online such as body positioning and space-time configurations (Poster 2001). Yet the issue of new technologies and civil society is at least worth considering. One might contend, along with Jodi Dean (2001), that media afford contexts for differential public spheres, ones not limited by the Western regime of rationality. The absence of this question in Hardt and Negri's book is regrettable.

POSTMODERN IDENTITIES

An index of the ambivalence of Hardt and Negri about the role of new information technologies in control society is the opposing depictions the reader finds in *Empire* of the postmodern self. Hardt and Negri first assume the familiar Marxist stance against the liberatory potentials of the postmodern figure of multiple subjectivity. Hardt and Negri compliment postmodern theory for its critique of modernity but fault it as being confused about "the forms of power that today have come to supplant it." The postmodernists, in their eyes, "are still waging battle against the shadows of old enemies" (142). Hardt and Negri continue with a strong judgment against postmodern theory: "The affirmation of hybridities and the free play of differences across boundaries, however, is liberatory only in a context where power poses hierarchy exclusively through essential identities, binary divisions, and stable oppositions. The structures and logics of power in the contemporary world are entirely immune to the 'libera-tory' weapons of the postmodernist politics of difference. In fact, Empire too is bent on doing away with those modern forms of sovereignty and on setting differences to play across boundaries" (142). In other words, post-modern theory's affirmation of contingent identities is just what the doc-tor ordered for Empire. In the new "flexible" post-Fordist regime of "just in time" production with zero inventories, the traditional stable identi-ties characteristic of workers with long careers with one firm no longer make sense. Capitalism now requires workers to retool their skills, change careers, move to new locations, migrate from their homelands as the eco-nomic moment requires. For Hardt and Negri, postmodern identities are a happy coincidence that matches the new conditions of production.

If postmodern identities are conservative in the context of Empire, then why, one might ask, do Hardt and Negri pin their hopes of resistance on precisely such mobile, fragmented selves? In their controversial and hotly disputed concept of the multitude as revolutionary agent, they para-doxically include as characteristics of this agent none other than typically postmodern traits.[19] First, they make the very postmodern move of privi-leging language in the question of politics: "The first aspect of the telos of the multitude has to do with the senses of language and communi-cation. . . . The control over linguistic sense and meaning and the net-works of communication becomes an ever more central issue for political struggle" (404). Hardt and Negri then characterize the new revolution-ary subject, "the multitude," in the postmodern terms of Homi Bhabha as hybrid: "The hybridization of human and machine is no longer a process that takes place only on the margins of society; rather, it is a fundamental episode at the center of the constitution of the multitude and its power" (405). What emerges in *Empire*, then, is a most confusing picture of the multitude or revolutionary agent as both symptoms of postmodern con-ditions and the cause of the future transformation of Empire.[20]

This confusion, I contend, stems from the inability of Hardt and Ne-gri adequately to theorize networked digital information and human as-semblages (and media more generally). Their understanding of Empire continually verges toward an analysis of new media but splits into an iden-tification of the Internet with Empire and a utopian attribution of cyber-space to the multitude. *Empire* fails, in my view, to open a double analysis of the work of new media in global processes, one that would indicate how existing forces such as the nation-state and the globalizing economy attempt to appropriate new media to their ends, and at the same time analyze how the unique communicational architecture of the Internet affords potentials for global forms of political organization from below.

In the end, Samuel Beckett's "What does it matter who speaks?" poses the challenge of a planetary system of networked information machines and human assemblages. Until we develop a critical theory that is able to raise this question in our media context, we cannot expect to contribute significantly to the formation of a discourse of postnational democratic forms of power.

MULTITUDES: A CONCLUSION

Hardt and Negri search for resistance to Empire in the countenance of a subject: the multitude. They write: "The new transversal mobility of disciplined labor power is significant because it indicates a real and powerful search for freedom and the formation of new, nomadic desires that cannot be contained and controlled within the disciplinary regime" (253). A critical theory of globalization, I argue to the contrary, to the extent that it explores media, must look not for a revolutionary subject but for a matrix of dispositifs, for a cluster of technologies of power that constructs networked computing and human assemblages that might, after they are extensively deployed, act in a fashion that transforms Empire into a planetary system outside the nation-state and capitalist market and toward what might still be labeled radical democracy (Laclau 1990). Hardt and Negri have given us instead an updated Jacobinism or Leninism, the movements that overthrew precapitalist regimes and brought us into modern society. The question of how to get beyond modern society can by no means simply assume that a new subject needs to be designated that replaces les sans culottes of the eighteenth century and the workers' councils of the twentieth. Instead the issue rests with information machine–human assemblages and their historical trajectory.

In *Multitude* they admit freely that the revolutionary subject that will transform Empire into "an absolute democracy" does not yet exist. It requires a project, radical democracy, to bring it into existence: "The multitude needs a political project to bring it into existence" (Hardt and Negri

2004, 212). In response to the numerous criticisms directed at the concept of multitude in *Empire*, the follow-up volume of 2004 attempts to clarify how resistance to Empire might emerge. To this end, Hardt and Negri present an extensive analysis to prove that the multitude is unlike "the people" or the revolutionary agent of modernity. The multitude is for them specific to the global regime of Empire and to current conditions of capitalist production.

One important example they use to illustrate the postmodern qualities of the multitude is relevant to my analysis of new media and globalization. Hardt and Negri turn to the phenomenon of open-source software as an example of how "an open-source society" might come into being. They write in *Multitude*: "One approach to understanding the democracy of the multitude . . . is open source society, that is, a society whose source code is revealed so that we all can work collaboratively to solve its bugs and create new, better social programs" (340). Instead of closed software programs on the model of Microsoft and Apple, programs may include their "source" so that any programmer can introduce changes and redistribute the altered version. The Linux operating system, the Apache server program, and Mozilla's Firefox Web browser are a few successful examples of open-source software. As Pierre Lévy (1997) argues, the Internet as a whole is the best example of "collective intelligence," of the creation of a vast cultural object primarily from the bottom up, from the contribution of potentially all human beings. Hardt and Negri's example of open-source software moves in the right direction for an analysis of the relation of new media to the multitude but clearly does not go far enough in exploring the radical potentials of the Internet as a locus of resistance to Empire.

Yet Hardt and Negri have opened the door to a critical theory of cyberspace and a trenchant critique of the emergence of a new form of power, Empire, in the context of globalization. In the next chapter, I will assess, in the spirit of a revised Hardt and Negri understanding of globalization, the figure of the citizen, drawing attention to its limits as a subject position appropriate to a networked planetary democracy.

4

CITIZENS, DIGITAL MEDIA, AND GLOBALIZATION

Paradoxical as it may appear, isn't it through the rights of man that transpires today—
at a planetary level—the worst discriminations?
—Jean Baudrillard, *Mots de passe*

With these words, Jean Baudrillard suggests that the doctrine of the rights of man, which intends to empower individuals in relation to governments, becomes, in the context of globalization, a discourse that legitimizes the hegemony of the Western nations, especially the United States, in relation to non-Western societies. "The worst discriminations," to use his phrase, are those that enable the West to impose its economic leverage and political will against nations with less-developed industrial structures and weaker systems of military protection. Western activists in the human rights movement deploy the doctrine of natural rights to rescue victims primarily in non-Western societies. From the non-Western point of view, it may appear that the human rights movement is yet another imposition from the dominant other. Certainly Baudrillard does not wish to diminish the importance of the work of human rights activists. Yet he calls attention to the way this same doctrine may also work to undermine the ability of non-Western governments to stem the process of globalization in which, perhaps as a secondary effect, the West imposes its culture on the rest. Baudrillard sounds a warning: with the increasing integration of economic activity and the increasing exchange of cultural forms and practices, the conventional political wisdom of liberal societies may no longer hold sway.

Here I revisit another hallmark of Western political ideology—the concept of the citizen—and ask if this mainstay of democratization also has effects today that tarnish its antiauthoritarian credentials. The concepts of the citizen and natural rights are closely connected and derive from the same democratizing movements that arose in the eighteenth century. The Declaration of the Rights of Man and the Citizen is a monument from the French Revolution of 1789 that binds natural rights discourse with the idea of citizenship in a partnership that has proved its worth against monarchical tyrannies during the past two centuries not only in the United States and Europe but in Latin America and other locations. Human rights and citizenship are tied together and reinforce each other in the battle against the ruling classes. If rights are asserted in simply being human, the Declaration also posits that this is not enough: there must also be something called "citizenship." Human rights, as Jacques Derrida (1986) argued in the case of the American Declaration of Independence of 1776, come into existence in their enunciation, but also with the practical force of the mobilized population of "commoners." These rights are ensured by their inscription in constitutions that found governments, and they persist in their association with those governments as the ground of political authority.

Human rights, as a term, seems excessive: why not just rights of French people or Americans? The claim to the "human" by the French revolutionaries appears entirely unjustified and, indeed, unnecessary, except for a number of important considerations. First, "French rights" was a term in practice already occupied. Formally, the rights of France were the monarch's rights, true enough modified to ensure some provisions for certain other groups. French rights could be interpreted in a radical way: to contrast with rights actually possessed by the population at large or rights asserted as future possibilities by the population at large. This, after all, was the spirit of Abbé Sieyès's intervention in the revolutionary process when he claimed, in *What Is the Third Estate?* that the "people," not the king, were the referent of the term "France" or "the nation" (Sieyès 1789). But, second, the sum of particular existing or possible rights of French individuals did not serve the purpose of a revolution, did not constitute enough of a break with the past. It did not clean the slate of all the injuries and inequities that accumulated for the millennial reign of the ancien régime. Something was needed that would wipe away the regulations through which French people were defined as subjects of the monarchy and of the complex network of other authorities that crisscrossed the territory of France (in its various incarnations) during the ancien régime. The problem is that there was no basis in practice to assert and to institute a theory of rights that named any "real" group. One therefore had to leap beyond oneself, to become "human." Only by being human—not French, not Christian, not Burgundian—could rights be grounded. "Human" served as the foundation, but as an impossible foundation. The unfortunate fact of 1789 was that the referent to the signifier "human" existed in no more a substantial form (and perhaps even less so) than the term "god." Numerous, tragic exclusions were prescribed in the term "human" in 1789—as feminists, antirace theorists, and animal rights theorists have properly insisted. Two centuries later, the referent is returning.

The term "citizen" was required to be appended to the term "human" in 1789 for all these reasons. And for at least one more: the citizen was required both to produce in practice human rights and to contain those rights. The practice of the citizen realized human rights, which, once installed, filled in the content of citizenship. Karl Marx argued that the duality of the human and the citizen reflected in politics the split between the private and the public, between the bourgeois individual and the person engaged in political affairs.

> The rights of man as such are distinguished from the rights of the citizen. Who is this man distinguished from the citizen? None other than the member of civil society. Why is the member of civil society called "man," man without qualification, and why are his rights called the rights of man? How can we explain this? By the relation of the political state to civil society and by the nature of political emancipation. (Marx 1967, 234–35)

Marx goes on to show how private property, the economic relation, structures the political relation, rendering "man" not the "human" but the bourgeois (Balibar 1994, chapter 9, "What Is a Politics of the Rights of Man?"). Here I stress instead the inherent problem in the term "human rights": that it requires a string of supplements to account for its impossibility, and among these in 1789 is the "citizen" as practical realization of the human.

Étienne Balibar objects to Marx's understanding of the split between man and the citizen as one between the private person of civil society and the public person of political rights and practices. Instead Balibar argues that "man" points to the same referents as "citizen," that the two are really one. He contends that the conjunctive "and" standing between the two terms in the document signifies an identity, not a difference, an identity in what Balibar calls "equaliberty," a simultaneous proclamation that equality and liberty exist only together (Balibar 1994, 46–47). For Balibar, The Declaration of the Rights of Man and the Citizen announces a new, unified anthropology, a demand that the human emerge in the stage of world politics *with the rights of the citizen* and at the same time. This "reopening of the question of the identity between 'man' and 'citizen'" has as its purpose "to progress toward a citizenship overdetermined by anthropological difference, explicitly toward its transformation" (56). Balibar radicalizes the Declaration beyond its bourgeois determinations (as Marx saw them) into a general concept of "equaliberty" in the age of globalization. There is, he claims, "universal truth contained in the *Declaration* of 1789," that betokens "a *postmodern* epoch in which the question of going beyond the abstract or generic concept of man on the basis of generalized citizenship is posed" (59). He would have the term "citizen" labor greatly to signify democracy in the age of globalization. I wonder if it is up to the task.

In the present context, one must tread lightly and carefully in any critique of the limitations of these bulwarks of human freedom. Yet circumstances today present an extraordinary case of transcultural and planetary mixing. Although human beings have long ago migrated all over the planet and long ago engaged in travels and exchanges across localities, the density of global transactions today transmutes quantity into quality. A threshold has been passed, perhaps never to be reversed, in which the human species transacts among itself as never before, however unequally and unevenly, the spread of these practices. The conditions of globalization and networked media present a new register in which the human is recast and along with it the citizen. I now explore the question of the suitability of this term today as a democratizing sign, as a figure for the practice of the human.

Critical discourse currently locates an antagonism between globalization and citizenship. The deepening of globalizing processes strips the citizen of power, this position maintains. As economic processes become globalized, the nation-state loses its ability to protect its population. The citizen thereby loses her ability to elect leaders who effectively pursue her interests. When production facilities are dispersed beyond the nation, jobs are lost to foreigners, labor markets are affected by conditions in countries with highly unequal living standards, and capital flows, at the speed of light, to places of optimum returns, regardless of the disruptions and sufferings thereby enacted on the local population. Consumption is also planetary in scope, bringing across borders alien cultural assumptions as embodied in the flows of commodities. The popular need no longer be the local. Although foreign goods are inflected with community values and easily adapted to local conditions, they retain to some extent their quality as indexes of otherness. More dramatically still than production and consumption, nation-states are losing their cultural coherence because of planetary communications systems. Much of contemporary music is global music or at least a fusion of diverse musical cultures. Satellite technology and the Internet bring all media (especially television from the United States) across national boundaries as if those borders did not exist. Global processes run deep and wide, rendering problematic the figure of the citizen as a member of a limited national community. Such a critical discourse is difficult to refute.

In this conjuncture, the figure of the citizen is placed in a defensive position. If freedom inheres only to the citizen, then we must admit that in all likelihood freedom is lost or soon to be lost. I urge us to consider, against the defensive posture, an offensive one. We need to reconfigure the political individual in relation to conditions of globalization, to discover amid the troubling inequalities of North and South, and the unlimited appetite of corporate greed, a means to define a new form of power and a new means of association, perhaps, as Jacques Derrida writes, "a new international," one that is able to open a new horizon of freedom in the space of the Earth (Derrida 1994).

I want to suggest, in the spirit of this chapter's epigraph from Baudrillard, that Western concepts and political principles such as the rights of man and the citizen, however progressive a role they may have played in history, may not provide an adequate basis of critique in our current, increasingly global, condition. They may not provide, that is, a vehicle for thinking through and mobilizing a planetary democratic movement. This is so for several reasons. First is the simple fact that these principles derive from the West, and the West is responsible for an imperialist and capitalist form of globalization, a condition that detracts from the ability of these principles to catalyze truly global movements against domination and renders many suspicious of them from the start. Second, the situation today calls for democratic principles that include difference with universality, that cover the peoples of the Earth but acknowledge situational differences. Enlightenment principles are deficient here because they move to the universal too quickly, forgetting their conditions of possibility in an emergent bourgeoisie of the eighteenth century. In the rush to insist on democracy and humanity, in the intoxication with the idea of democracy, in the irrefutable radical quality of such ideas in the context of the waning of the ancien régime in Europe, the principles of natural rights required one to extract oneself from the social in order to proclaim the universal as natural. Third, today the natural no longer exists as an autonomous realm of self-determination. Today science and technology, as they are implemented through social institutions, constitute a "humanized" nature and in so doing bring forth a population of machines. The conditions of globalization are not only capitalism and imperialism: they include the coupling of human and machine. New democratizing principles must take into account the cultural construction of the human-machine interface. In short, we may build new political structures outside the nation-state only in collaboration with machines. The new "community" will not be a replica of the agora but will be mediated by information machines. What is required therefore is a doctrine of the rights of the human-machine interface.

Fourth, linked with machines in a global network, the citizen has become something else. The term is no longer a purely political designation. As Nestor Garcia Canclini argues, acts of consumption and acts of citizenship have, through the advance of the media, become increasingly merged:

> Men and women increasingly feel that many of the questions proper to citizenship—where do I belong, what rights accrue to me, how can I get information, who represents my interests?—are being answered in the private realm of commodity consumption and the mass media more than in the abstract rules of democracy or collective participation in public spaces.[1]

The separation between consumption and political activity characteristic of modern society has dissolved, and a new political culture emerges in which the two are combined. The strategies that individuals use in defining themselves as subjects occur, as Paul Mazursky shows in *Scenes from a Mall* (1991), in acts of consumption, as Nick (played by Woody Allen) and Deborah (played by Bette Midler) continually change after emerging from each store. Self-constitution of consumers spills over into politics as citizenship becomes an extension of consumption (Bratich et al. 2003).

What is more, as consumption has become political, so politics has become a mode of consumption. Candidates in election campaigns increasingly rely on media to reach their constituents. Political advertisements are the chief means of conducting campaigns. The primary means by which citizens obtain information about candidates is the television set, bringing politics to individuals in the same way they experience entertainment. The deep consumer culture of the television medium is merged with the electoral process. And celebrities from the domain of entertainment, a major aspect of consumption, become credible candidates for high office with no particular training or experience, as evidenced by the election of Ronald Reagan and Arnold Schwarzenegger as governors of California. We are indeed in a postmodern world of the consumer citizen.

INTERLUDE ON IDENTITY

One vision of a new form of citizenship, one joined with cultural and social difference, is offered by Steven Spielberg in his 1997 film *Amistad*. Let me explain what I mean by this surprising assertion and indicate why I think Spielberg's is not an adequate vision of new citizenship.

FIGURE 10. Busts of John Adams, George Washington, Thomas Jefferson, and Benjamin Franklin surround John Quincy Adams in court (still from *Amistad*)

Near the end of the film, John Quincy Adams (played by Anthony Hopkins) pleads before the Supreme Court of the United States for the lives of the African mutineers by arguing, against John Calhoun, a Southern advocate of slavery, that men are free by nature (see figure 10). Adams eloquently argues a liberal position while pointing for emphasis to a copy of the Declaration of Independence that hangs in the chambers. Resistance to slavery, he says, such as that of the accused and that which is inscribed in the historic document, is proof enough that men are free. Continuing his oration, Adams then switches to another line of argument, one provided him by Cinque (played by Djimon Hounsou), a member of the accused group. Shortly before the trial, Adams and Cinque speak to each other (through an interpreter). Upon learning from Adams that their case will be difficult to win, Cinque announces that he will invoke the tradition of all his ancestors in order to give him strength. The African, faced with an extreme danger, merges his identity with those of his forebears to achieve maximum solidity of self, or even a collective self.

The surprising move in the film is that Adams reproduces Cinque's traditionalism in the court. As he speaks to the justices about the natural freedom of humanity, he walks around the room gesturing to busts of past presidents, including that of his father, John Adams. John Quincy Adams supplements rational arguments for freedom with the traditions of liberty in the still young United States, amplifying the power of his own position by incorporating those of past leaders of democracy. These leaders, the audience hardly needs reminding, resisted slavery to England just as Cinque resisted and committed mutiny. Adams warns the justices that the identity of American citizens is at stake in the trial, that they must acquit the Africans in order to renew the nation in its commitment to freedom. What I find remarkable in this scene is its blending of liberal citizenship and traditional identity formation. In the magic of the movies, with its practice of montage, of making links that are difficult to experience outside the theater, Spielberg has his cake of natural-rights freedom and eats it too as individualist identity politics. We might say that today the figure of the citizen joins together the autonomous individuality of modernity with the postmodern neotraditionalism of identity politics. Is this most unseemly blend, we might ask, suitable to conditions of an emerging planetary politics of the twenty-first century? In particular, what is the fate of modern and postmodern political identity when communication takes place in the borderless world of the Internet?

NATION AND CITIZEN

The citizen as an autonomous being had been articulated as the nature of man in the Enlightenment, achieving its best expression in Descartes. A being separate from the world of material objects, defined by rationality, outside any social integument—this Cartesian subject was the prerequisite of the citizen. The complexities, difficulties, and ironies of this historic change are captured well by Balibar in his term "citizen subject." This subject was a transformation of the older "subject" of the monarchy, a relative and subordinated being, into an active, independent, and universal agent. The argument for such a radical redefinition of the term was accompanied, however, by the historical need to exclude women, children, slaves, and nonwhites more generally. The citizen subject, then, was of necessity somewhat indeterminate, a category between the universal and the empirical, at once real and effective enough to promote the making of a revolution but also contingent and empty enough a sign to remain a possibility for realization in the future.[2] The citizen subject came into being not as an emanation of a Cartesian idea but in the dilatory, imperfect forge of massive political transformation. Balibar defines the contingent element in the category of citizen as follows:

> That which appeared to us as the indetermination of the citizen . . . also manifests itself as the opening of a *possibility*: the possibility for any *given* realization of the citizen to be placed in question and destroyed by a

struggle for equality and thus for civil rights. But this possibility is not in the least a promise, much less an inevitability. Its concretization and explication depend entirely on an encounter between a statement and situations or movements that, from the point of view of the concept, are contingent. (Balibar 1991, 53)

To demonstrate the contingent nature of the figure of the citizen, Balibar traces the dialectical history of the citizen through its transformation during the period of the national welfare state. He depicts the expansion of the civil rights of the citizen during the twentieth century, through the class conflicts that come under the term *socialism*. What in the nineteenth century may have been the private domain of "man"—labor contracts, old-age benefits, health conditions, family reproductive practices—became in the twentieth century in much of Europe and the United States a question of citizenship. Balibar holds up this history to the mirror of the present, where the issue of immigration is hotly contested in France around the question of sub-Saharan Africans and North Africans from former colonies. He calls for a new expansion of citizenship, paradoxically, that is "without community." He urges a politics of citizenship for the global age in which no one could be excluded from citizenship and its rights owing to the community of their birth (Balibar 2001). But, notwithstanding Balibar's argument, I wonder if the term *citizen*, contingent though it has been, may continue to serve as the sign of the democratizing subject in the current conjuncture. While Balibar would reanimate the citizen against the gatekeeping tendency of the nation-state, I would question the continued viability of the term. Does the term *citizen* carry with it a baggage of connotations from Western history that render it parochial in the globalized present?

The issue of immigration, although general around the planet, is played out differently in each instance. Europe takes down its national borders to form a larger European Union that can compete economically with the United States and Japan. At the same time, regional struggles in the former Yugoslavia, the former Soviet Union, Ireland, the Basque region, Belgium, and elsewhere indicate tendencies toward new and smaller national units. In Western Europe, however, history introduces a new form of the return of the repressed: peoples of former European colonies tread on European soil in a reversal of the invasion by conquistadors and imperialists of the past half millennium. The irony in this phenomenon is lost on most Europeans, on the conservative nationalists, of course, but even on many on the left, who might argue that Europe is now reaping its due returns. If one switches focuses to the United States, the picture is far different. Here a nation of immigrants is now so "mixed"—the population of California is more than half of non-European origin—that the term *nation* no longer refers to a homogeneous people in any meaningful sense. In Taiwan, again by contrast, the waves of Chinese immigrants, who marginalized the native Hakka population and could think of themselves only as Chinese wistfully imagining a return to, and recapture of, the mainland, now proclaim themselves "Taiwanese," as if national identity is created by acts of a legislature or executive fiat. One could go on to enumerate at length the paradoxes of national identity and citizenship. But the question is clear: how much liberty can governments take in defining their national referent before the term itself becomes laughable?

The nation, one important support of the citizen, is now being superseded, challenged, and displaced by processes of globalization, as Saskia Sassen convincingly argues, both in its territoriality and in its sovereignty (Sassen 1998, 81). Multinational and transnational corporations cause nation-states to adjust to their profit-oriented imperatives. New global organizations like the World Bank, the World Trade Organization, and the World Intellectual Property Organization, however much they are influenced by the United States and other powerful nations, bypass to some degree national juridical institutions in the regulation of trade. Similarly, international rights organizations like Greenpeace, Doctors without Borders, human rights organizations, and other NGOs instantiate political relations outside national control. Could it be that in this process the citizen will be surpassed by the person, and earthlings will be recognized as a determinate human grouping more than as a figure in science fiction novels and films? In this context, when claims for human rights are being at least somewhat successfully constructed as a global norm, we need to examine the role of the media in globalizing practices that construct new subjects. We need especially to examine those media that cross national boundaries and to inquire if they form or may form the basis for a new set of political relations.

In this endeavor, one must be careful to avoid the perspective of existing political formations, such as the nation as well as political movements outside the nation that are opposed to it and bound to it at the same time. The new media, from these perspectives, merely reinforce or threaten territorial political relations. The important questions, rather, are these: Can the new media promote the construction of new political forms not tied to historical, territorial powers? What are the characteristics of new media that promote new political relations and new political subjects? How can these be furthered or enhanced by political action?[3]

NETIZEN AND CITIZEN

In contrast to the citizen of the nation, the name often given to the political subject constituted in cyberspace is "netizen." Netizen may only be a partial term, because no one lives in the Net permanently, at least not yet (who knows what may emerge from the genome project and experiments with virtual life?). Yet the netizen might be the formative figure in a new kind of political relation, one that shares allegiance to the nation with allegiance to the Net and to the planetary political spaces it inaugurates. Certain structural features of the Internet encourage, promote, or at least allow exchanges across national borders.

Like other media such as the telephone, radio, and television, the Internet deterritorializes exchanges, extracting them from bodily location. But the Internet reterritorializes exchanges in a manner different from those other media. Broadcast media such as radio and television are centralized at points of emission. These points are located in national space and may be regulated and controlled by nation-states. The architecture of the Internet, by contrast, is that of a decentralized web. Any point may establish exchanges with any other point or points, a configuration that makes the Internet very difficult, if not impossible, to control by the nation-state. The telephone system, by contrast with broadcast media, is bidirectional, reterritorializing exchanges as point-to-point voices. The Internet differs from the telephone by including text (admittedly, fax does this) as well as images, expanding the dimensions of the exchange. Also on the Internet the exchange is digital, affording considerable advantages over the analog telephone conversation. On the Internet, one may access not simply phone numbers as with telephone but vast stores of information, information that, in digital form, may also be altered in its reception and retransmitted. Unlike the telephone, the Internet encourages a new cultural practice of resignification, something possible in the small agricultural communities of the past, but then limited to the immediate members of the group. Folk music exemplified this form of cultural practice that now may have become general. Further, the Internet makes it far easier to send messages to multiple recipients, like broadcast media, but also to afford multiple emitters, unlike broadcast media. In all these ways, the Internet contains the potential of new practices. The process of realizing these potentials is, it must be emphasized, a political one.

THE NET AS A TOOL

The objection to the argument for the netizen might be raised that the Internet promotes, even enhances, existing political formations. The Zapatistas and the neo-Nazis alike further their political ambitions by means of Web sites, Listservs, blogs, e-mail, chat rooms, and so forth. In heavily mediatized societies, political candidates of all stripes deploy the Net to their advantage. Reform movements in China and Eastern Europe depended on the Net, as well as other media such as fax and television, to spread their word and foster political change. Countless experiments could be named, such as the City of Santa Monica's Public Electronic Network (Rheingold 1993, 268), which use the Net to extend democratic processes. The demonstrations in Seattle early in the year 2000 against the World Trade Organization and the World Bank, as well as the general process of globalization, benefited in addition by the ability of the Net to aid the work of organizing political protest. These examples all bespeak the ways in which the Internet can function within existing political structures.

Many examples might also be cited in which the Net functions to affect new types of political movements that are unique to it. Laura Gurak (1997) shows how the protests in the 1990s against Lotus Marketplace and the Clipper Chip introduced new forms of political action that relied on features particular to cyberspace. In these cases, opposition to corporate actions and government policies was organized primarily on the Net. A simple e-mail to friends by someone who drew attention to privacy questions related to a database of consumers in production at Lotus Corporation grew into a heavy flurry of e-mail protests, eventually, after the president of Lotus Corporation figured out how to access his e-mail, leading him to drop the project. The case of the Clipper Chip was somewhat different. Here several organizations concerned with the Internet, such as the Electronic Frontier Foundation, organized an e-mail protest against the Clinton administration's effort to grab control of communications on the Net by deploying a special computer chip that would allow it and it alone to decode all messages. In this instance, the protest was somewhat successful.

These cases illustrate the ways that the speed, the rhetorical traits, and the connectivity of the Net can be used to organize social movements. Gurak suggests that the Net affords the possibility of new forms of political mobilization. In both instances she studies, however, what is at issue is protest against modern institutions, the corporation and the state, not the development of new political bonds inscribed in the new human-machine interface.

THE MATERIALITY OF MEDIA

A second objection to my argument for the netizen might be that media merely mediate. One might point to the long history of sanguine expectations surrounding the introduction of new media only to end in disappointment in the results of their dissemination. At least since the telegraph, observers have argued for utopian consequences—global peace, the harmony of mankind, the elimination of inequality—from the invention and spread of media of communication. Many conclude from the history of these dashed rosy expectations that media are simply tools, neutral devices that change nothing of the structures of domination prevailing before them. These skeptical positions overlook the deep cultural and social changes ensuing from the media, even if these are regrettable rather than utopian. Who can doubt the role of print and television in the formation of modern society, each producing through myriad practices of appropriation profound alterations in the way people think, fantasize, and act?

The brunt of the argument against the importance of the media does not concern their effects. These are beyond doubt. Rather, it has to do with the ontology of symbolization in general. If the motor of cultural existence is consciousness, then media are merely facilitators, playing little role in the form of exchange. As long as a metaphysic of consciousness is maintained, the media are secondary, almost insignificant phenomena.

If, on the contrary, language is the basis of culture, then there are two possible positions: either language mediates symbol formation in a material process of alteration, or the specific wrapping of language affects the structuring of cultural subjects. I follow the line of thought of Marshall McLuhan in arguing for the latter position. I cannot here fully develop this assertion, but to a readership that includes literary critics and humanists more generally, I maintain that a novel does not constitute subjects in the same manner as digitized narratives inscribed in the Net. If you harbor any doubts about this, I ask that you think about copyright law and its current dissolution in cyberspace. Or perhaps inquire of an executive in the music industry if there exists any difference between their commodities (LPs, tapes, CDs) and MP3 files. Or perhaps ask an executive in the film industry, which is zealously digitizing its products and disseminating them as DVDs, if he or she thinks that the Internet raises anxiety about the differences among media.

NEW MEDIA AND GLOBALIZATION

A final objection to the proposal of netizenship concerns the response of peoples around the world to the introduction of Internet technology. Internet use is spreading, however unevenly, around the globe. Servers, domains, Web pages, and users outside the United States surpassed those within the United States around the beginning of the twenty-first century. While use remains skewed within the United States and even more within North America and Europe, there is no question of the spread of networked computing across the globe. In the late 1990s, over one-third of the population of Trinidad, a nation not routinely associated with the rapid adoption of new technology, were users (Miller and Slater 2000). In this context, some researchers are concerned that the Internet, a Western technology, will destroy other cultures. They assume that a "global village" must "preserve and enhance" what they regard as "cultural differences" (Ess 2001, 5). I am not sure what is meant by "enhance" in this context, or how enhancement might relate to, or conflict with, preservation. Surely visibility on the Net might globally extend the presence of local cultural values. But such promotion might not be seen as preservation and might well incur alteration by the mere requirement to advertise one's mores and customs. If a relatively autochthonous culture presents itself on the global stage, it thereby introduces a change in its relations with the outside world. In addition, there has never been a guarantee of eternity to cultural values, which have no doubt been in continual flux even when they have not been so perceived. Moreover, the simple existence of certain values by no means justifies or ensures their worth.

Scholars have begun to explore the fascinating and urgent question of the introduction of Internet technology outside the United States.[4] The results of such studies so far have been mixed and can only be regarded as tentative, since transcultural research is so problematic and difficult. An ethnographic study of Trinidad suggests that, from the point of view of the local population, some Internet functions match closely and harmonize easily with preexisting cultural values and practices (Miller and Slater 2000). In the discipline of philosophy in Germany, Listservs and similar communications facilities used in the 1990s were only marginally successful in furthering prevailing dialogue and discussion (Hrachovec 2001). Among women in Kuwait in the 1990s, Internet use was at the highest level in the Arabic world, despite a strong patriarchal culture. There researchers found women seated apart from men in gender-segregated Internet cafes. Nonetheless the women simultaneously mingled with men freely in chat rooms (Wheeler 1998; Wheeler 2001, 198). In South Africa, learning centers were rapidly erected to teach Internet use to those interested (Postma 2001). A study of new media in Thailand concludes that Thai values are not endangered by global exposure. Instead a reciprocal play of influences is set up, promoting Thai culture while opening it to wider perspectives (Hongladarom 2001). Finally, in Singapore, gay individuals were able to socialize and to organize on the Internet while meeting face-to-face was forbidden by law and incurred harsh penalties. Here new media come in direct conflict with existing culture, at least as defined by the government (Ho 2000).

These examples of Internet use around the world are surely spotty and inconclusive. Even the methodology for studying global Internet use is only beginning to be elaborated. One can anticipate the deployment of a great variety of strategies of adaptation as diverse groups explore networked computing. And one can anticipate a great variety of strategies of adaptation by researchers in examining the phenomenon. The field of postcolonial studies and transcultural studies will surely take the lead in the exploration of global technocultures. One danger to be avoided in this process is to configure the non-Western societies as victims of advanced technology. Quite the reverse can be argued: those who benefit most from the dissemination of global media are those whose local values are most put in question (Chow 1996). They are the ones who might gain significantly from the foreign "invasion" in having the opportunity of critical self-reflection and developing the most innovative responses and adaptations for the benefit of all. Yet one critical argument to keep in mind is that the integration of networked computing in human societies is a novelty for everyone, an experience that will likely change the relations of force around the globe. In such an eventuality, the figure of the netizen might serve as a critical concept in the politics of democratization.

CONCLUSION

I am not suggesting that the political space that is opening or may be opened on the Internet is a utopian realm of equality and freedom. Far from it. Each area of the Internet, from e-mail to chat rooms to MOOS to Web pages to Listservs to databases, contains its own forms of hierarchy and control, manipulations and risks. In chat rooms, as Katherine Hayles reminds me,[5] many forms of political presence characteristic of the nation-state are reproduced. In electronic messages, one must sustain one's identity, even if it is invented for the purpose of the online encounter. In the same vein, chat rooms provide a means for the assignment of responsibilities. These echoes of the world of territorial politics are nonetheless mediated in various ways by networked information machines and do not reproduce exactly the politics of earlier epochs.[6]

Nor am I suggesting that the emergence of netizenship is the leading tendency or even the most salutary eventuality in the current process of transnational developments. Saskia Sassen is surely correct to remind us that one of the most prevalent forms of postnational or extranational Internet use is the development of global finance markets, many of which derive from the public electronic space of the Internet but produce private networks inaccessible to the general user. As Saskia Sassen argues, "The enormous growth of private digital networks—especially the case of the global financial markets—rather than the Internet . . . is having the greater impact on national sovereignty and indeed transforming particular features of it" (Sassen 2000, 19). The massive flows of capital that course through the fiber-optic tentacles and radio waves of these intranets and extranets are far more influential in undermining the power of the nation-state than the fledgling steps of netizen politics. Tracking the vicissitudes of finance capital, however, is not the only function of critical intelligence. One must as well be vigilant about new opportunities for democratizing entrenched powers. And this is perhaps the main function of the category of the netizen.

There is, then, at least one political novelty specific to the Internet that I choose to highlight. The Internet holds the prospect of introducing postnational political forms because of its internal architecture, its new register of time and space, its new relation of human to machine, body to mind, its new imaginary, and its new articulation of culture to reality. Despite what may appear in the media of newsprint and television as a celebration of the Internet's harmony with the institutions of the nation-state and the globalizing economy, new media offer possibilities for the construction of planetary political subjects, netizens who will be multiple, dispersed, and virtual, nodes of a network of collective intelligence (Lévy 1997). They may resemble neither the autonomous agent of citizenship, beholden to print, nor the identity of postmodernity, beholden to broadcast media. The political formation of the netizen is already well under way, bringing forth, as Heidegger might say, a humanity adhering not to nature alone but also to machines, not to geographically local identity alone but also to the digitized packets of its own electronic communications.

The import of these speculations is not to assert the existence of an ideal domain of human communication in cyberspace, nor is it even to suggest that the prospects for improving the human condition are significantly enhanced by this network. It is rather to call attention to the possibility for the establishment of global communications, one that is more practically dispersed across the globe than previous systems, one that is inherently bidirectional and ungovernable by existing political structures. And it is to call attention to the need to rethink our understanding of terms like the citizen that derive from cultural worlds in which information machines were limited to books, periodicals, paintings, and mechanical clocks—in short, to take into account what Félix Guattari (1933) felicitously terms "the machinic heterogenesis" of the human.

PART II.
THE CULTURE OF THE DIGITAL SELF

5

IDENTITY THEFT AND MEDIA

The relationships we have with ourselves are not ones of identity, rather they must be
relationships of differentiation, of creation, of innovation.
—Michel Foucault, "Sex, Power and the Politics of Identity"

The fate of the humachine is played out not only on the grand scale of
global political and cultural relations but also in the truly local spaces of
individual self-constitution. In the second part of this book, I examine
new formations of human and machine with regard to identity, aesthetics, ethics, and psychology. In these domains, the innovation of the digital
emerges as the mediation of new cultural forms.

The recent construction of the crime of identity theft raises the paradoxical question of the security of identity. How can actions in the world
impinge on and even destabilize an individual's identity? Is not identity
threatened primarily from interior upheavals such as crises of identity,
traumatic loss of memory, disintegration of the personality as a consequence of mental breakdowns, psychoses, and the like? If one's identity is
subject to the felony of theft (grand theft identity, one would surmise), is
not the nature of identity itself called into question? When identity can be
stolen like an automobile, a purse, or a credit card, then it must be a thing
of this world, a piece of private property, an asset of some sort, a material
possession. If that is the case, we must account for the construction of
identity both as an object and as a subject.

American culture generally regards identity as the basis of subjectivity,
as the center of the self, its spiritual core. If that were true or the entirety
of the issue, then "identity theft" would clearly not be possible. When

individuals construct their own identities, as current liberal ideology proclaims, the theft of identity is not even conceivable. Since the crime of identity theft is quite real, we need then to account for a change in the nature of identity, its exteriorization and materialization, its becoming vulnerable to theft, its emergence as insecure—within the ideology of individualism itself. To achieve such an analysis, I propose two steps. The first is to place the alteration of the construction of identity squarely within a Foucauldian framework of a technology of power. This affords the advantage of comprehending identity in its exteriorization to begin with, as a phenomenon instituted by discourses and practices, as a form of "subjectivation." Next we need to account for the role of information machines or media—what I call "the mode of information"—in the process. Such a double strategy of interpretation allows "identity" to emerge as a historical process, one neither naturalized nor universalized within the ideology of liberalism and its insistence on the always already given figure of identity within the individual. The innovation of identity theft as the materialization of identity thus appears not as a fall from the grace of interior identity, as some malign feature of new media, but as the potential of every construction of identity, as the dangerous supplement to the positing of identity as the core of the self. Before discussing the important cultural implications of identity theft, I present an overview of its social and historical emergence, paying particular attention to the place of information machines.

IDENTITY THEFT AS SOCIAL FACT

One of the noteworthy aspects of identity theft is its sudden appearance in print media. On August 22, 2003, I searched for the term in several online databases and received surprising results. The Modern Language Association bibliography returned a result sum of zero. As of that date, we can conclude that no humanistic inquiry had been published on the topic. Two other bibliographic databases yielded the following figures:

	1987 to 1999	2000 to August 2003
The Expanded Academic ASAP/Gale	39	144
Computer-related magazines	18	56
Proquest ABI/INFORM	10	328

Almost none of the references dated before 1995, and through 1999 there were very few. Beginning in 2000 there is a flurry of articles that have "identity theft" in the title, mostly in newspapers and popular weekly magazines and newsletters. It is clear that "identity theft" is a twenty-first-century phenomenon. This fact is significant especially since it indicates a cultural lag in the use of the term because it includes both digital crimes on the Internet and the theft of credit card information that occurs in more conventional public spaces. It took some time before the term "identity theft" was adopted in the print media to apply to situations of stolen personal credit information. One had first to distinguish "identity theft" from ordinary forms of fraud.

The popular media definition of identity theft specifies the appropriation of an individual's personal information to provide access for the criminal to credit lines, purchases, and cash. The thief does not take material objects that belong to someone else, only "information." Here is one definition: "With identity theft, a thief takes over a consumer's entire identity by stealing critical private information, such as the Social Security number, driver's license number, address, credit card number or bank account number. The thief can then use the stolen information to obtain illegal loans or credit lines to buy goods and services under the stolen name" (McNamara 2003, 40). Identity theft, then, does not refer to the familiar theft of credit cards and their use by the perpetrator. The crime might include taking a credit card, but it is taken only for the information it provides the criminal, in particular account numbers. The false use of credit cards constitutes fraud (presenting oneself in a store as someone else and forging their signature on the credit slip) and is not included in the category "identity theft."

Other writers define the term somewhat differently. Jennifer Lee, writing in the New York Times, makes an interesting distinction between illegally using existing accounts or funds and creating new ones: "Unlike identity theft, in which the criminal uses personal information to open and use accounts that are in the victim's name, account theft entails using stolen credit or A.T.M. cards, or financial records, to steal from the victim's existing accounts." Identity theft is more serious, she continues, because "the scope of the problem is moving international and moving to larger rings of criminals" (Lee 2003). What Lee terms "account theft" is thus a more tra-

ditional form of robbery, while "identity theft" designates acting in someone else's place to create financial instruments for illegal gain. Lee's distinction tends to hold in most of the media discussions of the crime, but
it fails to discriminate between various uses of digital media in the crime.

Some reporters limit identity theft to cases where the Internet is used to
obtain personal information and restrict the illegal use of found or stolen
credit cards to more traditional categories of transgression. The difficulty
in sustaining this distinction is that even in cases where a physical credit
card is misappropriated, criminals often use the card as information on
the Internet to purchase goods, obtain loans, or secure new credit cards
(Mihm 2003, 44). In either case, identity theft refers to stolen information that is deployed in a digital network illegally to obtain money and
goods. In one of the few books devoted to the topic, Katalina Bianco defines identity theft as follows: "Identity theft is a term used to refer to all
types of crime in which someone wrongfully obtains and uses another person's personal data in a way that involves fraud or deception, typically for
economic gain" (Bianco 2001, 1). She also fails to distinguish the type of
media used to accomplish the crime.

We may now return to the question of why the term "identity theft"
was not used until the twenty-first century. "Identity theft," like so many
other practices on digital networks, was until recently not recognized as a
crime. No one, before the widespread use of the Internet, committed the
crime, nor was there a law against it. Thieves certainly used other people's
personal documents, but they did not, until recently, extract personal information from these papers and cards to act economically in another's
place. As Stephen Mihm explains: "Existing federal legislation addressed
only the fraudulent creation, use and transfer of identification documents,
not the theft and criminal use of the underlying personal information, particularly Social Security numbers and dates of birth" (2003, 44). It was not
until October 30, 1998, that the U.S. legislature enacted the Identity Theft
and Assumption Deterrence Act, which covered the practices in question.[1]
Only after that date could one prosecute someone for identity theft. Newspapers began to discuss identity theft by and large only after it was designated a crime. There was thus something very new about identity theft.
Only with digital networks could the crime of using someone's personal
information for economic gain become a widespread practice. Digital in-

formation machines were thus coupled with criminal intent to produce the innovation of identity theft.

And steal they did. In the short space of two or three years, identity theft went from an unrecognized practice to the fastest-growing crime in the United States. In 2002, for example, there were 418,000 robberies in the country but 700,000 identity thefts, almost twice the number. One periodical reported that no less than seven million Americans thought they had been victims of identity theft (Livingston 2003). The statistics are astounding and frightening. Judging from newspaper and periodical reports, the likelihood is great that many if not most individuals will have their identity stolen in their lifetime.[2] The commonality of identity theft leads to some amusing and interesting speculations concerning the future of "identity." With the high frequency of the crime, even the criminal cannot be certain of the security of his or her own identity, or that the identity he steals is not already stolen.[3]

PERPETRATORS AND THEIR VICTIMS

Who commits the crime of identity theft? One might guess that such a high-tech crime would be the métier of computer specialists such as hackers. But this is not at all the case, judging from newspaper reports. Here is a list of categories of perpetrators gleaned from periodicals: a former college official, a former state worker, a former H&R Block manager, high-tech insiders, an Orange County couple, prison workers, a student, the wife of an imprisoned gang leader, automobile dealership employees (with 1,700 complaints in 2001), and, of course, al-Qaeda terrorists. One article argued that identity theft is not normally the act of a lone individual but requires the complicity of major financial institutions like banks and credit agencies. Sheila Cherry (2002) writes: "Identity theft is only possible with the full cooperation of three major participants: the impostor, the creditor and the credit bureau. All are coconspirators and equally guilty of identity theft." So much information is needed to carry out the felony that lax security procedures by large financial institutions are a condition for the crime. Insiders are naturally blamed for information leakage, not only from banks but also from government agencies. As one critic notes, "There is widespread use of Social Security numbers in government and business databases, which hackers access illegally" ("Identity

Theft" 2003). Sheila Cherry continues: "Others say the technology that gave government easier access to private information is in fact responsible for the epidemic of identity theft. Even the Department of Justice (DOJ) has warned of the insider problem caused by too many employees having too much access to personal information on citizens" (Cherry 2002). The institutions that are responsible for our security—banks, insurance companies, government offices—turn out to be a major source of criminal activity in the area of identity theft.

Although obstacles can be placed between one's computer and the global network, the basic architecture of the Internet is designed for open and rapid connections between all online computers. Firewalls and other techniques to limit outside access to one's local machine are means of partial isolation and protection. Many instances of identity theft are a consequence of the open structure of the Internet. Scott Bradner (2003) observes: "A major reason for the dramatic increase in the threat [of identity theft] stems from the all-too-easy availability of personal information on computer systems connected to the Internet." We can conclude from this that identity theft is a result of the new relation between humans and digital information machines, an interface that couples carbon-based and silicon-based beings in a new synergy. In the context of the human-computer interface, identity takes on a different configuration from the common-sense view that it is an interior state of consciousness, bounded by the skin of the individual. The security of identity in the digital world is, as a consequence, a different matter from safety in the physical world of extended objects. What is stolen is not one's consciousness but one's self as it is embedded in (increasingly digital) databases. The self constituted in these databases, beyond the ken of individuals, may be considered the digital unconscious. If the list of perpetrators is long, the list of victims is even longer. Just about anyone who has credit is vulnerable to identity theft: surprising, perhaps, on the list are doctors and patients, army troops, even a UC Irvine faculty housing resident. The police department crime log of the University of California, Irvine, reports under the category "grand theft" the following: "UCI affiliate reports credit card fraud by theft of identity in University Hills. Disposition: Report Taken." One is apparently not safe anywhere, even in the academic district of peaceful "village Irvine." Many of the victims are accosted not in the street or in physical space but in the virtual realm of the Internet. Cyberspace is a realm that cancels the borders between public and private, rendering all communications and all data on one's hard drive part of a shared electronic space.

IDENTITY THEFT AND ITS DISCONTENTS

Victims Assistance of America, Inc., maintains a Web site that allows victims of identity theft to upload their stories. As one browses through the tales of loss, it becomes clear that identity theft turns people's lives upside down. After someone has amassed huge unpaid bills, all in your name, you often cannot get a mortgage or refinance your house for months while you try to clear your credit history. Meanwhile you are harassed by collection agencies insisting you pay for charges you swear to them you did not make. A couple of incidents printed in *Consumer Reports* will suffice to give a feeling for the trials one undergoes as a victim of identity theft. "Frances Green, a beautician from Jamaica, N.Y., discovered that the house she was about to buy had already been sold — to an ID thief posing as Green who, with a phony seller and fake lawyers, defrauded the mortgage company and ruined Green's credit" ("Stop Thieves from Stealing You" 2003, 12). More typical of identity theft is the story of Bob Hartle of Phoenix, Arizona: "Hartle spent nearly four years and $15,000 to restore his good name after an identity thief borrowed more than $100,000 in his name and then filed for bankruptcy. The impostor had also obtained five driver's licenses (and a speeding ticket) in Hartle's name, opened bank accounts, was hired and fired as Bob Hartle, and failed to pay state and federal taxes. The real Hartle says he contacted more than 100 people in his quest to repair the damage, including local law-enforcement agencies, the FBI and the U.S. Secret Service's financial-crimes division" (K. Davis 1998). Stories like these are abundant in print and broadcast media as well as online.

The inconvenience and economic loss suffered by victims is enormous. It can take a victim several years to straighten out his or her situation. Often one does not discover the problem until months after the perpetrator has carried out the crime, an indication that the theft of identity is unconscious to the individual. And the loss is paid for by all consumers, amounting to an estimated $4.2 billion in 2003 ("Stop Thieves from Stealing You" 2003, 12). Identity theft is thus far from a trivial problem, but one that increasingly characterizes digitally mediated society.

IDENTITY THEFT AS MEDIA CONSTRUCTION

Everyone in the United States now knows about identity theft and probably has some degree of fear and insecurity because of it. People know about it and are anxious about it not necessarily because they have directly experienced identity theft but because the media have relentlessly informed them about it. The situation regarding identity theft is typical of insecurity in a heavily mediated age. Information machines—newspapers, magazines, television, radio, the Internet—constitute the discourses that (in)form subjects as participants in culture. Far more than oral, face-to-face networks, media disseminate cultural meanings and give shape to our insecurities. In the case of identity theft, Americans have seen television shows, heard radio newscasts, and read magazines, all of which present themselves as educating the public about events and situations, while at the same time these media produce a hyperreal effect that makes all too present a certain danger.

I analyze a set of advertisements by Citicorp in print and television media to illustrate the way identity theft has become recognized in popular culture. These advertisements are an example of media-induced anxiety, but they also reveal the complexities of identity in the era of the digital machine. Citibank published an advertisement in *People* magazine on December 8, 2003. Video versions of similar material were broadcast on many television networks in late November and early December 2003, continuing well into the summer of 2004. Three photos in *People* showed images of individuals juxtaposed with text that somehow does not fit their appearance (see figures 11–13).

In figure 11, a middle-aged, conservatively dressed woman of color says, "I spent $2,342 on violent and suggestive video games." In figure 12, a portly, middle-aged white man says, "I had $23,000 worth of liposuction." In figure 13, a young white woman, a girl-next-door type, says, "There are 3 warrants for my arrest. One of them involves smuggling." In each case, the image does not fit the quote. This discordance is explained in figure 14.

Figure 14 for the first time designates the source of the advertisement as Citibank. It reads, from the top: "Identity theft. It can take your good

FIGURE 11. Citibank advertisement in *People* magazine, December 8, 2003

FIGURE 12. Citibank advertisement in *People* magazine, December 8, 2003

FIGURE 13. Citibank advertisement in *People* magazine, December 8, 2003

FIGURE 14. Citibank advertisement in *People* magazine, December 8, 2003

credit rating. Never mind your good name." At this point, the reader may be able to decode the apparent contradiction in figures 11 to 13 between the image and the text. The identities of the three people have been stolen, and the money was spent not by them but by the thieves. The advertisement, it might be noted, appropriates an artistic device made famous by René Magritte's *Ceci n'est pas une pipe* (1926), one that was widely used in conceptual art (see figure 15). The technique exploits the media specificity and difference between images and words, in Magritte's case to play with the opposing meanings or contradiction within the image, thereby destabilizing the viewer's reading and rendering impossible, some would say undecidable, a unified interpretation. The word, in this case "pipe," can never be identical to the image of a pipe or to the referent pipe. Yet the image *is* that of a pipe. The text and the image refute each other (Foucault 1983). The indexicality of the image and the referentiality of the text resist and work against each other. This oppositional tension, however, points to the nonidentity of word, image, and thing. It suggests both their mutual relation (words and images do refer to things) and their media specificity (as different media, they are able to operate against each other).

FIGURE 15. René Magritte, *La trahison des images (Ceci n'est pas une pipe)*, 1929. Oil on canvas, 60 x 81 cm. Los Angeles County Museum of Art. © 2005 C. Herscovici, Brussels/Artists Rights Society (ARS), New York. Photo Credit: Banque d'Images, ADAGP/Art Resource, New York.

Citibank's advertisement deploys, more modestly and with less artistic creativity than Magritte, the media specificity of word and image to indicate the consequence of identity theft: a person's life may be taken away from him or her if someone else is able to use the victim's personal information for the thief's own benefit. Thus in figure 11, $2,342 dollars was spent by a teenage boy to buy video games, not the woman pictured in the ad; in figure 12, $23,000 was used by a woman for plastic surgery to improve her appearance, not by the man in the image; in figure 13, a convicted smuggler stole the identity of a prim-looking young woman. The advertisement works its scary operations by stereotyping the texts and images, especially in relation to gender, ethnicity, and age. It could be that the woman in figure 11 is a fan of video games, that the fat man in figure 12 was much fatter before liposuction, and that the innocent-looking young woman in figure 13 was indeed a felon. Only the reader's cultural biases prevent an incorrect interpretation.

With figure 14, not only is the source of the advertisement made explicit, but the insecurity generated in the narrative of figures 11 to 13 is dissipated: Citibank will protect the reader from identity theft, guaranteeing one's safety as a consumer. The fear that was aroused in figures 11 to 13 through the contradiction of image and text is happily resolved. All one need do to achieve peace of mind and security of identity is to obtain a Citibank credit card. The financial corporation has made the world that much better and safer. And all of this happens on December 8, just in time for Christmas shopping. Happy holidays!

In the televised versions (directed by Steve Driggs), the promotion is more easily effective in producing the "correct" interpretation by the viewer. In one of some dozen of these, a young black woman speaks about spending a lot of money, but the voice one hears is that of a still younger man, synchronized with the lip movements of the person in the video image.[4] Of course, the "woman" might be a transsexual with a baritone voice. This possibility is not registered by the advertisement, working as it does with commonplace stereotypes. Granted this potential difficulty, the televised version deploys voice instead of text, with the specificity of the media resulting in a more obvious representation of contradiction and mismatched identity.

Although the ad, as moving image with sound, arouses the audience to immediate recognition of the double identity, thief and victim combined, it also generates in the viewer a strong feeling of the uncanny, together with some degree of amusement that may conceal anxiety, as Freud says (Freud 1960b). To unify the image with the sound, the picture must express emotions that are consonant with the voice. In this case, the voice (of the thief) is gleeful. He has pulled off a successful robbery and is enjoying his stolen merchandise. But the woman in the image, synchronously mouthing the same words the male thief speaks, is also smiling, even though she has no reason to be happy. There is a double contradiction in the advertisement: the man's voice speaks in the woman's body, and the woman is smiling while the words she mouths indicate unfortunate circumstances. The second contradiction is rendered necessary to achieve the verisimilitude of the first contradiction. If the woman's expression was one of unhappiness, the identity of the thief would not fold into the identity of the victim. The result for the viewer is intense discomfort at the discordance being performed.

The televised advertisement deploys a technique familiar in science fiction films such as Don Siegel's Invasion of the Body Snatchers (1956). The victim's body has been taken over by the identity thief, although in the case of the Citibank ad, the voice of the thief substitutes for the voice of the victim. The uncanny feeling in the audience results from the hybrid of the victim's body and the thief's voice. In the science fiction film, the victim's voice remains in the victim's body, with only a slight but important change in the tone of the voice, eerie and emotionless.[5] In the televised ad, the voice (of the thief) and the facial expression (of the victim) retain their demonstrative qualities. The media-specific merger of voice and body produces a discomforting illusion of the theft not only of identity but of the body as well. The thief's trace, however, is present in his or her voice. Identity theft is here represented visually and aurally not as a substitution of consciousnesses or information from one person to another but as a voice in the wrong body.[6]

If the print advertisement suffers from the limitations of its media constraints, so the televised advertisement, in some ways more effective than the former, also cannot quite pull off the representation of identity theft. For instance, the "theft" is not really a theft in the conventional sense of taking something away from someone so that the original owner no longer possesses it. The victim, in the crime of identity theft, still has his or her identity. What can be said about the crime is that the identity has doubled or been cloned by the thief. After the crime, at least two persons share the same identity. This aspect of identity theft is captured in neither the print nor the television advertisements. These media "failures" suggest the difficulty of the cultural issue of identity theft: the term "identity" contains so many irreconcilable fragments that its rupture through theft is not easily expressed in analog media. Given the difficulties of print and broadcast media to represent identity theft, one might well conclude that identity theft (and identity itself) may be culturally inscribed only in digital media or networked computing. Only in that domain can the social markers of the physical world—gender, ethnicity, age—be nullified; only in that domain can theft of identity be represented and practiced.

INSECURITY IN A DIGITAL AGE

Although the general vulnerability of humans to questions of security may be a feature of human beings in general, and some would argue that the problem of security is "timeless," the forms, degrees, and contents of security are certainly historically constituted. Foucault, for example, mentions in *Discipline and Punish* that the great productivity of industrial capitalism brought with it an amassing of enormous heaps of manufactured objects, and accordingly new questions of security and new illegalities concerning their unauthorized removal: "The economy of illegalities was restructured with the development of capitalist society" (Foucault 1977, 87). And Marx wrote in the introduction of the *Grundrisse*: "The mode of pillage is itself in turn determined by the mode of production. A stock job-bing nation, for example, cannot be pillaged in the same manner as a na-tion of cow-herds" (1973, 98). It should come as no surprise, then, that the rapid, global dissemination of networked computing and the concomi-tant spread of digital culture also provide an occasion for a new regime of insecurities. The massive migration to the Internet of financial and business transactions, records and archives of institutions of all kinds, personal communications, diaries, and family memorabilia gives rise to a new realm of social and cultural life that may be hacked, intruded on, defaced and mutilated, appropriated or destroyed. If the commodities of early industrial capitalism became vulnerable through their mere ubiq-uity, the age of digital networks finds a displacement of data into a pub-lic arena of what had hitherto been sequestered in "safe," private places. Early industrial capitalism presumed the equivalence of public and inse-curity, private and security. With digital culture, there occurs a shift into an exterior social space of information in all its forms — texts, images, and sounds.

In the nineteenth century, capitalism regarded the material contents of its warehouses and storage places as "private" and hence vulnerable to misappropriation; but digital culture extends this "private" domain to the intimate details of all cultural forms, making insecure everything that can be put into such a medium of traces. Anyone who has sent an e-mail to the wrong addressee or inadvertently "replied to all" or, as a result of a computer virus, had a sensitive message involuntarily and without one's knowledge sent to everyone in one's address book knows full well that communications in a predigital age that had been secure in their privacy are now subject to new forms of vulnerability and dangers. If individuals in a networked world are open to new dangers, so equally are large in-stitutions. Anyone or any company that digitizes cultural objects — texts, images, and sounds — may have them inserted into the Internet. The music and film industries in particular have learned this lesson, perhaps at the cost of their viability as economic institutions. Components of the publishing industry—encyclopedia and book-publishing presses in particular—also find themselves burdened with new threats of obsolescence.

Digital networks thus extend the domain of insecurity to objects that had previously been relatively safe. These newly endangered objects are cultural in nature. When their material character metamorphoses to the digital level from the analog realms of paper, film, tape, and the like, they step into the dangerous world of insecurity that had previously affected only large material objects. Here I examine only one such cultural object, and it is one that is not often regarded as being subject to this type of vulnerability. I speak of "identity."

MODERNITY'S DOUBLE:
IDENTITY AND IDENTIFICATION

Surely it must be considered a paradox that identity might be stolen, and yet, as we will see, so profound are the transformations of culture by digital networks that what is termed "identity theft" is no paradox at all.

Perhaps it is best to begin on common ground with the *Oxford English Dictionary*'s definition of the term. The venerable OED says of identity that it is "the sameness of a person or thing at all times or in all circumstances; the condition or fact that a person or thing is itself and not something else; individuality or personality." The OED definition harks back to Aristotle's logic of the excluded middle: that a thing is what it is and not what it is not. To have an identity means that one cannot at the same time and in the same place be what one is and what one is not. But the OED goes beyond classic Western logic to a more modern sense of the term that is psychological in nature. It speaks of "individuality or personality." The dictionary provides a psychological definition of identity as "the condition or fact of remaining the same person throughout the various phases of existence; continuity of the personality." In the move from logic to psychology, identity becomes an attribute of consciousness. The aspect of the self that endures, aside from the discovery in the twentieth century of the configuration of our fingerprints or our genes, is consciousness. Consciousness, that interior state of awareness or intentionality, is the key to identity. And this has been so throughout modernity, from John Locke up to and including Erik Erikson.

I argue that identity in modernity has been caught between two opposing directions: one that attempts to contain it within consciousness,
and another tendency that associates it, by dint of information media, with
the body. This Cartesian dualism of extended and thinking things, bodies
and minds, that so complicates the effort to configure identity at a cultural
and social level runs aground as information media overtake the earlier
figure of the individual as rational, autonomous, and centered.

GENEALOGY OF IDENTITY

An understanding of "identity theft" requires a clarification of the term
"identity." To this end, I will attempt a genealogy of the cultural figure of
"identity." Genealogies are best carried out, if Foucault and Nietzsche are
our guides, by going back to a point in history when the phenomenon in
question appears to contemporary eyes as monstrous, as in the punish-
ment of Damiens, the regicide, in eighteenth-century France.

In relation to the theft of identity, one might begin with an apparent case of identity theft in sixteenth-century France. *The Return of Martin
Guerre*, a book by Natalie Davis (1983) and a film by the same name directed by Daniel Vigne (1982), recounts the history of an "imposture" in
rural southwestern France. The story is well known of the disappearance
of Martin Guerre from his family and village, and his return first by an impostor, one Arnaud du Tilh, then by himself, with a trial and execution of
the impostor and the great fascination the case elicited in contemporaries.
Natalie Davis represents the crime of Arnaud as "identity fraud," never
using the expression "identity theft." She explains how identity might be
confused in the sixteenth century:

> Was it so unusual for a man in sixteenth-century villages and burgs to
> change his name and fashion a new identity? Some of this went on all
> the time. . . . At carnival time and at other feastdays, a young peasant
> might dress as an animal or as a person of another estate or sex and
> speak through that disguise. In a charivari, one villager might play an-
> other, might serve as a stand-in for the person being humiliated for his or
> her inappropriate marriage or bad marital conduct. But these were tem-
> porary masks and intended for the common good.
>
> There was also more self-interested deception: healthy beggars pre-
> tending to be lame or blind and people counterfeiting an identity to col-

lect an inheritance or otherwise gain some economic advantage. (Davis 1983, 40)

But none of these examples constitutes identity theft in the twenty-first-century sense. Although these are cases of representing oneself as another, the conditions of sixteenth-century society are fundamentally different from those of today. Davis's text convinces one that the case of Martin Guerre is not one of "identity theft" because the "lies" of Arnaud are entangled with village customs and family traditions, unlike in the situation in the present. In the sixteenth century, one might deceive some people and pull off an imposture, but the fraud depended on the memory of villagers and family members, their ability to match the physical traits of the impostor with their recollection of the original individual. Davis asks, "But how, in a time without photographs, with few portraits, without tape recorders, without fingerprinting, without identity cards, without birth certificates, with parish records still irregular if kept at all—how did one establish a person's identity beyond doubt?" (63). How indeed to do this when the media of self-representation were overwhelmingly proximate, territorial presence and memory?

A more serious issue concerns Davis's main question in her study. Her thesis is that the case of Martin Guerre allows the historian to examine "the significance of identity in the sixteenth century" (viii). Yet the term "identity" is the historian's, not that of contemporaries. Status, kinship, métier, and place defined individuals in early modern Europe, not identity. If identity theft was impossible at that time, so, more importantly, was the self defined as "identity."[7] Such a cultural representation would have to wait until modernity for inscription into social practice. The case of the return of Martin Guerre offers a point of difference, a time when identity and identity theft were, as Lucien Febvre (1982) says of unbelief in the same era, simply impossible.

We may then examine the transformation necessary as a prerequisite for the cultural construction of identity and the legal establishment of the crime of identity theft. To this end, I first explore the representation of the individual as one having an identity, then trace the changes in the media that afford the possibility of maintaining an identity, as well as the political and cultural alterations in the cultural figure of the self as one with an identity, finally turning to the place of digital media in the rise of identity theft. What I present is not a comprehensive or exhaustive genealogy of identity but a sketch that indicates the main lines of its cultural construction, enough of a picture to afford a better clarification of how identity theft is connected to media and how the current situation suggests the need for a critique of identity and an effort to formulate figures of the self that allow resistance to hegemonic institutions, especially the state and the transnational corporation.

LOCKE AND IDENTITY AS CONSCIOUSNESS

In the modern philosophical tradition there is a remarkably consistent use of the term "identity" as an attribute of consciousness, a discursive line that begins quite abruptly with John Locke and continues in Hegel and many others.[8] In "Of Identity and Diversity," chapter 27 of volume 1 of *An Essay concerning Human Understanding*, Locke first considers the question of identity or sameness in relation to all beings, not only humans. He argues that the sameness of anything is "something that existed such a time in such a place, which it was certain, at that instant, was the same with itself, and no other" (Locke 1959, 438–39). Here, as Alexander Koyré (1958) has so nicely demonstrated, is the coordinated Cartesian world of time and space, where any being can be fixed in its location. The world is here represented as a three-dimensional grid with each element or body occupying a unique and definite bit of space-time. For Locke, this condition applies equally to humans: "For man it is the same as with everything else: [identity is] a participation of the same continued life, by constantly fleeting particles of matter, in succession vitally united to the same organized body" (444). Humans have an identity precisely because they can endure through time and in space.

As an aside, I note that such a modern configuration of identity as sameness in time and space systematically excludes the dimension of time as change. Objects, after all, and contra Locke, do not subsist in time. They alter in appearance, decay, and disappear. Identity in Locke's sense persists only for the moment and, from a longer-term point of view, is illusory. Indeed, digital technology introduces the morph as a visual refutation of the Descartes-Locke model of identity. As extended objects, digital morphs alter seemingly at will (Fisher 2000), confounding the eye of the beholder with infinitely changing shapes, anticipated in imagination by

Ovid's *Metamorphoses*. The modern Western concept of identity is in this sense a remarkable cultural construction that, when the time dimension is considered, appears most unlikely.

But Locke, like his French forebear René Descartes, recognizes the special quality of the human as a rational, self-conscious being whose identity must reflect this all-important attribute. So Locke contends that identity must include the *recognition* of sameness. He writes that a person is "a thinking intelligent being, that has reason and reflection, and can consider itself as itself, the same thinking thing, in different times and places; which it does only by that consciousness which is inseparable from thinking, and, as it seems to me, essential to it" (448–49). Unlike Descartes, for whom it is enough that a human think in order to be and have its essence in reason, Locke conceptualizes identity as only secured through its enduring recognition by the self. Locke improves considerably on Descartes for making identity central to the human self.

In addition, Locke insists that identity requires not only recognition but, perhaps by dint of that, consciousness. Identity is an attribute of consciousness for him. In a remarkable passage, he formulates the cornerstone of the modern concept of identity:

> For, it being the same consciousness that makes a man be himself to himself, personal identity depends on that only, whether it be annexed solely to one individual substance, or can be continued in a succession of several substances. . . . For it is by the consciousness it has of its present thoughts and actions, that it is *self to itself* now, and so will be the same self, as far as the same consciousness can extend to actions past or to come; and would be by distance of time, or change of substance, no more two persons, than a man be two men by wearing other clothes to-day than he did yesterday, with a long or a short sleep between; the same consciousness uniting those distant actions into the same person, whatever substances contributed to their production. (450–52)

Regardless of changes in what he calls secondary attributes such as clothing, Locke defines identity as an interior quality of awareness. In this respect, the notion of sameness is not the same for all beings, he argues against his earlier claim, but is unique for humans as distinct from other substances with respect to its property of consciousness. He writes: "This may show us wherein personal identity consists: not in the identity of substance, but, as I have said, in the identity of consciousness" (460).

A further complication of Locke's theory of identity, especially as it relates to the question of identity theft, is the connection he draws between the self and property (MacPherson 1962). In *The Second Treatise of Civil Government*, Locke grounds the basis of property in social wealth in the relation one has to oneself. In the first instance, property is ownership of the self by the self. He writes: "Every man has a property in his own person; this nobody has any right to but himself" (Locke 1937, 19). Acts of labor expand the domain of property to the objects worked on, such as land. These practices include as part of the self, Locke indicates, "my horse," "my servant," and "the ore I have digged."[9] Identity theft is therefore a violation of the primary relation one has to oneself, removing the ground for all subsequent forms of accumulation brought about through labor. If one's self has been stolen, one cannot, given Locke's logic, amplify one's property through labor because there is no agent or ground for the addition. Identity theft undermines the capitalist basis for property and presents the paradoxical state of a body with no ability to accumulate wealth.

Locke considers several objections to his concept of identity, dismissing each one in turn with arguments based in logic. The classic conditions of unreason that Descartes had noted are also debated by Locke, those of drunkenness and dreaming, for instance. Locke also, it might be noted as something of a remarkable curiosity, takes up the question of multiple personality, of "two distinct incommunicable consciousnesses acting in the same body" (464). I will not pursue in any detail here Locke's analysis of two consciousnesses in one body, each quite unconscious of the other's existence. Suffice it to say that the question of multiple selves has been a major point of contention in many areas of discourse for the past three decades. Psychologists still ponder the possibility of multiple personalities without firmly resolving the question (Hacking 1995). Philosophers too have continued to debate the point, with postmodernists like Gilles Deleuze and Félix Guattari outrageously announcing in the first lines of their celebrated work *A Thousand Plateaus* their own multiplicity: "The two of us wrote *Anti-Oedipus* together. Since each of us was several, there was already quite a crowd" (Deleuze and Guattari 1987, 3). Multiple identities certainly complicate the question of identity theft. How many identities does a thief have to steal in order fully to render the robbery complete? And what would Citibank have to say about the issue?

John Locke, then, articulated with great subtlety a concept of identity as consciousness. His ideas were, of course, only one dimension of a much broader set of historical developments such as the spread of print, urban life, the nation-state, European imperialism, and commerce, all of which, each in its own way, fostered both the cultural figure of the person as one having an identity and as that identity being in the first instance internal consciousness. The concept of identity as internal consciousness was written, as Lyndon Barrett has pointed out to me, in a mediascape that already included other, "external" forms of identity. And although Locke was the first to outline an understanding of the self as conscious identity, he was followed by many other thinkers. Instead of tracing this intellectual history, I turn to the concept of identity not in philosophy but in psychology.

ERIKSON AND IDENTITY AS EGO

If John Locke linked identity with consciousness, the psychological implications of the move were not systematically developed until the work of Erik Erikson, for whom identity became, extending and replacing the Freudian concept of the ego, the central feature of individual psychology. Starting with *Childhood and Society* (1950), continuing in *Young Man Luther* (1958), and culminating in *Identity: Youth and Crisis* (1968), Erikson developed a concept of identity that was widely influential in the social sciences and in the general culture. If anyone can be said to have authored the term in twentieth-century American society, Erikson must be given credit for the accomplishment.

Erikson's position within the psychoanalytic community was associated with the ego psychology whose leading theorist was Heinz Hartmann (1964). Briefly, ego psychology altered psychoanalytic theory by diminishing the importance of the instincts, marginalizing the role of the unconscious, stressing position of the ego, and introducing a new preoccupation with social aspects of individual psychology. Each of these revisions of psychoanalysis contributed to the emergence of the question of identity. In post–World War II America, the leading psychological issue was no longer, as it was in Victorian Europe, sexuality and its etiology but the coherence of the self. Americans, it would appear, felt lost, dazed, and confused perhaps by the incredible success of the United States in world affairs, by their country's boundless power, by the rapid changes that were being introduced in society and culture.

Erikson theorized identity explicitly as an addition to, and revision of, psychoanalysis, complaining that the lack of a concept of identity was a serious failure. With the goal of opening space in psychoanalytic theory for a concept of identity, he lambasted classic Freudian thought for its inadequate recognition of the social. He contended that the absence of a concept of identity in psychoanalysis is a direct consequence of its preoccupation with interior mental life at the expense of understanding the individual as immersed in a wider world: "The traditional psychoanalytic method . . . cannot quite grasp identity because it has not developed terms to conceptualize the environment. Certain habits of psychoanalytic theorizing, habits of designating the environment as 'outer world' or 'object world,' cannot take account of the environment as a pervasive reality" (Erikson 1968, 24).

From his first formulations of the concept, Erikson characterized identity as an attribute of the ego. He wrote in 1950: "The sense of ego identity . . . is the accrued confidence that the inner sameness and continuity prepared in the past are matched by the sameness and continuity of one's meaning for others" (Erikson 1963, 261). In 1968, almost twenty years later, he confirmed his earlier notion of identity, defining it in remarkably similar terms: "Ego identity . . . is the awareness of the fact that there is a self-sameness and continuity to the ego's synthesizing methods, the *style of one's individuality*, and that this style coincides with the sameness and continuity of one's *meaning for significant others* in the immediate community" (Erikson 1968, 50). One might quip that there is an identity to Erikson's concept of identity. One might also note the strong resonances of Locke's thinking in Erikson's notion of identity. "Sameness," "continuity"—these are the terms through which Locke theorized identity.

Ego identity was, for Erikson, not an easy accomplishment but a stage of life fraught with dangers. There was no assurance that identity would be achieved; fragmentation and confusion were equally possible as fates for the individual. Identity, for him, was a persistent issue throughout life but was especially acute during an individual's youth or adolescence. It was this time of life that marked a "crisis" of identity. The individual was challenged to synthesize earlier psychic developments and achieve a stability of self that a century before might have been called "character." Erikson writes regarding the period of youth: "It is the ego's function to integrate the psychosexual and psychosocial aspects on a given level of development and at the same time to integrate the relation of newly added identity elements with those already in existence" (162). If this task is successfully negotiated, the individual emerges with an identity enjoying three psychic strengths: "a conscious sense of individual uniqueness," "an unconscious striving for continuity," and "a solidarity with a group's ideals" (208). The American discourse on identity, by dint of the popularity of Erikson's writing, reinforced the Lockean version of identity as consciousness.

Identity in the United States is secure, despite the psychic issues of crisis that Erikson raised, since it refers by definition to a quality of self-consciousness, an interior sense of unity, integrity, autonomy, and determination. This notion of identity carried over into the political realm in the 1970s and 1980s, just before the origin of the crime of identity theft.

IDENTITY AND THEFT

Although the main current of the modern definition of identity was associated with interior consciousness, there was a second cultural inscription of the term, one far less dominant than the first, but nonetheless increasingly important as certain changes occurred in the configuration of political power beginning in the late eighteenth century. Starting at that time, the technology of power of sovereignty began to be supplemented with a new technology of power of governmentality, as Foucault (1991) names it. "Governmentality" refers to the policing of the population, the institution of surveillance mechanisms, the construction of extensive bureaucracies and social science disciplines to monitor many aspects of the health and welfare of all citizens. A new kind of power was thereby established that constructed each individual as a case. Potentially all individuals would have a dossier filled with information that tracked them through their life course, recording significant events and changes in their circumstances. In other words, databases were set in place that identified individuals and traced their comings and goings. Each individual took on an additional identity, one inscribed in the ledgers of governments, insurance companies, workplaces, schools, prisons, the military, libraries—every institutionalized space in modern urban environments. In the words of Nikolas Rose, "The ideas of identity and its cognates have acquired an increased salience in so many of the practices in which human beings engage. In political life, in work, in conjugal and domestic arrangements, in consumption, marketing, and advertising, in television and cinema, in the legal complex and the practices of the police, and in the apparatuses of medicine and health, human beings are addressed, represented, and acted on *as if they were selves* of a particular type: suffused with an individualized subjectivity, motivated by anxieties and aspirations concerning their self-fulfillment, committed to finding their true identities and maximizing their authentic expression in their life-styles" (Rose 1998, 169–70). The self as "identity" thus spread throughout the spaces of modern society.

But for governmentality to be effective, media were necessary, media in the form of records that first were handwritten, later took the shape of print, and finally were digitized and computerized. In the nineteenth century, means were sought in new technologies to link the record of the individual to his or her body. Mechanisms of identification were needed to suture the individual with the record, an early effort at biometrics. At first, simple records were generated in the form of identity cards and passports, but later photography was adapted by police, and the uncertain science of fingerprinting was added to the arsenal of practices of criminal investigation (Cole 2003), for the most important individuals to be fixed into the media of record keeping were criminals. Crimes against persons and especially against property militated strongly for apparatuses of identification.

With the emergence in the nineteenth century of a degree of anonymity in urban crowds, the state was in desperate need of methods to gain knowledge of individuals. Personal networks (communities) such as those that decided the fate of Martin Guerre in the sixteenth century no longer functioned adequately. In the urban spaces of nineteenth-century Europe and the United States, Tom Gunning observes, "Bureaucratic means to trace and identify [were developed], such as medical documentation and the growing use of photographs in identity cards and passports, all of which demarcate a person as a unique entity." Gunning argues that the new medium of the photograph was central to constituting the individual as a unique identity and therefore to the origin of the modern individual. "Such techniques of identification became necessary in the new world of rapid circulation and facilitated the circulation of the newly constituted individual through its circuits with a traceable accountability" (Gunning 1995, 23). The body (of the criminal) might now more easily be identified. Gunning concludes: "The vulnerability of one's body to recording and classification developed into fantasies of universal observation not only through being photographed while under arrest but also through being caught in the act by photography" (35). From the outset of modernity, then, media were coupled with identity, and criminals were the leading figures in the new play of forces. As soon as an effort was made to identify individuals, the focus on interior consciousness was inadvertently dislocated into the exterior mechanisms of analog traces—as photographs, as fingerprints, eventually as DNA. In a similar vein Celia Lury (1998), writing on the experimentation with self and identity in what she calls "prosthetic culture," asks "how the photographic image may have contributed to novel configurations of personhood, self-knowledge and truth" (2). She argues that "photography, more than merely representing, has taught us a way of seeing . . . that . . . has transformed contemporary self-knowledge" (3). What needs special emphasis in the context of my effort to make sense of the new crime of identity theft is that individual identity is being transformed, by dint of information media, into something that both captures individuality and yet exists in forms of external traces.

IDENTITY AS RESISTANCE

The prehistory of identity theft cannot, however, be written as a linear evolution from the region of consciousness culminating in the realm of the media. The narrative is much more complex. Just as highly sophisticated and fine-grained media were able to identify individuals by the merest traces left behind by their bodies or in the notations inscribed in extensive databases, a new current developed that combined both earlier tendencies in Locke and Erikson to understand identity as consciousness, and the more recent practices of identity as material, bodily trace.

In the new social movements of the 1970s and 1980s and in the popular culture of the postmodern era, to pick somewhat arbitrarily two examples, identity was reconfigured both as exterior sign or mediated trace and as intentional consciousness. In the protest movements that contested gender and race hierarchies, visible features of the individual such as body shape and skin color were linked with rebellious consciousness against forms of discrimination and oppression that were targeted to those traces. Identity politics were born. Ethnicity and race, gender, and sexual orientation became pivots of resistance against discrimination, marginalization, and social injustice operating insidiously in countless forms. In some cases, privileged positions of radicality were claimed in many of these movements in the form of assertions that one was especially able to recognize injustice and to struggle against it *because* of one's identity as an Asian American (Lowe 1996), a woman (Hartsock 1997), a black woman (Collins 2000), a queer (Warner 1993), and so on. In each case, critical consciousness is coupled with some aspect of bodily identity. A unity is fashioned from both the "interior" of consciousness as identity and the "exterior" of bodily characteristic. What is of special interest in the context of identity theft is that such unity is, in many cases, regarded as unproblematic: resistive identity consciousness fits all too easily with bodily characteristics *and* modes of oppression.[10] Identity is thus a double operation of material trace and consciousness bound together in a configuration that solidifies the figure of identity even as one enunciates opposition to its subjugation. Both the oppressor and the oppressed rely on the same figure of the self.

It is perhaps ironic that popular culture took a similar path in the 1980s, also combining interior consciousness and external trace in a happy confluence of identity formation. Consumers and fans of celebrities began to link their identities with their purchases and their favorite pop stars. Consumers ostentatiously displayed the labels of their apparel, often purchased especially for the cultural capital afforded by the names of designers. In a parallel move, fans, mostly young ones, draped themselves in the trappings of favorite rock bands, sports teams, movie stars, television shows, and the like. In both cases, individuals sought public recognition of their identity in the objects they wore on their body. More modestly perhaps than the aspiration to critique assumed by identity politics, popular culture modes of identity generally aspired merely to attach the individual to the brand or band, claiming with pride primarily the cultural value or taste of the selection. Consumers, then, did not organize their resistance into political forms in order to celebrate their branded identities as focuses of opposition. True enough, there certainly were anticapitalist and anticorporate consumer protests, perhaps most commonly associated with Ralph Nader and the cooperative movement. Moreover, some critical theorists located resistance in all acts of consumption (de Certeau 1984). Yet the pattern of consumer identity construction was not deeply political in orientation.

The inscription of identity into the general culture of postmodernity entailed a mixture of materiality and consciousness. But this composite identity remained a construction for which the individual alone was regarded as responsible. The bodily aspect of identity folded into the conscious component. Identity remained the property of the individual, bordered and guarded by the skin and wrappings intentionally chosen by him or her. I return now to the question of identity theft and examine the ways identity begins to crumble and to disintegrate as the cultural form of the self.

THE PHENOMENON OF IDENTITY
THEFT IN DIGITAL NETWORKS

After this review of the concept of identity and an examination of the practice of identity theft over the past decade, we may return to the media representation of identity theft and inquire about the consequences of identity theft for the formation of the subject. We have seen that identity theft posits identity as external to the consciousness of the self, altering a long-accepted usage of the term in modern society. Identity theft implies that identity consists of a series of numerical indicators (social security numbers, credit card numbers, driver's license numbers, bank account numbers, birth dates) and a series of personal information (name, address, mother's maiden name). These may be known to the consciousness of an individual, but they exist regardless of that knowledge in computer databases, Internet sites, plastic cards, and other documents. The constituents of identity in the sense of identity theft exist, therefore, in information media, and these media are dispersed across the globe.

With the emergence of the phenomenon of identity theft, the meaning of identity and its cultural instantiation is now doubled. Identity fragments into an aspect of consciousness (an awareness of continuity in time and space) and a complex of media content contained in information machines that combine to define an individual. This duality of identity, I contend, has not been adequately recognized in cultural discourse, and its implications have not been fully explored. Instead the media representation of identity theft—and this is one of my chief arguments here—works to foreclose the duality, to conceal the difficulty of reconciling the definition of identity as consciousness with the definition of identity as digitized information, to expose the danger of the latter for the former and to defuse that danger, to familiarize the population with the phenomenon of identity theft, and to normalize that phenomenon so that it appears as always already in the social fabric. In other words, the media representation of identity theft constitutes the crime as a new basis for insecurity and provides a solution to neutralize the threat through a subscription to the bank's credit card. The media discourse of the Citibank advertisement, in both its print and its television examples, performs the difficult, seemingly impossible cultural work of raising the specter of identity outside consciousness while confirming the security of identity within consciousness.

Yet the cat has escaped the bag. The recognition is dawning of a new mediascape with profound implications for the position of the self in culture, society, and politics. The practice of identity theft is conditional on the heterogeneity of identity, the inextricable mixing of consciousness with information machines, the dispersal of the self across the spaces of culture, its fragmentation into bits and bytes, the nonidentical identity or better identities that link machines with human bodies in new configurations or assemblages, the suturing or coupling of pieces of information in disjunctive time and scattered spaces. Some argue that such a figure of the self, often termed "postmodern," is congruent with the exigencies of global capitalism. This may in part be so. But the terms of emerging cultural struggles must be fought not on the ground of returning to the conveniences of identity as interior consciousness. Instead critical discourse must find the bases for a happier inscription of the self in its conditions of coupling with machines, in its media unconscious, precisely against the effort of trajectories of globalization that would prefer the Citibank solution of an admission of multiplicity of the self, but one shrouded in the comfort of unity and security within consciousness. We might then discover that the term "identity" is not of much use as a critical category but rather designates the construction of the self in our current conjuncture, including our modes of subjectivation, the ways we practice the self on ourselves. And we might search for new configurations of selfhood that keep open spaces of resistance, finding them especially in the human-machine mediascapes of networked computing.

6

THE AESTHETICS OF DISTRACTING MEDIA

The practices of artists using digital networked technology suggest a new subject-object relation in which identity is put into question far more radically than in the case of identity theft and its corporate-media appropriation by the likes of Citicorp. In this chapter, I explore the cultural theory of the media object, especially in Benjamin's analysis of cinema, and then turn to digital art, inquiring if it illustrates a break from the aesthetics of the analog cultural object. I argue that digital media, especially computerized databases, instantiate a culture of underdetermination that constitutes a break from the past.

BENJAMIN'S CHALLENGE

Mankind's "self alienation has reached such a degree that it can experience its own destruction as an aesthetic pleasure of the first order. This is the situation of politics which Fascism is rendering aesthetic. Communism responds by politicizing art" (Benjamin 1969b, 242). With these words, Walter Benjamin ends his pathbreaking, stimulating, confusing, and contradictory essay "The Work of Art in the Age of Mechanical Reproduction." And so begins a question that has of late become more and more persistently posed: what is the relation today of aesthetics to politics? Can one simply draw an inverse parallel between fascism and communism, the Right and the Left, as Benjamin appears to argue, with fascism aestheticizing politics and communism politicizing aesthetics? Does mankind, again as Benjamin writes, continue to derive aesthetic pleasure from the experience of its own destruction? Recent films like The Day after Tomorrow (2004), Armageddon (1998), and Independence Day (1996) would seem to offer up for the moviegoer just such apocalyptic fare. They provide the cake of visualizing the destruction of the Earth while in the end preserving it so that one may still have it to enjoy upon leaving the theater.

In this chapter, I look at Benjamin's quote and draw attention to something that is often forgotten: I place his quote about the relation of aesthetics to politics within the context of the rest of his essay "The Work of Art," which, after all, concerns the relation of technology to art, or film, and to a lesser extent photography as media.[1] I then sketch a history of several media in relation to art and to politics, bearing in mind the general thesis of this book concerning the relation of the human to information machines.

The reassuring smell and touch of book pages, the anticipatory crackle of opening a new music CD, the cozy comfort of surrendering oneself to broadcast television's scheduling, the magical darkness enjoyed by a cinema audience watching a film, the warm community feeling of listening to radio—these aesthetics of media might soon become little more than memories. And the politics that accompany them—the liberal, autonomous individual of print and film, the pacified consumer of broadcast media—might also now gradually dissipate with the advent of new media, with their different aesthetics and politics. The screen-network interface of living online absorbs these earlier media (Turkle 1995), restructures or remediates them into the realm of the virtual (Bolter and Grusin 1996). The subject position of the user has become a human-machine assemblage and a node, a cyborgian point (Haraway 1985) in a global network of collective intelligence (Lévy 1997). What are the politics and aesthetics of this allegedly haptic regime?

THE LIMITS OF FILM AS CRITIQUE

Benjamin sees the new methods of mechanically reproducing art in his day as contradictory to fascism and promoting revolution: "creativity and genius, eternal value and mystery," authenticity and aura, tradition and cultural heritage, are principles that he thinks will be brushed away by the cinema (218). Mechanical reproduction, he argues, adjusts culture to the increasing importance of the masses in "reality." In the case of film, art for the first time is produced without an original, is created specifically for mechanical reproduction, thereby destroying the link of art to ritual. The reproduction of the filmic work of art is possible because it is recorded, he contends, by a camera. Cameras intervene between the actor and the audience, destroying aura first because the actor cannot adjust to the audience's response in the manner of a feedback loop, and second because the camera takes up positions for the recording that are also later composed through a cutting process by an editor, with the result that the audience views what the camera allows, not what the actor intends. The camera thus enacts a "thoroughgoing permeation of reality with mechanical equipment" (234). The mediation of the recording machine, for Benjamin, destroys aura by defeating presence (229). Instead of aura, the actor's performance, enhanced outside the work of art by the culture industry's promotional efforts, elicits merely "the spell of the personality, the phony spell of a commodity" (231).

In addition to "shriveling" the artwork's aura, mechanical reproduction changes the audience. First it brings the work of art to the audience, dispersing copies throughout society, as compared with auratic art, which must, as an original, be attended in its own space (museums, concert halls, theaters). Film, therefore, is part of society, having little distance from it, easy to experience for people regardless of class. Second, in place of a "reactionary attitude" of the viewer toward an auratic artwork, the response of the movie audience is "progressive." This is so because the audience for a film, unlike a painting, enjoys a "collective experience" and finds itself in the position of a critic. Audience reaction is progressive also because of the "shock effect" of film, its continuous alteration of viewpoints. The viewer of film must have a "heightened presence of mind" to follow the shifts in perspective afforded by montage and shifts in the position of the camera. If film is received by the audience in a distracted mode, as compared with the contemplative stance evoked by traditional art, Benjamin stubbornly turns this highbrow dismissal of film into an argument for its politically revolutionary effect. Distracted by the movies, the masses become "an absent-minded examiner" (241).

Samuel Weber reminds us that the German term used by Benjamin for "distraction" and "absent-mindedness" is *Zerstreuung*.[2] This word comes from the root *streuen*, which is closest in meaning in English to "strewn" and gives the best sense of the word's German meaning of "dispersed" (Weber 1995, 92). Weber goes on to explore the lexicographic aspects of the term in relation to Benjamin's use of it in *The Origin of the German Mourning Play*, where it also suggests the physical dispersion of the *flâneur*, the person strolling in a modern city, subject to the surprises and serendipitous events of urban agglomerations. More than simply a wayward consciousness or a shifting intentionality, "distraction" suggests a fragmentation of the self, a physical coming-apart or falling into pieces in which multiplicity and heterogeneity become characteristic of the self. Weber's subtle analysis of the use of *Zerstreuung* is most helpful, but it does not acknowledge the context of its use by Benjamin in "The Work of Art."

Benjamin's first use of the term "distraction" appears directly after a quotation from the noted contemporary French critic Georges Duhamel, who in *Scènes de la vie future* excoriates cinema in purely ethical terms, calling it a "pastime" (*une passe-temps*), a "diversion" (*divertissement*) requiring no "concentration" (*aucun effort*) or "intelligence" (*aucune suite dans les idées*) (Duhamel 1930, 58). Immediately subsequent to this citation from Duhamel, Benjamin invokes the term "distraction" as an antonym to "concentration": "Distraction and concentration form polar opposites which may be stated as follows: A man who concentrates before a work of art is absorbed by it. He enters into this work of art. . . . In contrast, the distracted mass absorbs the work of art" (239). In each case, distraction and concentration, the body is displaced: in contemplation, it bleeds into the artwork; in distraction, the artwork enters into the body. Benjamin disrupts Duhamel's moral attack on film by relativizing the terms: in both cases, the person is physically altered.

Benjamin continues by linking distraction to practices of encountering buildings, as Weber suggests in his urban associations of the term. But Benjamin does not connect the reception of buildings with dispersion. Instead he emphasizes the "tactile appropriation" of buildings through "habit." He opposes the habituated urban dweller with the tourist who stands before buildings with rapt concentration in a *visual* relation to them. For Benjamin, the cinema is distracting in its tactile quality and its habitual mode of attention. This manner of reception pertains, he thinks, to all historical changes that are abrupt: "For the tasks which face the human apparatus of perception at the turning points of history cannot be solved by optical means, that is, by contemplation, alone. They are mastered gradually by habit, under the guidance of tactile appropriation"

(240). Benjamin shifts the register of critique from Duhamel's ethical level to that of the sense ratio, as in Marshall McLuhan. He rehabilitates the distraction of the masses, not so much by calling attention to their dispersion, as Weber would have it, but by discovering a critical component in the almost passive deflection of their experience, suggesting Jean Baudrillard's notion of the critical element in the "silence of the masses" in the face of mass media (Baudrillard 1983). For Benjamin, the cinema-going public may become revolutionary by their deflection of the shock of the new into a distanced perception of culture, not by a focused attention, but by absorbing the work of art into their bodies.

The media effect of film—to dissolve aura and to promote critique—is not to be equated with the appropriation of film by political movements. Fascists aestheticize politics—they film their rallies—in order, Benjamin insists, to keep property intact, and communists turn art into politics, favoring realist styles as a means of extending education about reality. In neither case do these movements intentionally deploy the media effect of art. The surrealists, Benjamin notes, may be revolutionary in politics, but their artistic practice is decidedly retrograde, relying on the aura of the artwork. The one exception in this essay mentioned by Benjamin is the films of Sergei Eisenstein. The media criticism offered by "The Work of Art" proposes not to reproduce contemporary modes of aesthetics and politics but to introduce a principle of analysis that lies at a level outside the intentions of political and artistic movements. Benjamin's argument for a progressive role of film intervenes at the level of unconscious effects, suggesting that the spread of movies throughout society will gradually produce a more critical and progressive population. This, of course, is the opposite position from that of his friends Adorno and Horkheimer, whose "culture industry" chapter in *Dialectic of Enlightenment*, written a decade after "The Work of Art," proposes that the democratic potential of the working class has been eviscerated by popular culture in all its forms— film, radio, and so forth.

Judged by the history of the past fifty years, Benjamin was clearly wrong, although Adorno and Horkheimer may not have been correct, either. There has surely been no massive swing to the left during this period in the United States, the country where film viewing is perhaps most widespread, although France and India are also high on the list. To the extent that there have been radical politics such as the antiwar movement, the New Left, and the counterculture of the 1960s and 1970s, these have been far more influenced by rock-and-roll music and even television than by film. The civil rights movement of the sixties, the feminist movement of the seventies and eighties, and the antiracism and antiheterosexism movements of the eighties and nineties cannot be tied convincingly to any particular medium of popular culture. Film, then, does not promote socialist revolution in any consistent way. But in another sense, Benjamin was clearly correct or at least insightful about the analysis of the media: he heeded the emergence of the machine as a condition of culture. He paid attention as did few if any others up to his day to the structure of the mediation of cultural objects (phenomena formerly known as art).[3]

MACHINE MEDIATIONS

Benjamin was wrong about more than the possible political effects of film. Although he presciently paid attention to the mediation of the information machine, he remained tied to the binary opposition of presence and absence. For him, presence was associated with aura and conservatism; absence with distraction and radicalism. This contrast does not work. High or traditional art like painting forecloses its media effect; it is, for Benjamin, pure presence: the painting constitutes a direct line back to the artist, one that enhances tradition and authority and reanimates ritual. Arts that sustain aura do not, for Benjamin, have a media effect. The spirit of the artist goes through the material in which his or her work is presented, touching the viewer. For the actor it is the same: the presence of the actor to the audience is what counts, affording the actor authority. For Benjamin, then, machine mediations begin only with lithography and reach their fruition in cinema. This conceptualization of the relation of art to technology fails to account for the differential effects of media, for the always already mediated nature of art. It erects a false opposition between art and technology that spills over into the opposition between fascism and communism, aesthetics and politics.

Benjamin does not want to encourage this opposition; at least his text begins with an assertion that "a work of art has always been reproducible" (218). But he quickly loses this insight by arguing that "mechanical reproduction of a work of art . . . represents something new" (218). A difficulty

Benjamin has introduced into his text derives from taking a secondary difference and making it primary. Reproducibility is his criterion for technology. Its opposite is the original, such as a painting, which cannot truly be reproduced, although there can be copies, prints, photocopies, forgeries, et cetera. But aside from the question of reproducibility, art requires technology: the work of art is always mediated, as are all cultural objects, a lesson that deconstruction has taught us well. Reproducibility, that is to say, the absence of an original, is a secondary difference within the technology of culture. Certainly mechanical reproduction marks an important break in the history of culture, a break that leads progressively to Baudrillard's concept of simulacra, to a culture in which originals, properly speaking, do not play a role in the work of art.

Benjamin's "mistake," if I can call it that, is nonetheless productive. His mistake brings into the foreground a leading problem in the theorization of the relation of culture to technology. This problem is made increasingly exigent as art becomes digitized. It is the question of the relative significance of different aspects of technology. How are we to understand the place of technology in the formation, dissemination, and reception of cultural objects? Once we acknowledge that technological mediation is a general condition of culture and recognize that this mediation is not neutral, not to be understood under the sign of the tool, we are compelled to look seriously at the object as a material construct. We are urged to consider the multiple dimensions of the materiality of the object and to assess their relative importance. Such an approach to culture goes against deeply ingrained habits of mind that give prominence primarily to the subject, to the creator, to the heroic individual, to his or her genius. With the advent of ever more capable, interesting, and intelligent technologies, we are advised not to heed the object in a simple reversal but to put forth and conceptually to develop a multiplex standpoint in which both the traditional subject and the traditional object are displaced in new registers of understanding.

SENSIBLE MEDIA THEORY

McLuhan began this theoretical reorganization but did not carry it far enough. For him the media were themselves a message but one that was limited to the all-too-human faculty of sensation. McLuhan theorized media in relation to what he called the sense ratio: the relative prominence of a single sensory organ. Books intensified the visual sense, reducing the senses of smell and hearing that were dominant before Gutenberg's invention. Electronic media reversed the situation, bringing especially touch into play. For McLuhan, media had their effect on the human being as it was conceived in the seventeenth and eighteenth centuries. Locke and Condillac theorized the human as a machine for receiving and processing sensory information. Condillac's famous statue of clay metamorphosed into human life as sense capacities were added one by one, albeit with the additional requirement of movement (Brigham 1997). These Enlightenment thinkers were determined to root the human essence in the natural and material world, far from the otherworldly imaginings of the priests. McLuhan's innovation was simply to insert media, information machines, into the world of the Enlightenment's figure of the human. The great resistance to McLuhan during his lifetime concerned the apparent agency he gave to information machines, an agency that threatened to swamp or to displace the reign of reason over the senses. Yet McLuhan did not reach far enough into this Enlightenment worldview to question the human at the level of culture, the issue of the constitution of the subject.

If McLuhan's media theory failed to open the question of the subject, it also fell short in its theory of the object, the media themselves. McLuhan conceived media as "extensions of man." Each medium allowed humans to expand the limits of their sensory capacities. Books were excellent memory devices; radio amplified the voice across space; film and television extended the eye's reach throughout the globe. Media for him were thus anthropomorphized. They were theorized as human senses and little more. In this view, the Internet would be understood no doubt as extensions of the nervous system and the brain combined. Information machines in McLuhan's theory had no specificity as machines. It is hard to imagine, for instance, what McLuhan would make of the computer screen as interface. His famous "global village" was a space in which highly extended sense organs attained local presence. Because of television, all human beings, in principle, could experience the same sights and sounds, the same events, and do so at the same time. What better definition of a village community?

The otherness of information machines and the destabilization of the subject when interacting with them is lost on McLuhan. Despite the extraordinary prescience of his understanding of media, McLuhan cannot be our guide in questioning the relation of aesthetics to politics in the era of networked computing.

UNDERDETERMINED ART

The question of aesthetics and politics takes on surprising new turns in relation to the medium of the computer. In 1985 the Centre Pompidou opened an exhibit, "The Immaterials," curated by Jean-François Lyotard, featuring the use of computers in art. The goal of the installation was to destabilize accepted meanings and to explore the polysemy and "immateriality" of language. Lyotard was interested at the time in presenting an exhibition that might set into play his concept of the postmodern. He spoke not of "indoctrinating" the visitor but of introducing the new technocultural conditions (Lyotard 1985). The content and display of the exhibit were designed to set the visitors along their own courses through the galleries, but at the same time to put into question "established cultural" norms, to open the visitor to a position of critique, to complicate the reception of art, to multiply "rationalities." Thanks to the prestige of Lyotard and as a result of the emerging fascination with information technologies, the Centre Pompidou enjoyed great success with this exhibition.

One installation consisted of several Minitel computers, each containing a document in which intellectuals, writers, and artists responded to the curator's request to define certain words (such as *freedom, matter, maternal*, and so forth). While computers were not necessary for the exhibit, they did allow a form of browsing that amplified the exhibit's purpose. On the screen, words were electronic and presumably became less material. In another room, an installation wired each square of the floor, which was activated by the movement of the participant. As one walked through the space of the installation, one's body movements provided inputs to a computer. Sounds and lights changed based on an algorithm programmed into a computer, transforming the participants' input into data, and then into sound and light configurations. (When I was in the room, there were technical problems that aborted the installation, not an uncommon experience in early applications of computers to art.) In both cases, the use of computers facilitated the questioning of the stability or materiality of cultural forms and automatically included the audience in the work of art. Already the position of the audience had changed from the disinterested contemplation of the traditional gallery of paintings to the distracted participation in computerized art. Already the work of art was losing its fixed and delimited characteristics and becoming less of an object than an experience, less determinate and more changeable.

A decade or two later, artists have become far more sophisticated in the application of computers to art projects. Above all, recent installations employ not stand-alone computers but networked computing. The installation is displaced into cyberspace as well as embedded in traditional sites. An exhibit at the Centre Pompidou in 2001 by George Legrady illustrates the new configuration of aesthetics and politics in relation to the media. Legrady's installation *Pockets Full of Memories* calls for visitors to input in digital form some object they regard as important. Visitors to Beaubourg are greeted by a phalanx of scanners, machines that enable the digitization of any object in the visitor's pocket that may be significant, loaded with memories. Those attending the exhibit via the Internet may upload images from their computer. The visitor may also add text to the image of the object. These inputs are composed by the computer into a database. After so contributing to the work of art, the visitor passes, by foot or, if online, by computer, into a room with a large wall on which the digitized objects appear. Before objects appear on the wall, however, a computer program decides on their placement based on a complex set of criteria. Interest in the exhibit depends to a great extent on the relation of objects to one another drawn by the computer. The work of art, the wall, is a collective work formed by visitors in person, visitors on the Internet, and the computer program that arrays the images. Once again the mediation of networked computers allows the artist to experiment with including the audience and the machine in the composition of the work. Far from disinterested contemplation or aura, the work appears to the audience as in part its own creation. The clear separation of artist and audience, subject and object, is broken in a new relation of aesthetics and politics.

A final example of the new relation of art and politics is Sharon Daniel's online piece *Narrative Contingencies*. It reveals a still more elaborate relation of media to the work of art. Unlike Legrady's art, Daniel's exists exclusively on the Internet, removing art completely from traditional spaces of exhibition. The displacement of art from museums, galleries, and other places of presence was in part anticipated by Benjamin, who wrote, "In the same way, by the absolute emphasis on its exhibition value the work of art becomes a creation with entirely new functions, among which the one we are conscious of, the artistic function, later may be recognized as incidental" (225). For Benjamin, film showings throughout society eroded the centrality of the artist. This tendency is developed still further when an artwork is placed in cyberspace, where it can be viewed at any time by anyone who is online.

Narrative Contingencies consists of passages from certain published works that may be commented on by the online user. The user may add his or her texts and images to the work. A key feature of the work is that the database includes operations that randomly rearrange and alter the texts initially inscribed, as well as those added by participants. The resulting work combines the conception of the overall design and selection of initial texts by the artist, the database application by the programmer, texts added by the participant, and the transformation of texts by the computer program. In this case, the work of art is a collective creation combining information machines with engineers, artists, and participants in a manner that reconfigures the role of each. Art is thus not a delimited object but an underdetermined space in which subject and object, human and machine, body and mind, space and time all receive new cultural forms.

Sharon Daniel's essay "The Aesthetics of Databases," explaining her work, draws directly on the media and makes explicit links with the politics of art. One finds in it many echoes of the "Immaterials" exhibit:

> Narrative Contingencies was built based on the assumption, or belief, that—while it is impossible to escape the image and language of the existing symbolic order—it may be possible to restructure them by circumvention and dislocation. It is hoped that a participant—who is able to find a meaningful interpretation of images and texts that she herself brought together and altered using random or chance operations—may conclude that relations of meaning are not dependent upon the ordering intention of a single author but inherently contingent upon the subjective location of the reader or viewer. (Daniel 2000, 209)

Digitized, networked art installs a new relation of art to politics, one in which the stable positions of artist and consumer are erased. Aesthetics of beauty and practices of contemplation are subverted.

The deep rupture introduced into art by the medium of networked computing calls on critics and theorists to rethink aesthetics and its relation to politics. One critic, Janez Strehovec, proposes that given the rise of artworks such as those of Legrady and Daniel, we can no longer speak of art but must instead speak of "would-be-works-of-art." He defines this conjunctive term as the art of the "extraordinary": "The key concept of the new aesthetic is therefore not contemplation but immersion based upon atmospheres of the extraordinary" (Strehovec 2000). Acknowledging that theorists such as Heidegger, Benjamin, Baudrillard, Adorno, Barthes, and Hegel anticipated the transformation or even the disappearance of art, Strehovec argues convincingly that the practice of art in recent years has introduced science and technology in a manner that requires new aesthetic theory.

In my view, Strehovec's concept of the extraordinary does not specify clearly enough the nature of the transformation introduced by new media. I prefer the term "underdetermination" to suggest the unsettling of basic components of culture in the art of networked computing. From the perspective of new media, art of the modern era preserves features of social practice as much as it sets itself in opposition to them. The critical value of modern art is limited by the form of its objective presentation; that is, it appears as an object that may become a commodity and that reinforces the hegemonic relation of subject to object characteristic of modernity. The art of Legrady and Daniel, by contrast, opens a space of transformation, a complex object that remains incomplete, requiring the viewer to change the object in the process of experiencing it. As such, the art of networked computing brings forth a culture that highlights its future transformation rather than confirming the completeness of the real. This art insists on the virtuality of the real, its openness to possibility. It solicits the participant not simply to admire the real, or even imagine a critique of the real in the sense of a future happiness (Marcuse 1964). Instead the art of networked computing invites the participant to change the real. If Marx called for philosophy not simply to interpret the world but to change it, the new art, more forcefully perhaps than he imagined, fulfills his own purpose.[4]

DATABASE NARRATIVES

Whatever formal properties of the cultural object one may wish to designate as the central feature of narrative—the discussion of this issue is complex, as in Genette (1980), Bal (1997), and Chatman (1978)—in the end, narrative must to some extent be understood in relation to a culture's inscription of temporality. Members of society must be able to narrate the story of themselves, their world, and the way the two fit together. In this sense, there is no question that narrative is a central component in culture. And it has often been recognized as such, as for example in Barthes:

> The narratives of the world are numberless. Narrative is first and foremost a prodigious variety of genres, themselves distributed amongst different substances. . . . Able to be carried by articulated language, spoken or written, fixed or moving images, gestures, and the ordered mixture of all these substances; narrative is present in myth, legend, fable, tale, novella, epic, history, tragedy, drama, comedy, mime, painting . . . stained glass windows, cinema, comics, news item, conversation. Moreover . . . narrative is present in every age, in every place, in every society; it begins with the very history of mankind and there nowhere is nor has been a people without narrative. All classes, all human groups, have their narratives . . . narrative is international, transhistorical, transcultural: it is simply there, like life itself. (Barthes 1977, 79)

Such a paean to narrative, by no means unusual in literary and theoretical discourse, must not dissuade us from questioning whether narrative persists in the "substance," as Barthes writes, of digital culture.

There are, of course, enormous variations in the content and form of the narrative in different cultures. More than that, there are large differences in what might be termed the agent of the narrative. This figure might be the society as a whole, part of the society, or an individual. The narrator might be acting or reciting as an instance of the narrative, like a Greimasian actant in a novel, or, at the other extreme, solely for herself, like the author of a diary. The entire community might be the addressee and audience, or the narration might enter the uninhabited, dark space of a desk drawer. Today, it might be recalled, in our heavily mediated environment, the narrator might be not a person at all but a computer agent, telling a story that is nonetheless indistinguishable from that of an organic individual. And there are equally large differences in what might be called the agency of the narrative, the extent to which the narrative is expected to repeat preexisting narratives or invent new ones, to represent the life of the community or the cosmos as a whole or nothing more than the vicissitudes of one person's experience. We might say that in modern society, individuals are expected to narrate their own lives, connecting their stories more or less closely to preexisting narratives, such as the idea of progress. Modern society imposes on individuals the task of taking account of themselves, of forming or directing their lives, of intermittently taking stock of where they are at a given point in life's journey, and, at base, knowing their own story. Just as Rousseau supposed in *The Social Contract*, modern individuals are forced to be free. That is, they regard themselves as freely constructing their own narrative, but this function is at the same time required of them. It might also be noted that only some individuals are designated as free or self-narrating. The following groups at different times in the modern era and in different nations were disqualified from the position of narrator: the poor, the insane, women, children, nonwhites, nonheterosexuals, and others.

The issue I raise is that of the significance of the medium to narrative. Does the medium in which narrative appears affect the nature of the narrative? Does it matter at all that a certain narrative is uttered in proximate relations, broadcast on radio or television, printed in a newspaper or book, or formatted graphically on a Web page? Although narrative is always mediated by language and often by ritual practices, modern society might be distinguished by the use of media in narrative. From handwritten diaries and printed books to the latest of the new media, modern society is characterized by media that supplement and displace speech. The question of media in narrative derives its urgency from the pervasive trend to digitize all cultural forms—text, image, and sound—enabling and indeed promoting a distanced reception of narrative. The digitization of narrative enables an extreme separation in space between narrator and listener, as well as an instantaneity of transmission of the narrative and response to it, and requires a globally networked machine mediation that envelopes the narrative. What is the effect of these conditions on the nature of narrative and its place in culture?

MODERNISM AND POSTMODERNISM AGAIN

The dominant tendency in modernist cultural theory is to regard narrative as universal. In a classic essay on the subject, Hayden White writes: "Far from being one code among many that a culture may utilize for endowing experience with meaning, narrative is a metacode, a human universal on the basis of which transcultural messages about the nature of a shared reality can be transmitted" (White 1981, 1–2). White excludes from narrative those records of events like chronicles and annals that contain a certain coherence or unity. He makes the case nonetheless for a comprehensive notion of narrative. Narrative for him is a foundation of culture, one without limit or exception. Not every discourse qualifies as narrative, but narrative is everywhere.

In another classic discussion of narrative, J. Hillis Miller continues the claim for the universality and naturalness of narrative (Miller 1995, 66). But Miller, like White and many others, theorizes narrative as if the medium in which the narrative appears matters not at all. By medium I do not mean literary form such as novel, drama, poem, and so forth. Miller argues effectively for the ubiquity of narrative across all of these. I refer instead to the material form in which the narrative is presented: whether the narrative is spoken, written, printed, presented as a play, televised, shown in a cinema, on video or DVD, or available for viewing on a Web page, to name only a few of the many possibilities that the presentation of narrative might take. In his essay on narrative, Miller's list of important theories is exhaustive—from Russian formalism to deconstruction—but he omits media theory. His list of theorists of narrative is equally comprehensive—from Chicago Aristotelians to Sigmund Freud and Paul de Man—but he excludes Walter Benjamin, Marshall McLuhan, Mary Ann Doane, N. Katherine Hayles, Paul Virilio, and others who explore the relation of narrative to media. And Miller is hardly exceptional. In fact, in more recent writings, he is quite attentive to the impact of media on literature (Miller and Asensi 1999).

This modernist or humanist view of narrative has come under sharp attack from many quarters in the past few decades. Critics have pointed out that narrative requires closure, that it betrays a certain link to patriarchy and other forms of domination in modern society, that it positions an author in a stance of command (Darley 2000, 141), that it inscribes an unbridgeable distinction between artist and reader or audience (Ryan 2001), that it contains desire in a narrow Oedipal circle (de Lauretis 1984), and so forth. The critique of narrative arose also in the debates over postmodernism. In this discussion, the issue of the media began to emerge as a significant problem for narrative theory. Before approaching the question of media in relation to narrative, it is necessary to situate briefly the question of narrative in the debates over postmodern theory. For many literary theorists and scholars, postmodern theory appeared to challenge the place of narrative in culture. John Carlos Rowe writes: "This complaint—that the postmodern trivialization of the subject and its culture is accompanied by the destruction of *narrative*—is common in critical interpretations of postmodern culture" (Rowe 1994, 99). Theorists and critics in the 1980s and 1990s lined up as either defenders of narratives and modernism or as advocates of postmodernism and some alternative to narrative. William Paulson's analysis of this debate moves to place technology as the missing term that substitutes for narrative. He explores the possibility that "computer media" or "electronic media" interrupt both narrative and canon: "One thing that changes decisively is that the experience of reading and simulation becomes more labile, at once interactive and transitory. In a possible future, to paraphrase Andy Warhol, every text will be canonical for fifteen minutes" (Paulson 1997, 231). From this point on, modernity and postmodernity, narrative and technology, would be mixed in a discussion of the future of literature, indeed of writing itself.

The postmodern assault on narrative reflects the critique by Jean-François Lyotard in *The Postmodern Condition* of what he termed "grand narratives" (Lyotard 1984). While Lyotard did suggest that grand narratives, such as the idea of progress in modern discourse, might be losing their credibility, he was far from dismissive about narrative in general. In fact, Lyotard detected a reemergence of "the small story" or "language games" (later "the differend") from the premodern period of European history as the basis, ironically, for a postmodern culture. All of this is familiar. What is often less noted is that Lyotard attempted to associate the postmodern small story with new media. For Lyotard, media play a crucial role in the unfolding of a postmodern culture based on small stories. Postmodern society, for him, is beset by an oppositional duality of grand narratives that have migrated into instrumental rationality or performativity and small narratives that have become heterogeneous and multiple. The medium of the computer is the key to the outcome of this struggle. Here is Lyotard's dramatic formulation of the politics of the narrative:

We are finally in a position to understand how the computerization of society affects this problematic. It could become the "dream" instrument for controlling and regulating the market system, extended to include knowledge itself and governed exclusively by the performativity principle. In that case, it would inevitably involve the use of terror. But it could also aid groups discussing metaprescriptives by supplying them with the information they usually lack for making knowledgeable decisions. The line to follow for computerization to take the second of these two paths is, in principle, quite simple: give the public free access to the memory and data banks. Language games would then be games of perfect information at any given moment. (Lyotard 1984, 67)

The alternative for Lyotard is clear: terror or freedom.[5]

For our purposes, the medium, here the computer, is a tool that might be deployed for better—the postmodern small story—or for worse, the system's performative terror. Lyotard, writing in the late 1970s, understood the computer as a stand-alone recording system, not connected to the Internet, a globally networked communication system. The role of networked computing in deciding the fate of narrative in postmodern culture might then be reformulated as the "terror" of ubiquitous monitoring or the freedom of infinitely dispersed positions of speech. In the latter instance, public access to information is only a small part of the story, for the Internet enables, in principle, the unbounded proliferation of the creation of narratives: on Web pages, in chat rooms, in networked gaming, in MOOs, and so forth.

A decade after *The Postmodern Condition*, Lyotard began to recognize the importance of networked computing for narrative. In *The Inhuman*, Lyotard sees the cosmic novelty of the Internet: "The electronic and information network spread over the earth gives rise to a global capacity for memorizing which must be estimated at the cosmic scale, without common measure with that of traditional cultures" (Lyotard 1991, 64). The unprecedented nature of the new media apparatus registers for him a break of unparalleled proportions with previous history and with narrative hitherto. The crucial impact of the media, as he conceived it, was on time and space. Narrative relies on time for its inscription, but the computer erases time, he thinks: "The question raised by the new technologies in connection with their relation to art is that of the here-and-now. What does 'here' mean on the phone, on television, at the receiver of an electronic telescope? And the 'now'? Does not the 'tele-'element necessarily destroy presence, the 'here-and-now' of the forms and their 'carnal' reception? . . . Is a computer in any way here and now?" (118). Disrupting the basic elements of culture, the Internet—not quite named even in 1988 by Lyotard—scrambles the foundations of narrative. The "inhuman" in the work's title represents the new media conjuncture. Rather than explore in depth this new invasion of the body snatchers, this new disembodiment or lack of presence and carnality, to use his terms, Lyotard instead frames the cultural moment in relation to what he calls "the unpresentable" and urges an art of the unpresentable as a counterforce to the terrorism of the system's rationality. To my thinking, Lyotard's project preserves too much of an opposition of art/narrative and media, failing to embrace the "inhuman" assemblage of human and machine to test the possibility of narrativity within media.

HYPERTEXT NARRATIVE

Within literary studies, the discussion of narrative and media has focused on a type of digital work known as hypertext. An extensive body of important work has already appeared addressing this issue.[6] While I cannot here explore in detail or with systematicity the question of hypertext, I will at least relate the question of hypertext to that of narrative.

Hypertexts are digital writings consisting of nodes and links. The nodes are passages of texts that are in most cases fixed by authors, and the links are connections between nodes or pathways from one node to another that are made by readers. The extent to which the reader may select a link varies with each hypertext, although at the extreme, any point in any node may be linked to any other. In hypertext, then, the reader determines, or appears to determine, the sequence of texts to a greater extent than in a printed book, with some notable exceptions from Laurence Sterne to Jorge Luis Borges and beyond. To a certain degree, the contrast between printed texts and hypertexts has been argued in terms of linear and non-linear logics. To my mind, Nancy Kaplan draws the distinction best when she contends that the important difference between print and hypertext rests with a shift from the node to the link. When hypertexts are viewed merely as nodes with non-print-like links, critics may well find the difference minor and the preference resting with turning a page rather than clicking a mouse. But as Kaplan points out, a perspective that places links at the center of the issue of narrative reveals that hypertexts offer a very different practice of reading. "Links force readers out of one mode of cognitive activity and into another, at least for a time. . . . The moments during which readers recognize and consider the offered link cues should be understood . . . as moments of especially deep engagement with meanings. . . . The repeated acts of choosing links by succumbing to each one's cue creates a contingent order, a linearity perceived in tension and against the possibility of other lines" (Kaplan 2000, 222, 227). For Kaplan, reading by links places at the forefront the multiplicity of possible narratives, while reading by nodes underscores the salience of a single narrative. In Stuart Moulthrop's Deleuzian reading, "hypertextual writing seduces narrative over or away from a certain Line, thus into a space where the sanctioned repetitions of conventional narrative explode or expand, no longer at the command of a *logos* or form, but driven instead by *nomos* or itinerant desire" (Moulthrop 1997, 273). For both critics, hypertext shifts the text's emphasis away from direct or even multiple lines of plot toward a relatively heterogeneous field where the next step is above all contingent.

If hypertext is a different inscription of writing from printed books, containing a logic that moves away from propulsive coherence, then the hypertext's effects on the reader might also diverge from that of the book. Katherine Hayles offers just this argument in her studies of hypertext. But her position is complicated by her recognition that in some cases, printed books might be hypertexts (Hayles 2002b). If books are organized as nodes or lexia with no particular ordering except that imposed by the sequencing proximity of the pages and their numbering, it is possible to "read" a book by jumping haphazardly, say, from one node to another, disregarding page number and proximity.[7] Yet Hayles goes on to show in a subtle and fascinating analysis of Shelley Jackson's hypertext *Patchwork Girl* that this work could exist only in a computer hypertext because the "patchwork girl" is composed of body parts with lexia embedded within them, folding the signifying structures within the computer-generated body (Hayles 2000). While it is difficult to represent in textual form the (non)narrative qualities of *Patchwork Girl*, Hayles concludes, rightly, I believe, that a hypertext located on a network of computers reconfigures all positions in the literary act—author, narrator, text, reader—to such an extent that perhaps the term *narrative* does not adequately capture or indicate the new positions. The ontology and epistemology of the text no longer resemble that of the printed book.

If we switch perspectives and move not from the printed text to the hypertext but directly to the World Wide Web as a whole and consider it for what it properly is, a single hypertext of enormous complexity, the difficulty of deploying the term *narrative* becomes clearer. At two different levels, the Internet may be considered a hypertext: first, Web pages are linked to one another in a haphazard tangle without center or obvious organizational principle; and second, locations on the Internet, as distinct from the Web (IP addresses, domain names, etc.), are also linked, though at a machine level rather than a textual level. Web pages directly constitute a text of sorts, what Pierre Lévy (1995) terms "collective intelligence." With millions of pages already constructed and millions more no doubt on the horizon, the Web consists of inputs from users. Its authors are its readers. Negotiating the Web with Firefox, Explorer, or Navigator (note the effort to code reading as "surfing" or moving through physical space), the "user" enters a culture without any of the markers of the "normal" physical world. In the world consisting of electrons and light pulses, the virtual space of the Internet, narrative and narrator are impossible to specify. The hypertext of the Internet and the Web evacuates all meaning from the term *narrative*.

TELEVISION AND NARRATIVE

Lyotard opened the discussion of the relation of narrative to media but was more interested in the possibility of new (postmodern) narrative forms than in exploring the vexed question of the media. Yet television itself poses challenges to narrative theory. Some critics complain that television has no defining narrative (Rowe 1994, 100). One critic points out that the application of narrative theory to television produces more problems than it solves. James Hay observes that "narrative theory's emergence out of literary studies often increases its tendency to analyze television in critical terms better suited to the kind of *discrete* narrative text that is commonly associated with literature, film, or even oral folk tales. . . . For this reason, the most convenient objects of study for narratological criticism of television have often been episodic series or serials . . . rather than the 'flow' qualities that critics . . . have associated with television and radio" (Hay 1992, 358). Narrative theory is skewed toward what might be called stand-alone cultural objects, a bias that seriously misses the salient features of television. Narrative theory transforms television programs into a set of "works" such as novels or films.

But television does not easily lend itself to such framing. As many theorists of television have noted, notions of authorship do not apply to television, whether one speaks of news, quiz shows, serials, late-night talk shows, and so forth. In addition, the modes of reception characteristic of novels, paintings, and even films are not well suited to understanding television: the deep imaginary constructed by the world of the novel, the contemplative gaze associated with painting, and the intense fascination that draws viewers of cinema into the diegesis are unlike the distracted absorption with which audiences receive television broadcasts. Also, television offers not one piece of cultural work at a time, as in film, but a continuous flow of hundreds of programs that are interrupted by commercials from the sender, by remote-control switching on the part of the receiver, time shifting with VCRs, and even picture-in-picture double viewing. Then, too, the position of the camera, which directs film viewers in a cinematic apparatus to a relatively fixed point of view, is very different in television, which offers not a directed scene but a constant shifting of images without a consistent vantage point. Psychoanalytically inclined scholars characterize television as unlike the dreamlike "regression" induced by cinema and the concomitant styles of identification it encourages. Television, they contend, effects "numerous partial identifications" in its "liveness and directness" of image (Flitterman-Lewis 1992, 219). In all these ways (and others too numerous to list here), television resists narrative theory. It foreshadows a further drift away from narrative that I argue characterizes the culture of digital media.

At a second level of television's place in the larger culture, it is possible to recuperate narrative theory. In John Rowe's view, "Television is merely participating in the larger rhetoric of an economy of representation, in which the principal aim is not the marketing of commodities but the production of narratives capable of being retold by their viewers" (Rowe 1994, 101). In this account, television is a sort of supernarrator, spinning tales that viewers then recount as if they were Lyotard's *petits récits*, the basis for conversation in daily life. At this level, Rowe celebrates the culture of television precisely for its narrative function:

> As a *narrative*, television is the most complicated and influential mode of constructing and judging experience that we have had, however trivial we may find its individual narratological "units." It is as a complex narrative that television must now be interpreted, along with them means by which it constructs its own implied readers, whose "competencies" more than any other discursive standard constitute the terms through which our social consensus is structured *and* retold in our conversations, our behaviors, our dreams, and even our representations of ourselves. (Rowe 1994, 118)

A difficulty with considering television narratives in this way is that it separates the viewer too much from the transmission. Baudrillard (1994) has argued convincingly of the simulacra effect of television, by which it constructs its own world and viewers along with it. While Rowe's argument certainly has some merit, it ignores the specific culture of television as experienced, the "hyperreal" culture it generates. And again, this will be a major concern when I discuss new media hereafter: their tendency to inscribe human-machine interfaces at such a profound level that one can no longer speak of a narrative with distinct functions of enunciation and reception.

OPEN TEXT CULTURE

The innovation of digital media in relation to narrativity derives from an unexpected place: the practice of computer programmers to present their work in the form of open source. Standard procedure for professional programming, as studied in computer science departments, called for a computer program's execution file to be accompanied by a text file (source code) that made the program's code readily available for editing and alteration. The most conspicuous program today that maintains that tradition is the Linux operating system, but it is also true of Netscape, Firefox, and peer-to-peer programs like Gnutella and BitTorrent. The open-source movement in computer programming presumes that the user is also a producer, that the reader is also a writer. It takes advantage of the computer's ability to store, copy, and transmit code at high speeds and little cost. Open source introduces a new principle as basic to mediated culture: the reversibility of all positions of writing and reading. It is in sharp opposition to previous media that, in different ways, introduced stability into cultural objects, be they books, radio or television broadcasts, movies, sound recordings, and so forth.

The implications of open source for cultural objects other than computer programs emerge in "open content." This is the position that all cultural objects that are digitized may be transformed in their reception, that any entity consisting of text, images, sound, or their combination may be edited, revised, amended, or abridged in the process of being read. The implications of this aspect of networked computing for narrative are devastating: culture becomes malleable, unfixed, and fluid. With open content, it becomes clear that narrative theory has presumed a stability and endurance to its objects that is related to the material form of their appearance and may be contingent on that material form. If cultural objects, developed in the context of networked computing, come to be characterized by continual transformation, they no longer sustain a narrative. At best, narrative moves to another level: that of the process of the changes itself. One might discern a narrative to the transformations the object undergoes. However, since this transformation is likely to be the result of the collaborative effort of all readers, the coherence of anything like a linear narrative may be lost.

But I speak in the science fiction mode of the future at a time when several generations have grown up in a media ecology of networked computing, albeit including earlier media such as print and film. Today's reader might be disturbed by, or skeptical of, a cultural practice that does not depart from the material affordances and constraints habitually and unconsciously associated with objects like books and films. At this time, one may only imagine a culture based on open-content digital code rather than paper and ink or celluloid and Mylar. Yet the handwriting is on at least the virtual wall. One direction for critical practice in the cultural sciences is to explore the potential of open content. If we do not, the development of a culture of networked computing is more likely to take forms that we might well find objectionable. Thus, it is important to discuss the implications of humachines for ethics.

7

THE GOOD, THE BAD, AND THE VIRTUAL

For what is morality, if not the practice of liberty, the deliberate practice of liberty?
—Michel Foucault, in *The Final Foucault*

The media have a complex relation with ethical practice. The introduction of each medium, from print to the Internet, has been greeted with howls of despair over the fate of morality. Critics complain that the new media will undermine the ethical basis of society. As late as 1880, readers of novels were warned of the dire consequences of print media: "Millions of young girls and hundreds of thousands of young men," the journal *The Hour* shrieked, "are *novelized* into absolute idiocy. Novel-readers are like opium-smokers; the more they have of it the more they want of it, and the publishers . . . go on . . . making fortunes out of this corruption."[1] The same concerns are often voiced today about the Internet with the same imagined threat of addiction. Of course, jeremiads like this one are commonplace and cannot be given too much importance. Yet they sound a note that is revealing: they register the force of the medium and its impact, as medium, on the ethical culture. The complaint in 1880 said nothing about the content of the novel. The same story told orally presumably would not raise hackles. Media, to employ Gilles Deleuze's term, deterritorializes culture and in doing so unsettles ethical certainties. And the Internet urges a rethinking of ethics, an innovation in the theory of ethics.

Sergio Leone's film *The Good, the Bad, and the Ugly* (1966), for instance, sets cinema in opposition to mainstream American values as it upsets the moral framework of the Western movie genre. Westerns, from the earliest days of cinema with Edwin Porter's *The Great Train Robbery* of 1903 through the 1950s, reenacted the American myth of the frontier (Wright 1975), the struggle against the Indians, the violence of life in the West, and, above all, the clear delineation of good and evil. The morality of liberal America is tested and performed in Western settings: the struggle for society based on law against the harsh natural landscape, against pagan "primitives" and Mexicans, against the lust, greed, and brutality of transplanted Europeans—instincts set loose in the wilderness. The oater presents in fantasy a replay of America's origin myth: the building of a New Jerusalem in a desolate world and its repeated rebuilding in the settling of the frontier. In the Western, the American movie audience was constructed as a moral agent with an unambiguous imperative. As an American, one knew right from wrong. To act morally meant progress and well-being, at least for white males with guts, brains, and brawn.

Leone's movie plays with the panorama of American morality. The protagonists—Eli Wallach as Tuco, Lee Van Cleef as Angel Eyes, and Clint Eastwood as Blondy—are introduced in turn at the outset of the film as the Ugly (il cattivo), the Bad (il brutto), and the Good (il buono) (see figure 16). In a long, almost three-hour, quest, the three men prove themselves morally bankrupt. Eastwood's "the Good" only marginally improves on the other two when near the end of the film he shows compassion for a dying soldier. In the main, however, the heroes pursue buried gold with no loftier ambition. As they romp and murder their way through the stark Western landscape, the Good, the Bad, and the Ugly find themselves amid the Civil War, one of America's most tortured ethical events. Again, in Leone's hands, the war appears without moral justification, only as senseless butchery, for instance in a battle costly of human life fought over a bridge that has no strategic value. A dying Union commander dreams of destroying the bridge, since so many men have been lost needlessly in quest of its prize. The Good and the Bad comply by blowing up the bridge, but not to redeem the captain's moral wish, only to allow themselves to pass through the battlefield to arrive at a cemetery where the gold lies interred in a grave.

The Good, the Bad, and the Ugly introduces into the binary of good and bad a third element, ugly, which destabilizes the opposition into a nonlogical list. The ugly is taken from an aesthetic binary, one that has no direct relation with good and bad. The good and the bad in the title both suggest the standard moral equation of the Western and deny it: all three char-

FIGURE 16. The search for gold (still from *The Good, the Bad, and the Ugly*)

acters are bad, in an obvious way. In this manner, the terms *good* and *bad* shift from their adjectival sense into nouns. The trio may be Tom, Dick, and Harry, or the Good, the Bad, and the Ugly. And by deploying these terms, Leone also suggests that his movie is a medieval morality play with characters given the names of virtues. In this chapter, I use the terms *the good, the bad,* and *the virtual* in a different way. I do not hypostatize them into characters. Instead I use the terms to suggest that the virtual may not fit into existing definitions of the good and the bad. For Leone, employing the medium of film in the mid-1960s, the genre of the Western affords the undoing of American ethical aspirations. The Italian director deploys American media and American narratives to question the core of American beliefs. And Americans loved it, judging by both critical and popular responses.[2] As the media extend their influence and multiply their forms, what might be the fate of ethics in what has been called "the age of information"?

ETHICS AS A PROBLEM

How can mediated cultural acts be evaluated? Can we apply the same norms, value judgments, and moral and ethical criteria that we use in evaluating face-to-face speech acts to acts that are distanced by information machines?[3] Do the standards deployed in real life serve us well in the virtual domains of cyberspace, film, radio, television, telephone, telegraph, and print, in short, in the media? I will explore the hypothesis that the emergence of an age of information may put established ethical principles into suspension. Perhaps ethics are limited in their range of applicability to what is now, after the vast dissemination of media, called real life. Perhaps the virtual imposes a species of cultural life that is, to use Nietzsche's phrase, beyond good and evil. The problem, then, would not be to determine a means to apply ethics to a recalcitrant and strange domain of the virtual but to invent new systems of valuation that adhere effectively to mediated life.

Another question arises just as the first is posed: if new ethical rules are required for mediated culture, perhaps the earlier system of ethics was flawed. Perhaps ethics as we have known them are put into question when the virtual complicates the real. Perhaps certain problems with the ethical emerge when one attempts to extend its reach to mediated acts. As long as the media are contained to particular times and spaces, ethics are arguably not in question.[4] To read a printed novel, newspaper, or treatise is a special act, easily delimited from real life and face-to-face relations by the very materiality of the printed page. It is simple to distinguish between talking to a person and reading a novel, even if the novel is more arresting than the conversant. The medium of film is similarly bounded by its reception and its form: films, at least until the advent of television, are shown in specific places at specific times; they are determined in time and place. After the credits have rolled, the audience leaves the theater and encounters other people, perhaps to discuss the film.

These familiar boundaries between relations among people and the media are now beginning to crumble. Walkmans and portable radios permit a person to listen to music regardless of location. The assignment of specific places, like concert halls, for listening to music has become obsolete. Television, with its continuous flow of programming, disrupts the sense that mediated culture is a collection of finite works. Twenty-four hours a day, over one hundred channels continue to broadcast, punctuated more by commercials than by boundaries between shows. Mobile phones enable connections between people regardless of location. Space is eliminated as an obstacle to conversation. The digital network of computers enables global connections that are interactive, like conversations. Teleconferencing adds voice and video to remote relations. Audio and video reproduction by the consumer undercuts the hegemony of network programming, time-shifting, as it is called, the enactment of cultural objects. Combinations of these technologies are further blurring the lines between real relations and virtual relations. The Internet incorporates malls, radio, film, television, fax, and other media. Mobile phones include e-mailing and limited Web browsing. Cars and home appliances "speak to" the consumer, and the computer "recognizes" the user's speech. It is possible that the domain of the ethical was context specific to cultures that at one end of a time scale were secularized and at the other end had not yet been immersed in virtual media. I turn now to the premodern period to inquire if ethics were possible before modernization.

The great ethical philosophers of the modern period presupposed an individual separated from webs of dependency that characterized premodern society in the West. There first had to exist a certain distance between individuals and political and religious authorities in order for the individual to raise the question of the nature of the good. When Kant formulated his categorical imperative for ethics ("Act only on that maxim whereby thou canst at the same time will that it should become a universal law"), he assumed a world in which individuals could choose how to act and in which the consequences of their acts would in some significant sense not be determined by institutional authorities (Kant 1949). Neither the peasant nor the priest nor the aristocrat could be the ethical person; only the bourgeois, the commoner bound not by personal ties of allegiance and obedience but by the impersonal rules of the market, could, from this perspective, be ethical. When these market rules were universalized, the universalization of the ethical domain followed in its path. Even then the process took ages to accomplish. Nonwhites, women, and the poor all were outside the ethical domain when Kant wrote in the late eighteenth century.

Religion, the cultural dominant of the premodern era, does not give ethics the pride of place they have in modern society. To be commanded by an almighty God is hardly to adopt an ethical criterion in an autonomous rational act. One might still have a narrow slice of choice between God and Satan, but this decision is theological, affecting the soul for eternity—not, properly speaking, ethical. Søren Kierkegaard put ethics in its rightful theological place, well beneath the religious, spiritual domain in import for individuals. Although the spiritual is for him separate from and above the ethical, some religious thinkers did address the question of ethics in relation to the media. In *The Present Age*, Kierkegaard himself, for instance, understands the challenge that the media present for ethics and for spiritual life in general. He regards the press as a danger to humanity because of the anonymity it introduces. For him "the powers of impersonality" of the press are nothing less than a "dreadful calamity." The media of print eviscerates responsibility on the reader's part, undermining the moral dimension of commitment characteristic of face-to-face relations. The press creates a phantom public realm in which everything is "reduced to the same level" (Dreyfus 1999, 16). Kierkegaard confines his critique of the print media to the level of the ethical, not the religious dimension. His complaint about the virtuality of print—what he calls its phantom quality—might raise more difficulties for him if he placed it at the spiritual level, where God himself might be regarded as a virtual being.

It is true that in the twentieth century, religious thinkers such as Martin Buber and Gabriel Marcel introduce ethical dimensions into theology. Perhaps this tendency is best illustrated by Emmanuel Levinas, who regards the ethical relation to the Other as deeply religious or at least spiritual. His notion of the Other serves to decenter the self, taking up familiar post-structuralist themes in a critique of philosophies of consciousness and of individualism more generally. The Other for Levinas is the moral ground of the self, disrupting all forms of Cartesian egoism. For our concern, it is especially interesting to note that Levinas presents the Other as a "face." [5] Although the face for him is surely metaphorical, its position as the foundation for ethics reminds us of the territorial assumptions of the ethical, even as late as 1963, when *Infinity and Otherness* appeared. One could still at this point presume the arena of the face-to-face as the horizon of human relations; one could still forget about the mediation of the information machine, the facelessness of relations that insist on the partiality and multiplicity of the self engaged in moral interactions. [6]

The philosopher's quest for the *summum bonum*, the ultimate good, with all its variations and definitions, is but one perspective from which to consider the ethical. [7] Another is the simple observation that individuals in their daily lives continuously make judgments of good and bad. Humans evaluate. This indisputable fact of social life, taken as a starting point to develop an ethics, is Nietzsche's approach. He develops a genealogy of morals by demonstrating the historicity of value systems (Nietzsche 1967). He outlines the pagan, noble ethics of good and bad, contrasting them with the Judeo-Christian, slave morality of good and evil. Nietz-sche's genealogy defines ethics as a historical construction. True enough, he overlays this history with a transcendental criterion of life affirmation, evaluating each moral system in relation to what he regards as its ability to promote great health (*grosse gesundheit*). And he closes his narrative of moral history with a future, utopian system of the transvaluation of all values, a Hegelian synthesis of earlier systems that combines the spon-taneity of judgment in the master morality with the depth of the slave morality, adding to the new moral regime an aesthetic dimension of cre-ativity by the free spirits, the overmen.

What is most pertinent to my argument concerning ethics in the age of information is that Nietzsche includes a sociological moment in the understanding of moral systems. The standpoint of the group is crucial to the type of morality it will create. The nobleman stands above other people, making valuations from a position of domination. Whatever the nobleman likes is the good because there is no one to tell him otherwise. By contrast the slave, who is in a subordinate position, must have values that first refute those of the rulers. To regard themselves as good, the slaves must negate the rulers' judgment. So the priest among the slaves invents an alternative world, a heaven, with a moral authority superior to that of the earthly rulers, and in this higher authority, the slaves are re-garded as the good, the slaves, that is, who attend to the higher authority and his rules. But the mediation of the higher world requires the slave to disavow all earthly judgments by elevating himself above that world. Dis-carded is the morality of flesh and blood, of territory, that is controlled by the lash of the earthly rulers' whip. Nietzsche's genealogy of ethics, then, goes through the circuit of sociocultural position, of territorial space, to understand historically instituted moral systems. Yet Nietzsche, writing in the 1870s and 1880s, attentive as he was to the typewriter (Kittler 1990), did not consider the role of the media, of information machines, in the problem of the ethical.

I shall then pick up from the place left off by Nietzsche and attempt to outline some directions for a genealogy of morals in an age populated not only by humans but also by information machines. I shall pay particular attention to the Internet since the term "Information Age" takes on new urgency after people began flocking to the Net in the mid-1990s.

TERRIBLE MACHINES

The incursion of information machines into daily life elicits considerable worry about ethics.[8] On the Internet itself there are many discussion groups in Usenet and in blogs devoted to the topic, and it is a constant issue in chat rooms across cyberspace. Until the Web was created in 1993, the culture of computer scientists and the ethos of the university community dominated the moral tone of communication on the Internet. A vague ethic of the sharing of information characterized exchanges on the Net. In fact, the architecture of networked computing promotes just such rapid, decentralized information flows. One of the basic functions of the Net, file transfer protocol (FTP), has no other purpose. The design of the Net maximized openness between users as if participants lived in a harmonious community, one where there is no need to lock one's door, surround one's property with fences, erect gates to keep out intruders. Civility was presumed and largely prevailed on the Net from 1969 to 1993. Users were for the most part convinced that a utopian communication device had been set in place that surpassed the moral tone of real-life meetings as well as encounters in other media. Howard Rheingold's discussion of the WELL, a bulletin board or electronic cafe located in the Bay Area, attests to the general goodwill and flourishing of mutual aid of this period (Rheingold 1993).

Yet even in this halcyon period of the Net, troubles emerged. Forms of conflict appeared that were possible just because of the technological design of the Net, forms of strife that had little parallel in real life. In particular spamming (sending unwanted messages) and flaming (insulting an addressee often with violent language) ruffled the equanimity of users (Spinello 1999). Spamming was promoted by the ease of sending messages in multiple copies to multiple addressees. Flaming was encouraged by the distance between sender and receiver and by the interface of the screen (Dery 1993). These flies in the ointment of open communication, users believed, could nevertheless be regulated by the Net itself. *Netiquette* was the term invented for proper online communication. Such protocols of civil communication spread quickly among users. New users were initiated into the mores of the Net by more experienced users. These "newbies" and "trolls" suffered from their inferior status at the hands of "wizards" and "masters" as part of the hazing process characteristic of the early years of the Web. Netiquette was an ethical system that did not eliminate inequalities. But in 1993 Web browsers were invented, making the use of the Internet easier and more attractive as graphics and sound were integrated into computer communications programs. The population of users grew quickly from 20 million to 200 million by the end of the decade, overwhelming the Net culture of the earlier period. In the new conditions of mass usage, the practice of coaching newbies in the ways of netiquette could not keep up.

The problem of the ethics of the Net attracted the attention of other media—newsprint, radio, film, and television—where the issue of inter-media rivalry must not be overlooked. These broadcast media (transmitting the same copy from the few to the many) presented the world of the Internet to society at large, to those who had never used the Net. The discussion of ethics on the Net escaped the confines of the Net itself and became news for everyone. If spamming and flaming besmirch the moral tone of conversation on the Net, newsprint and television arguably present even more degraded types of communication. Here the capitalist profit motive encourages gross, sensationalist strategies of information conveyance. Selling newspapers or movie tickets and attracting viewers and listeners lower the discussion to a deplorable level. When the topic of ethics on the Net turns to its presentation in the broadcast media, the medium is so coarse that the message, in this case, ethics, is difficult to discern. In newspaper and television reporting of Net ethics, it is impossible to separate motives of gain from evaluations of behavior in cyberspace. The ethics of broadcast media are a topic one may approach only with some touch of irony.

Acknowledging these problems, I will discuss the treatment in the press of ethics on the Internet, focusing on issues of content, censorship, and anonymity. In this discussion it is important to keep in mind the question of the private and the public, for what seems to arouse ethical concerns about the Internet is often the ease of access and global availability of what is posted there, just the features that the design of the medium promotes. In other words, what raises hackles for some is not that a particular act or statement is done or said but that it is so out there, so blatantly in one's face, so terribly, unashamedly available, so public. In the mid-1980s, Joshua Meyrowitz (1985) raised the issue of the media's ability to blur boundaries between public and private, especially in the case of television. The televised shooting of Oswald by Jack Ruby, news films depicting dead American soldiers and photographs of Vietnamese victims of American napalm bombs in the Vietnam War, the live broadcasts of the Gulf War and the O. J. Simpson trial and so many other cases are self-evident examples of the power of the media to change audiences by transporting what had previously been public actions right into the privacy of the home. In the early 1990s, Lynn Spigel (1992) made a similar case for television's impact on the public-private distinction in regard to gender. Broadcast media undermine modern culture's ability, she argues, to maintain a private realm separate from the outside, and with this loss of a private realm, so also disappears the ethical individual. In a media culture, individuals lose their distance from the public sphere, lose a sense of separateness from objects and events outside themselves, lose cultural distance that is essential to autonomous, ethical judgment. The Internet continues this trend but amplifies it considerably because its content is always and everywhere available, not limited by the programming controls of the broadcast corporations, and because it is interactive, fostering a deeper participation in the cultural event by the recipients of the message.

Take the example of a sex-change operation performed on a Webcam for everyone online to witness. The *Los Angeles Times* reported the event as an ethical question. The headline read, "Sex-Change Webcast Stirs E-thics Debate" (Ebnet 1999), emphasizing both the ethical and the media aspects of the event. The doctor performing the surgery was asked to defend himself on ethical grounds, not because he was performing a sex-change operation but because he was Webcasting it. The ethics of the transsexual may be objectionable to many people, but as long as the procedure is sequestered behind the walls of an operating room, it does not seem to incite moral emotions. In the newspaper report, the operation becomes ethical solely because of its media existence, its availability on the Internet. The important point is that acts which may be regarded as acceptable in certain contexts become moral issues owing to their media proximity. The media, in this case the Internet, change the ethical environment. They do so by juxtaposing actions, images, sounds, and texts from diverse subcultures. The media mix together what in real life were held separate. The media, in short, transform the cultural basis of ethics by erasing boundaries around local communities that subsist in time and space. The Internet demands that we acknowledge as morally acceptable things that we may prefer to disavow. Thereby the Internet brings to its users a wider spectrum of humanity than was accessible before. It reveals to us that our comfortable distinction of public and private permits us to tolerate experiences that we regard as bad or even evil.

The report of the event in the newspaper further complicates the ethics of new media. It ensures that those who do not use the Net will know about it. Those who are not familiar with new media and perhaps are somewhat anxious about them are confronted by information about an experience they judge without any sense of what happened. Newspaper readers are likely to make judgments not about the sex-change surgery as such but about the propriety of its appearance on the Internet. A similar complication occurred two months earlier when the *Los Angeles Times* ran a story about FBI agents who pose in chat rooms as underage girls to entrap would-be sex offenders. In this case, the ethical question was not about sex with thirteen-year-olds but about the authorities' behavior. Since on the Internet no one knows you are a dog, no one knows you are an FBI agent, either. Officers manipulated features of the medium (creating a "handle" or new identity) to encourage pedophiles and then to arrest them. A representative of the Electronic Frontier Foundation told the reporter, "At least half the 13-year-old girls in chat rooms are probably policemen" (G. Miller 1999b, A21). The content of chat room discussions is not in question in the newspaper report; only the ethics of police luring pedophiles.

If the ethics of the FBI become questionable when agents go online, print media find just as perplexing distinctions between the virtual and the real induced by the Net. It is well known that a good deal of downloaded content on the Web is erotic, a fact that says as much about the state of sexuality in postmodern puritan culture as it does about new media. And some of this material consists of images of children. But is it ethical to view or download child pornography? The *Los Angeles Times* wanted its readers to know that courts found computer images of naked children acceptable but analog photographs of those children illegal. A judge in a circuit court of appeals explained to the reporter: "The 1st Amendment prohibits Congress from enacting a statute that makes criminal the generation of images of fictitious children engaged in imaginary but explicit sexual conduct" (Weinstein and Miller 1999, A1). The judiciary determines that the Internet is the realm of the virtual, of the "fictitious" and "imaginary," quite distinct from the real where other laws apply. The newspaper disseminates information to all society that questions the ethics of a separate order of the virtual. The key is the criterion of the fictitious. If an erotic image of a child is digitized and some of the pixels are altered, the image is no longer that of an "actual" child. How many pixels have to be changed for the image to enter the register of the virtual? Or is the mere digitization and uploading of the image itself a conversion into the virtual? The reporter did not clarify the precise technology of networked computing that alters the ethical quality of an image.

With digital media, contents of actions and symbols no longer fall under ethical rules that apply in real life, and the print media disseminate this disturbance. Another example illustrates the difficulty of ethics in digital media more fully. Again the case involves FBI agents cum underage girls. This time the perpetrator raised the defense of virtuality: even though he showed up in real life for a meeting with an underage cybergirl, Patrick Naughton, the accused, argued in court that his actions "were grounded in an online fantasy world" and were not reprehensible morally or legally (G. Miller 1999a, C1). He won his case. The justice system accepted the distinction between real and virtual pedophilia.[9] And I rest mine that the media upset ethical certainties and alter the content of human experience, a condition that older media find troublesome.

ANONYMITY OF IDENTITY

In the early days of Internet messaging in the 1980s, the ethical problem of computer-mediated communication (CMC) already arose. The interface of the computer removes all traces of the embodied person, his or her voice, appearance, and gestures. The receiver of the message perceives only what is typed on the screen, and this is received from a username that is often fictional. Many users assume that the identity they are communicating with is a "real" individual, one whose e-mailed statements are equivalent to spoken words in proximate relations. Thus in an electronic community from the early 1980s, participants were dismayed to learn that their longtime friend whose online identity was "Joan" was revealed to be a male psychologist named Alex. Many participants were troubled by what they regarded as an ethical transgression: a person willfully misled others about their gender (Van Gelder 1996). To swap genders and to carry on years of exchanges posing as the "wrong" gender, was, for these users of electronic messaging, an ethical crime of identity fraud.

Networked computing is not the only medium in which such deceptions occur. It is possible to switch genders in written letters, in masquerades, in everyday life by cross-dressing, as the movie *Boys Don't Cry* (1999) demonstrates. Books may be published under a pseudonym; passports and identity papers may be forged or altered. Even before electronic and print media complicated personal relations, identity could be in question. The film *The Return of Martin Guerre* (1982), as we saw in chapter 5, depicts identity confusion in a preindustrial village community. One can never be absolutely certain, then, of the identity of one's interlocutor. While not unprecedented, the ethical issue of identity in online exchanges is new in its systematicity. The interface of the computer, coupled with the ease of communicating through the network, renders identity in question *in every case*. Messages sent through the Net *are always* suspect. What is the ethical value of this unrelenting suspicion?

One ethical question raised by online identity construction is the relation of responsibility to anonymity. Some observers argue that the easy anonymity of the Net promotes irresponsibility. On the Net, this position maintains, users may say or do what they like without suffering the consequences. If I insult someone I am "chatting" with, I may leave that "room" or return under a different handle or pseudonym. In a widely publicized case of cyber-rape, a participant in an online community performed on the screen unmentionable acts on other participants in the electronic space. The offended parties, that is, the individuals behind the online identities, were deeply affected by the outrageous acts and demanded that the operator of the system punish the offender, who, as far as anyone knows, had committed no such infractions in real life (Dibbell 1993). It would appear from this case that Net anonymity contributes to ethically questionable behavior. To decide this question, one would, I suppose, have to compare the ethical quality of conversations on the Net with those in proximate relations. Perhaps such a study would need to include a vast quantity of dialogues. There would be difficulties for the analyst, such as the availability after the fact for study of online dialogues in archives compared with the need of the analyst to be present, or have a recording device present, during proximate conversations. In each case, the analyst is in a different relation to the dialogue, a difference that some social scientists might find troublesome (Katz and Rice 2002).

If the role of anonymity in the ethical quality of online or proximate conversations is undecidable, the anxiety that Net dialogues elicit is revealing. Those who worry about the ethics of anonymous conversations impose two questionable assumptions. They presuppose the moral superiority of face-to-face relations, and they imply that online dialogues may be evaluated by the same criteria, are of the same order, as proximate relations. Each of these premises contains difficulties. The first leads to a contradiction: if people act morally, in part, because they are in certain physical relations, then the act, to the extent that its ethical value derives from the spatial arrangement, cannot be moral. If morality supposes choice or free will, then territorial qualities of acts are not moral. They are conditions within which acts may or may not be moral. It is true that the decision to place oneself in proximity to a conversant, as opposed to communicating online, might be a moral choice. But once one is in that position of nearness, the nearness is not volitional but a condition of the conversation.

The second premise—that the real and the virtual are equivalent—begs the question of their possible difference. A good case can be made that proximate relations and virtual ones invoke different ethical choices and even different criteria. Kant's ethical imperative might apply and be appropriate for bourgeois society, one where individuals have a great deal of choice (job, marriage, political affiliation, clothing style, etc.) and considerable social distance from authority figures. Yet the Kantian ethical individual is in the real: he or she meets with others in face-to-face relations. The Other for this individual is someone known and experienced proximately. As one moves away from this configuration of ethical choice, say toward the non-European Other, Kantian ethics work less well and seem harder to apply. "Act so that you may will the principle of your action to be universal" is difficult to consult when you know nothing about the subject of the universal and when you tend to regard the Other as the same as you (when Eurocentrism prevails). The Kantian principle governs the real as choices are continuously negotiated by Others who are proximate.

In virtual space, the Other is a configuration of pixels on a screen. Proximity to the Other may be emotionally and aesthetically compelling—one may fall in love with one's interlocutor—but the relation is not with an embodied presence. In cyberspace one may dump the Other with ease and little consequence. Simply turn off the machine, do not reply to e-mails, change one's handle, get a different Internet service provider or a different account, and the ethical relation is ended. The ease of disappearance requires a different type of moral obligation: the virtual invokes the ethical duty to maintain one's identity. Continuity of subject position in the virtual is an ethical requirement that makes no sense in real life. In real life, even the hint that one is multiple evokes psychological diagnosis and legal action. In the real, everything conspires to maintain the collective fantasy of the centered self. Only within that form of the self does the Kantian imperative come into play. The virtual realm shifts the register of the self's relation to itself. In cyberspace a practice emerges of continual self-definition. Ethics recedes into ontology. The Other has not vanished, and the practice of self-constitution is not that of liberal prescriptions about autonomous choices. In the virtual, the Other is just as exigent as in the real, only without physical embodiment. Self-constitution occurs in the virtual in language practices, just as in the real. The mechanisms of interpellation and misrecognition operate just as surely in the virtual as in the real. If one insists on ethical terms, it might be said that virtual ethics entail a different, perhaps more demanding, type of obligation. The moral imperative might be "act so that you will continue to maintain the identities you have constructed in relations with others."

OVERLOAD AND CENSORSHIP

There is a moral dimension to the political economy of information, one that has been intensified dramatically with the spread of use and awareness about the Internet. People object to having not enough information, to a lack of access to information, to exclusion from sources of information, to the unequal distribution of information. The assumption in this position is that information correlates directly with life chances. The more information one has, the better one can live. Surprisingly this position is held both in corporate discourse and in that of its left critics. Business ideology completely adopted the view that information access is the key to success: the more information one has at one's disposal, the more likely one can reap higher gains. Since the *summum bonum* of the capitalist is the bottom line, in a perverse way, information is morally good. And the same applies to critics of capitalism: for them, the high-tech wired and wireless world of telecommunications is immoral in its exclusion of the poor, nonwhites, and women. This charge is made rather harshly against the Internet, although the same complaints are often raised against television despite its almost universal dissemination. Regardless of these disagreements, surely open access to information on the Internet is a moral good and a political necessity.

Contrariwise others bemoan the flood of information, bewail information overload, complain of information saturation, protest being inundated by information (Gitlin 2001). The discourse of the data flood, we might call it, presumes a psychophysiological model that is questionable: humans must have a limited ability to absorb external sensations, and the Internet is hogging too much brain space. Anyone who has ever set foot in the Library of Congress must realize that the treasure of knowledge has long ago surpassed the individual's ability to survey it. Perhaps the ease of access afforded by the Internet to massive stores of cultural objects disturbs those in this category of moral positioning.

Even astute cultural critics often succumb to one or the other of these hypotheses. Jean Baudrillard, for instance, bemoans "the implosion of meaning in the media." He warns: "We live in a world where there is more and more information, and less and less meaning" (Baudrillard 1994, 79). Baudrillard argues the interesting proposition not that we are drowning in information but that an inverse relation exists between the quantity of information available and the quality of meaning in social life. The term *information* for him denotes electronic mass media (in short, television). Within this medium, information takes on the form of the simulation, the sign that is cut off from social exchange, from any object in the real. Information, for Baudrillard, constitutes an opposition to the real, one that eventually supplants it. Meaning persists only at the moral level of social life and cannot survive the mediation of electronic circuitry. Hence the more we communicate or receive signals through electronic media—the more information we have—the less meaning we have. Baudrillard's dire judgment about information was offered in 1981, before the Internet was a glimmer in his eye. His writings since the mid-1990s, however, simply extend the analysis of televised information to the new media (Baudrillard 1995b).

If the unprecedented quantity of cultural objects available in cyberspace has generated ethical discussions, so has the type of such information. Moral questions in the information age focus on what may be seen, read, and heard on the Internet. The censorship of what can be said and what material can be accessed on the Internet, as well as the sheer mass of available material, has stimulated debates over the moral quality of new media. Without question, one of the most lucrative Internet businesses is the provision of erotic materials. If the marketing success of videotape recorders depended on the demand for rentals of pornographic films, so the spread of the Internet has been motivated for many by access to erotica. In some cases, such images concern children, and we have seen how difficult it is in that case to apply laws designed for territorial space to cyberspace. Questions of free speech are also at stake. Obnoxious neo-Nazi home pages offend anyone with the faintest sense that racism is puerile and dangerous. Less controversial Web sites also raise moral questions. Parodic sites proliferate on the Web, often containing false information, deceptive images, misleading pastiches of text, image, and sound. Since these sites are easy to construct and cheap to maintain, the Net allows cranks of all stripes to vent their peculiar feelings, sometimes in damaging forms. With this newfound ease of presenting disturbing materials accessible worldwide, perhaps a new level of moral restraint is required.

DISCOURSE ON ETHICAL MACHINES

Scholars have begun to discuss the question of ethics in the information age. A journal began in 1999 entitled *Ethics and Information Technology*, and a bibliography on the subject is available both in print and online (Tavani 1996). The first annual meeting of the Association for Internet Researchers was held in Kansas in 2000, giving considerable attention to the question of ethics. The aspect of the problem often pursued by researchers on the ethics of the Internet is not "What is the good?" or even "What is the ground of ethics?" but a more primordial concern: "How can identity in cyberspace conform to identity in 'real life'?" The question of the nature of the good has become the question of the nature of the ethical subject. Computer-mediated communication places a thick interface between the phenomenological subject and the online subject, with the consequence that usual ethical issues must be set aside and another question raised in their place, that of identity. In Kant's ethics and even in Nietzsche's genealogy of morals there is, properly speaking, no question of the ethical subject. Researchers on the Internet enjoy no such assurance. They must first ascertain the nature of the communicating subject and its connection with the "real" subject. The ethical question thus shifts registers to the relation of mediated and immediate identity.

Many scholars simply assume that it is good if the identity of the online subject conforms to that of the phenomenological subject. In her study of Usenet identity, Judith Donath (1999) asserts the "unity" of the subject in the real and argues that cyberspace raises the question of "deception" about identity because the body is not present at the point of enunciation and because technical means of changing identity are readily available, even built into the communication situation. The Internet makes possible a new ethical concern: deception about identity. Donath thus registers the uniqueness of communications on the Internet but wants to impose on it what she regards as the standard or norm of "the real world." She does not explore ethics from the point of view of the new speech situation to ask what new issues might emerge for the older assumptions on the basis of the new circumstance.

Confusions over identity occur routinely in mediated communications with far less complex interfaces than the Internet. One research team reports on a medical technology in which patients are given advice by computers, "an intelligent interactive telephone system" known as Telephone-Linked Care. Scientists who studied the data were surprised to find that the reactions of patients to the computer program, which responds to patients' questions, were intense and emotional. Patients formed "personal relationships" with the voice on the phone, even though they knew it was machine generated. Strong ethical judgments were made by the patients about the machine. They loved and hated the machine (Kaplan et al. 1999). In this case, the character of the machine was altered by the patient. It was "humanized" and brought into the sphere of the ethical.

The study of Telephone-Linked Care suggests that mediated identities are by no means stable, that "identity deception" is not an adequate conceptual vehicle to understand ethics in the mode of information.

HABERMAS'S "DISCOURSE ETHICS"

One theory of ethics that requires attention in relation to the question of the information age is Jürgen Habermas's notion of "discourse ethics." Habermas grounds ethics in communicative practices where individuals reach consensus by recognizing the validity claims of others in the group. By looking for a basis of ethics in communications, it would appear that Habermas comes close to the issue of an informational ethics.

Discourse ethics, according to Habermas, "stands or falls with two assumptions: (a) that normative claims to validity have cognitive meaning and can be treated *like* claims to truth and (b) that the justification of norms and commands requires that a real discourse be carried out and thus cannot occur in a strictly monological form" (Habermas 1990, 68). The first requirement for a discourse ethics—that moral claims are *like* claims to truth—takes the argument back to Kant and the need to ground morality in reason, a claim that I have argued pertains to a situation of autonomy that is no longer pertinent. Nevertheless the bulk of Habermas's effort aims to clarify this issue: to ground discourse ethics in a truth claim that aims at universality. Lacking this principle, Habermas maintains, the speaker falls into performative contradiction. But one may object that performative contradiction pertains to the individual as speaker, isolating once again the position of speech from the intersubjective context and the possible reliance on machine mediation. It also presumes a field of discourse that is subject to rational resolution. Contra Habermas, there may be no individual who is separate from a machinic interface, as in mediated communication. In the speech situation of networked computing, no unitary individual faces another. Instead partial identities exchange cultural objects in a condition of paradox, that is, as if they were temporarily at least unitary subjects.

The second criterion sets ethics in relation to language and social interaction. Here we are closer to the problem at hand. Habermas, however, specifies the communication situation again without reference to the media. Discourse ethics occur for him in the "lifeworld": "The symbolic structures of every lifeworld are reproduced through three processes: cultural tradition, social integration, and socialization" (Habermas 1990, 102). These processes might be elaborated to include media, but Habermas does not venture in that direction. Without such an elaboration, the question of ethics in the age of information machines cannot even be posed. His promising move toward an ethical theory related to language ends in assuming only the context of face-to-face speech.

BEYOND GOOD AND EVIL

I have argued that a transcendental ethical principle is not possible, or at least that in the current conjuncture of mediated information society, its elaboration does not adequately constitute the conditions of ethics, does not illuminate the dynamics of good and bad in the various cultural contexts of cyberspace, broadcast, and print media. Instead I urge a Nietzschean perspective that explores the good and the bad in the culture of the virtual. The moral positions of the master and the slave, which Nietzsche analyzed so trenchantly, take as their communication context oral and print cultures. Moralities of good and bad, and good and evil, growing out of these contexts apply at best partially to information society. Even so, Nietzsche's critique of these moral postures is worth considering in relation to today's high-tech world. He proposed a "transvaluation of all values" with an eye to the enhancement of "life" (Nietzsche 1966). While his project contains many difficulties, his method of cultural transformation may serve as a starting point for rethinking ethics in an information age.

Nietzsche advocated, paradoxically, an aesthetic process of moral creation. His "free spirit" or "superman" resembles nothing so much as an artist, a spiritual warrior, one who wrestles with her own limitations in order to move beyond them, to get to a place where new values are possible. "One must still have chaos in one, to give birth to a dancing star," his Zarathustra urges (Nietzsche n.d.). The Nietzschean moral elite—for it is an elite—explores its own values, dissects them, rejects them, devalues them, purposefully seeks the pain of being lost, uncertain, without direction. In Herculean struggle with herself, the free spirit experiments with "living dangerously," risking her beliefs, deliberately placing herself amid the unfamiliar and the strange. This interior battle is Nietzsche's formula for cultural innovation. Only after such a self-reflective struggle is the individual in a position to find new values, new ways of valuing that he thought were less self-destructive than both the noble and the democratic or slave moral mechanisms. Having undergone a rigorous process of self-transformation, the free spirit is capable of expressing beautiful values, values that will attract others to join in their celebration. Nietzsche's moral elite *charismatically* and without force draws others within its moral circle, thereby enhancing the "life" or affirmation of life of all. This new will to power of the ethical requires for its appreciation the imagination of a constellation that has rarely if ever existed. In such a world, the good and the beautiful are not opposites; the good, the bad, and the ugly do not constitute an oxymoron; the elite and the demos are not in struggle against one another; power and submission or acceptance are not achieved by the exercise of brute force.

Nietzsche's utopia beyond good and evil may be impossible or wrongheaded or undesirable. Its interest, however, lies in the mechanics of cultural transformation that it delineates. Is there some analogy or resemblance between the process of moral transformation undertaken by Nietzsche's elite of supermen and the conditions of moral judgment in the age of mediated information? Does our submersion in print, broadcast, and computer-networked media provide us with anything like the conditions of estrangement, disorientation, and critical uncertainty that Nietzsche outlined as the basis of cultural questioning, of bringing "chaos to one's soul"? Well, there is one enormous difference between them. Nietzsche spoke of an elite few capable of undergoing self-exploration, self-examination, self-rejection. The media, by contrast, surround and solicit the many, involving multitudes in their web of remote cultural exchange. And the prospect is clearly that more and more will be so implicated, even to the extent of eventually enveloping a good deal of the world's population.

Contrariwise there are similarities in digital media and the overman's process of cultural creation. Networked, digitized information media cut across territorial boundaries of cultural groups. They juxtapose differences in a homogeneous medium. They bring together individuals with common interests but divergent nationalities and traditions. They shuffle us around, mixing and remixing the basic elements of cultural coherence. They form new agglomerations that make no sense in relation to proximate practices and norms. They interrupt the smooth flow of naturalized, legitimized mechanisms of constituting subjects, reconstituting them with bits and pieces of dissociated culture. They require a constant travel back and forth from the face-to-face, print, broadcast, and networked information flows. They disrupt the narcissism of the familiar, the identifications with the same. In these ways they perform a reorganization of the ethical subject, bringing chaos to the souls of those online. The Internet enacts a massive deterritorialization of cultural values and by so doing links or reterritorializes the ethical and the political. One innovation, then, of the Internet is a call for a new theory of the political as a collective determination of the good in a context where the ethical, the individual determination of the good, receives somewhat less prominence than in the modern or age of print.

The disruption of ethics as usual introduced by the Internet is enabled by its deterritorialization of information exchange both in the literal sense of reducing the significance of space in communication and in the figurative, Deleuzian sense of unhinging preexisting patterns of culture. As a consequence, ethics take on a political dimension, one that in some sense they perhaps always had. The establishment of ethical norms, for instance those of netiquette in cyberspace, occurs in the process of forming new relations of force, giving shape to the emergent zone of cyberspace. Ethics and politics appear mutually interleaved in networked computing. While ethical issues in the information age include topics of censorship and overload as these challenge existing norms and attitudes, the more serious issues point to the possibility of a transvaluation of values and the political aspects of forming subjects in the domain of the virtual. These latter questions provide the occasion for a rethinking of the ethical in terms that no longer postulate a circle of the transcendental and the individual. Instead ethics in virtual space might suggest multiple, relational patterns of immanence that at once invoke issues of power and of the good and the beautiful.

8

PSYCHOANALYSIS, THE BODY, AND INFORMATION MACHINES

The body is configured in practices (Butler 1993). It is constituted at the cultural level by ideas, attitudes, and values; at the emotional level by inscriptions of desire in the unconscious; and at the physical level by movements, postures, spaces. The body is inserted into multiple spaces and times that are always already socially given (although changing and polyvalent as well), positioned in relation to material objects, machines, other humans, animals and plants, represented in cultural artifacts of many kinds, and territorialized by desire, awakened and repressed at different points and in different ways. Certainly the body has natural limits, capacities, deficiencies, being finite and subject to gravity, requiring oxygen and nutrients of various kinds. For millennia these limits defined the human experience in varying yet surprisingly stable ways.

Now things are changing. Life span increases. Fatalities increasingly occur from social causes like car accidents, wars, pollution, and other dangerous alterations of the environment. Globalization invites marriages of previously distant individuals and groups, mixing bodies that in earlier epochs had little chance to commingle. Scientific advances in biochemistry open the body as a book to be rewritten, edited, and mixed with the "books" of parts of other bodies and even other species. Experiments in robotics and artificial intelligence redraw the line between the living and the dead, combining carbon- and silicon-based materials in new mixtures of machines and flesh. Arguments from the 1990s that the body is shaped, in part, by culture appear quaint and understated when confronted by somatic alterations on the horizon and already being put into practice. Many of these tendencies began centuries ago but seem to have reached, by the late twentieth century and the early twenty-first, a crisis point by which incipient changes in the body in the present and the future are likely far to surpass anything from the past, or indeed anything imagined in the past. Digital morphing programs, however trivial in themselves, represent this newfound plasticity to the human body.

In the context of such innovations, I consider the relation of networked computing to the human body, drawing on the reconceptualizations of the body initiated by poststructuralist feminist theory and continued by cultural studies, transgender studies, postcolonial studies, race studies, and queer theory. Originated perhaps by Michel Foucault in *The Birth of the Clinic* (1963), Gilles Deleuze and Félix Guattari in *Anti-Oedipus* (1972), Elaine Scarry in *The Body in Pain* (1985), Teresa de Lauretis in *Technologies of Gender* (1987), and Judith Butler in *Bodies That Matter* (1993), critical cultural studies have theorized the body both as resistant material substrate and as culturally constituted. The body is here understood as represented in the discourse of medicine through the gaze instituted in the early clinic; as a surface of desire inscribed upon, absorbing impressions, yet in the end undeterminable and capable of forming new patterns of energy and intensities; as gendered by binary heterosexual practices that bring to bear on it the vast resources of capital and the intimate privacy of the nuclear family; as racialized by hegemonic systems of prejudice; as brutalized, oppressed, and hybridized by Western imperialism; as a locus of pleasure, multifarious without visible limit, a point of heterotopian transgression; as a site of self-fashioning and self-constitution. Even before the genome project and the Internet, intellectuals have explored the complex mutual determinations of nature and culture as they impinge on the frail but magnificent human body. My examination of the body's relation to new media departs from these stunning advances in understanding how the apparent naturalness of the body is also historically shaped.

FREUD'S BODY

Before exploring the body in new media, I must return to what is still considered by many the major source of comprehending the body, Freudian psychoanalysis. In Freud's writing and practice, we find all the conditions for thinking about the body: the overture to the cultural conception of the body and its denial and naturalization; the perception of the body as situated in determinate practices and the misrecognition of those practices; the subordination of the understanding of the body in space to the need to grasp specific patterns of interior pain; the conflict of impulses between scientific critique and medical cure. One may assess the condition of the body immersed in new media only by first understanding how the body was understood without the least awareness of its intercourse with information machines. Let us not forget Freud's dismissive quip about the telephone and the progress of humanity it represented: that the telephone was like the pleasure received on a cold night by sticking one's leg out from under the covers in order to enjoy the warmth of returning it to where it was in the first place. Thanks to wired telephony, one can enjoy conversations at a distance, Freud seemed to say, but without such devices one might not take such long trips in the first place. Conditions today are such that many people, from businessmen to migrants and working women, no longer find the humor in such attitudes.

Psychoanalysis theorized the body as a development, as a process of formation through which functional zones and the pleasure inherent in the organs and nervous system were emotionally organized in particular patterns. The body for Freud is an input-output machine, taking in food, processing it for nutrients, and expelling waste. Associated with these functions are nervous excitation and release, pain and pleasure. At first the body is dependent on others to supply the food. This is the natural condition of the newborn human. Later the body would depend on the state of civilization for the same purpose. Freud, the scientist, understood three areas of the body as central to its early functioning: the mouth, the anus, and the genitalia. Highly intense nervous excitations beleaguer the three zones in the course of their early functioning. Accompanying these excitations are energy forms he termed libido. While undefined at first, libido undergoes a degree of organization in the course of the body's experience of its inputs and outputs. And while each individual develops unique patterns of the organization of libido, there are also general shapes of such organization. The question is how Freud understood the generalities at issue. I argue that in the interest of comprehending the specific libidinal organization of his patients and their pain associated with this organization, he played down the role of the situational practices of his day, his class, his place in the world. To comprehend the contemporary situation of the body and its current libidinal organization, one must rediscover the parallel elements in the Freudian scene of Victorian Europe.

When Freud studied the sexual etiology of neurosis, the group of individuals he encountered imposed quite specific practices on the newborn child. The oral phase was controlled by the birth mother's breasts, and feeding was rigidly scheduled. The anal phase featured very early toilet training with severe threats of the withdrawal of love from the child for inadequate performance. The genital phase was carried out with threats of castration if the child practiced what was called masturbation. The pattern imposed on the child was maximal denial of the pleasure in its body, compensated for by a high degree of affection from adults. The affection was, however, limited to the smallest possible circle of others: the immediate parents. Thus the child's body matured in the following way: its own body was not a source of pleasure, but links were inscribed on the child's body to the proximate adults. These were highly intense and highly ambivalent, intense because of the small number of possible "objects," and ambivalent because these adults severely restrained the child's access to pleasure of the body yet offered the child deep and sustained affection.

The social nexus of Freud's study thus figured the child in relation to a small circle of adults, organizing the child's libido in relation to these adults. For Freud the crucial aspect of the child's development was the emergence of the ego, which occurred after the body had been charged and marked. He theorized the child's options for ego development after the first three stages as consisting in a twofold path of libidinal discharge. Either the child could find objects toward which to orient the release of desire (object choice), or the child could incorporate the object into his or her own psyche (identification). Here at length is Freud's description of the situation of the child at the moment of the formation of the ego:

> The basis of the process is what is called "identification" — that is to say, the assimilation of one ego to another one, as a result of which the first ego behaves like the second in certain respects, imitates it and in a sense takes it up into itself. Identification has been not unsuitably compared with the oral, cannibalistic incorporation of the other person. It is a very important form of attachment to someone else, probably the very first, and not the same thing as the choice of an object. The difference between the two can be expressed in some such way as this. If a boy identifies him-

self with his father, he wants to *be like* his father; if he makes him the object of his choice, he wants to *have* him, to possess him. In the first case his ego is altered on the model of his father; in the second case that is not necessary. Identification and object-choice are to a large extent independent of each other; it is however possible to identify oneself with someone whom, for instance, one has taken as a sexual object, and to alter one's ego on this model. (Freud 1965, 62–63)

At stake in this process for Freud is the formation in the ego of a parental agency he calls the superego. Freud complicates the understanding of the process of superego formation by considering the place of earlier libidinal attachments (those of the first three stages discussed earlier) in relation to the superego: "The ego is formed to a great extent out of identifications which take the place of abandoned cathexes by the id; that the first of these identifications always behave as a special agency in the ego and stand apart from the ego in the form of a super-ego. . . . As the child was once under the compulsion to obey its parents, so the ego submits to the categorical imperative of its super-ego" (Freud 1960a, 38). In this way, Freud relates the superego, the internalized parental agency, to the relatively systematized bits and pieces of body energy organized from early infancy. The ego forms and along with it the superego as a synthesis of the child's libidinal experience.

THE HABITUS OF PSYCHOANALYSIS

There are many questions to raise about Freud's picture of the psyche and its relation to the body. First and often overlooked is the observation that "objects" for Freud are primary human beings (parents) or their body parts (Klein 1964). It is true that on occasion Freud discusses inert objects such as "the mystic writing pad" in relation to memory and the object thrown and retrieved in fascination by the child (the *fort-da* game) in connection with separation anxiety. Yet when writing about the basic formation of the personality, Freud gives overwhelming attention to living adults. He constructs the emotional universe of the child as consisting of adult characters who are the parents of the child. This limitation, while perhaps sensible in the context of the individuals whom Freud encountered, will need to be revised when we discuss the child's development in the early twenty-first century, when information machines play a vastly more significant role in the life experiences of small children. We will then have to consider what revision to make in the description we inherit from Freud.

The second problem I raise in connection with Freud's understanding of the body is a more familiar one: the strong sense in his writing of heteronormativity. Identification occurs only between the child and the parent of the same sex, leading to the passing on of heterosexual desire. Freud, as Teresa de Lauretis and others have noted, wrestles energetically with contradictory evidence. He recognizes the basic bisexuality of the human being but sees it as confusing the picture. He complains, "It is this complicating element introduced by bisexuality that makes it so difficult to obtain a clear view of the facts in connection with the earliest object-choices and identifications, and still more difficult to describe them intelligibly. It may even be that the ambivalence displayed in the relations to the parents should be attributed entirely to bisexuality and that it is not, as I have represented above, developed out of identification in consequence of rivalry" (Freud 1960a, 22–23). For Freud, one cannot "describe intelligibly" the basic parameters of the human psyche as long as one acknowledges, which one must, bisexuality. Here Freud negotiates with the heterosexual ideology of his day, recognizing its limits, yet conceding it pride of place. To render the bodily development of the child intelligible, the human, he thinks, must be heterosexual. Bisexuality gets lost in the shuffle of heterosexual science.

If heterosexuality is kept in place by Freud, so lamentably is patriarchy. The child's body, undergoing identification, now divides into two clear but unequal types: masculine and feminine. In Freud's words, "It is said that the influencing of the ego by the sexual object occurs particularly often with women and is characteristic of femininity" (Freud 1965, 63). In short, for women, object choice often regresses to identification. They cannot separate their own ego from the objects they choose to love, and so they reenact the process of identification from early childhood, something men, when making object choices, need not be bothered with. This, of course, is not the only way femininity and masculinity are distinguished by Freud, in every case to the advantage of the masculine, but it is enough to recognize that he generalizes what may have been the predominant (but certainly not universal) hierarchy of the sexes in his day in the West into nothing less than the fate of all humankind, in the past, the present, and the future.

The status of Freud's understanding of the child's body must then be understood as a description and analysis of a technology of power, the mechanism through which a cultural regime of the body is imposed on the self. This regime — bourgeois, masculinist, and heterosexist — must be taken as fragile and uncertain, historically contingent and ever at risk. Butler argues to this effect by pointing out that "the position[s] of 'masculine' and 'feminine' . . . are established in part through prohibitions which *demand the loss* of certain sexual attachments, and demand as well that those losses *not* be avowed, and *not* be grieved" (Butler 1997b, 135). As Freud argued, the crucial identification of the child with the parent of the same sex *substitutes for* the bodily attachments (cathexes) of the child's earlier emotional life. The father, as incorporated by the body of the child in a "successful" Oedipal resolution, includes mourning for the loss of all the attachments to the mother as well. The body of the "normal" bourgeois boy is thus an unstable amalgam of desires for both the mother and the father as they descend into unconsciousness, incorporated into the body from bits of desire for each of the parents. This incorporation, as Freud implies and as Butler insists (1997a, 136), occurs through threats, prohibitions, intimidations — all manner of force associated with the technology of Oedipal power.

Butler goes on to argue that the resulting masculine (and feminine) ego is so unstable that it exists only at the level of the imaginary:

> But where or how does identification occur? . . . Significantly, it never can be said to have taken place; identification does not belong to the world of events. Identification is constantly figured as a desired event or accomplishment, but one which finally is never achieved; identification is the phantasmatic staging of the event. In this sense, identifications belong to the imaginary; they are phantasmatic efforts of alignment, loyalty, ambiguous and cross-corporeal cohabitation; they unsettle the "I"; they are the sedimentation of the "we" in the constitution of any "I," the structuring presence of alterity in the very formulation of the "I." Identifications are never fully and finally made; they are incessantly reconstituted and, as such, are subject to the volatile logic of iterability. (Butler 1993, 105)

While I agree with Butler that to understand the instability of the ego, one requires "a logic of iterability," I cannot agree that identification "has never taken place." Rather, I would argue that it takes place the way all historical events take place: as a mixture of the real and the imaginary. And also that identification subsists in the way all cultural formations subsist: in their contingent iteration, but one that for long periods effectively cannot in practice be avoided. Victorian boys and girls became men and women in the regime of coerced heterosexuality, enduring it as they could, for better or for worse.

Yet another difficulty besets Freud's understanding of the child's body: the Eurocentrism of psychoanalysis is also recognized but disavowed by Freud. In the midst of a discussion of the formation of the child's personality in an obscure footnote in *An Outline of Psychoanalysis*, Freud acknowledges and dismisses the parochialism of his science: "No investigation has yet been made of the form taken by the events described above [childhood castration] among races and in civilizations which do not suppress masturbation among children" (Freud 1949, 93n). The issue in this passage is the practice of Western parents of discouraging with great vehemence, to say the least, their children from touching their genitals. The denial to the child of pleasure in the genital zone was a great battle of parents in their effort to impose proper behavior on their offspring. For Freud's theory of personality formation, this battle was crucial (even though he often intervened on the side of leniency). The castration threat was the emotional cauldron in which was brewed the fine drink of Oedipus, itself the discriminating taste of civilization, culture, and masculinity. Today one puts aside talk of the threat as an embarrassment, preferring to insist that the parents need only deny *something* for the operations of Oedipus to be effectuated. When I asked parents in Orange County, California, in a questionnaire in the mid-1980s if they threatened their children with castration, one responded by warning me that he would report me to the university administration for such a barbaric suggestion (Poster 1991). But Freud was not so timid. In the foregoing quote, he calls into question the scope of applicability of psychoanalysis "among races and in civilizations" where the threat is absent.[1] Imagine what might befall European culture if children freely touched their genitals, or even played with each other's.

Finally, Freud disavows forms of sexual preference that do not conform to the accepted views of his day. Homosexuality among women and men is simply not to be considered in understanding the process of identification and the consequent resolution of the Oedipal drama. He contends in *An Outline of Psychoanalysis* that these cases present confusions of the circumstances that can easily be dismissed as abnormal (Freud 1949, 121). Ruling out sexual attraction among individuals with the same genital organs sets in place the rigidly defined personality types of masculinity and femininity as the only legitimate outcomes of bodily formation. Such models are not simply restrictive and hierarchical in their binary opposition; they also insist on one set of libidinal preferences for each individual, centering the body in a unity and excluding multiplicity both in bodily preferences and in relation to nonhuman objects.

The image of the body we inherit from Freud is therefore highly delimited. It is human centered, unitary, binary, and hierarchical. Bodies of boys and girls are de-eroticized with narrowly defined zones designated for possible pleasures. Bodily desire is conscripted to the tasks of civilization in its bourgeois cultural form, with highly specialized, sex-specific etiologies. The men sublimate desire into the economy and imperial adventures; the women into the home. Both hystericize flows of desire they cannot manage into anal and oral fixations. Compulsive heterosexuality develops into stylized masculinity and femininity. Non-European societies, as they are being devastated by imperialist politics and economics during the career of psychoanalysis under Freud's aegis, are exoticized as the lubricious other. We might recall that this Victorian body is constituted through relations of force primarily with other humans. As we investigate the fate of the body in a context strewn with information machines, we would do well to note that a fully human organization of desire is not always and completely beneficent.

This image of the body rings true in relation to the circumstances of Freud's day but begins to lose its verisimilitude as we depart from those characteristic determinations. While psychoanalysis remains one of the most complex and rich understandings of the human body available, it bears the traces of its historicity. As we confront the world of contemporary technical conditions, we must rethink many of psychoanalysis's pronouncements and tendencies. In this spirit, I raise the question of the body in relation to the Internet.

MEDIA BODIES

Signs of difficulty with Freudian categories emerged clearly after 1945, a type of difficulty that also characterizes Marxist theory. Both theories position their truth value in relation to practices. In the case of Marx, the politics of the working class are a necessary component of the theory. If those politics differ from the expectations of the theory, at some point the theory must take this into account, either to explain away the anomaly or to alter itself to better connect with the circumstances. Neither Marxist nor Freudian theory is apodictic, claiming truth value transcendentally, in its own terms. With Freud, the problem emerges if patients express and display symptoms that have no relation to the theory. Freud acknowledged that his theory said little and could bring no therapeutic effect in the case of psychosis, for instance.

Increasingly since the mid-twentieth century, hysteria and neurasthenia have been displaced by a number of diagnoses and complaints ranging from identity confusions in Erikson's ego psychology, to schizophrenia in Laing's antipsychiatry, to narcissism in Kohut and Kernberg, to borderline disorders, multiple personality syndrome,[2] clinical depression, addiction, and an array of other designations of trouble discovered or invented by other clinicians. In these circumstances, psychoanalysis must do more than insist on the truth of its theory and methods. Indeed, the rogues' gallery of mental disorders just listed is related to changing circumstances, changing patient groups, and changing cultural norms.

I argue that one way to understand these changes is to study the disciplinary practices of embodiment. In the past fifty years, the body has become subject to disciplinary practices that differ from those of the Victorian nuclear family.[3] Patterns of feeding infants, toilet training them, and controlling their genital pleasures have drastically altered. Children of the middle class are no longer sequestered in apartments, away from the dangerous life in the streets, and confined to the tempestuous microsociety of parents and siblings. Instead, they are sent out to preschools within months of birth. Their bodies are tended by strange adults and engaged in play with their diminutive peers. Perhaps most significantly, their surroundings in the home have been revolutionized. Parents are more attentive to the requirements of young children in the design and furnishing of their rooms and even the shared areas of the home. Color schemes, decorations, and toys are selected to match the bodies of young people, even if the specific choices may arguably be no better suited to them than those of the past. And above all, media machines populate the home, even the child's room.

The child's space in the Victorian home lacked all the information technologies we assume today.[4] It consisted of furniture, bookcases perhaps, a bed, and few other articles. Decorating schemes concerned the education of the senses as well as reason. Parents were urged to fill the room (without overstuffing it) with prints from the great art of Europe and with books that reflected the highest values of that culture, such as (and especially) Chaucer and Le Morte d'Arthur (Wharton 1975, 177). Children from families who might later in life find themselves on a psychoanalytic couch were being readied for the cultural work of European civilization. In reading descriptions of children's space from this era, one is struck by the degree to which bourgeois parents were able to design and to control the world inhabited by their children. The meaning of privacy here emerges in a new light.[5] While the parents were surely influenced by their social world in selecting the child's environment, the child could say little about it. No technology or youth culture available through its means interfered with the wish of the adults in these matters. No external forces penetrated the bourgeois interior to provide alternatives for the child to the dictates of adults. Each object, however trivial, that appeared before the child was there at the discretion of the child's parents. Perhaps only the window in the child's room afforded an unmonitored glimpse of the world beyond the privacy of the nuclear family.

The situation today is dramatically altered. The outer world — corporations, media providers, schools — designates children as a market. Beyond the family, institutions recognize children of various ages as part of society in a manner quite different from earlier times and with diverse consequences. At issue are not simply toy manufacturers, advertisers, television and film producers — who prey on children and young people with greedy expectations of monetary reward. There are also theme parks, large spaces devoted to attracting children, and restaurant chains like Chuck E. Cheese and other fast-food corporations; there are manufacturers of clothing, from sneakers to jeans to T-shirts, who have attended to and captured the fashion aspirations of increasingly younger persons. For better or worse, general social institutions cater to what they regard as the desires and bodily needs of young people from birth to majority. Whatever the motivations of the providers of these objects and amusements, one consequence is clear: youth cultures now exist that are beyond the control and in many cases the understanding of parents. One might hazard the speculation that our postmodern culture is characterized not simply by the multiculturalism of ethnicity, race, gender, and sexual preference but also, and of equal importance, by age. Society is splintered into microcultures of groups determined by age. But the important question for this discussion of the body concerns the specific mechanisms through which the child connects with and experiences cultural patterns that are unique for him or her. At the center of this question, I submit, are information machines.

Freud's clients took photographs, sent telegraphs, listened to phonographs and radios, answered their telephones, and, what is often overlooked in such lists, read books and deployed typewriters and other writing implements. From the mid-nineteenth century onward, information machines increasingly took their place in the lives and the homes of the Western bourgeoisie. These machines produce cultural objects (cameras, typewriters), store cultural objects (books, phonographs), transmit cultural objects (telegraph, radio, telephone), and disperse cultural objects throughout urban space (films, books). These objects of mechanical reproduction (Benjamin 1969b) alter social relations by substituting machine mediation for face-to-face relations. They reconfigure space by altering the relation of the public sphere and the private sphere (Meyrowitz 1985), altering the configuration of the subject. The solid walls and locked doors of apartments are invaded as if by an army of foreign cultures, upsetting the ability of the nuclear family to sustain its degree of separation from the wider world. The cultures made available through these information machines may be remote but are also differentiated by age. In Freud's time, parents were still able to control the source and nature of these cultural objects. Books, phonograph records, prints, and other media remained within parents' dominion. Children were able to obtain only those cultural objects purchased by their parents. In studying the development of the child's body, Freud was thus still able to ignore the role of information machines and focus his attention on parents as the sole components of the family environment.

By the early twenty-first century, the number and variety of information machines installed in the home has increased remarkably. Televisions, answering machines, fax machines, computers, electronic games, network connections, and so many other devices have made entry into the residence. Each of these, along with the earlier technologies, has multiplied throughout the home and also become mobile with Walkmen, mobile phones, and personal digital assistants enabling the extension outward into the public sphere of the private world. Mechanical appliances, from refrigerators to microwave ovens, have added computer chips to their assemblage, rendering them "smart machines." The home has become infinitely permeable to the outside world, with the result that the coherence of the culture of the nuclear family has been fragmented into what I call the segmented family (Poster 1991). Each member of the family now sustains a separate cultural world within the family. Media provide programming for each person, with only a small proportion aimed at the family as a whole. The Kaiser Foundation, in a series of studies of media in children's bedrooms, has found an increasing presence of information machines. In 1999, televisions were found in one-quarter of the bedrooms of two- to four-year-olds, for instance. And for the age group of eight to thirteen, fully two-thirds of children had their own televisions in their rooms. The same study discovered an increasing presence of computers in youngsters' bedrooms, as well as VCRs, radios, video game players, and cable or satellite access.[6] The conclusion is clear that younger and younger children have more and more highly sophisticated media available for use in their bedrooms.

The Freudian body required as a necessary condition the privacy of the bourgeois home. The child needed to be nurtured by the parents in order for desire to implode and be sent reeling through its Oedipal course. The public world was a beyond, a remote place, to this child. As Thomas Keenan writes: "The public is not the realm of the subject, but of others, of all that is other to—and in—the subject itself. . . . The public is not a collection of private individuals experiencing their commonality. . . . The public is the experience, if we can call it that, of the interruption or the intrusion of all that is radically irreducible to the order of the individual human subject, the unavoidable entrance of alterity into the everyday life of the 'one' who would be human" (Keenan 1993, 133). When the windows onto the world opened by dint of information machines, the private space that cultivated the bourgeois body would be shattered forever.

If in the Victorian period, worker and bourgeois did not understand each other, Catholic and Protestant felt distant, and regional cultures were

barriers to communication, today men and women have separate subcultures, and children, if they do not understand adults, are equally opaque to
their elders. Media serve to heighten and to intensify what Durkheimian
sociologists term the structural and functional differentiation of modern
society.

MEDIA DISCOURSE FOR CHILDREN

A good example of the ability of children to find alternatives to the culture of their parents, to look outside the window of the family, is the story
of a boy who developed his gay sexual orientation through the Internet.
Growing up in a Southern Baptist town and finding only condemnation
for homosexuality, Jeffrey, at the age of fifteen, wrestled with his sense of
liking boys. His only outlet beyond his home environment was the Internet. With a simple search on the Web for "gay" and "teen," he was able
to contact a community of like-minded youths. In his words, "The Internet is the thing that has kept me sane. . . . I live constantly in fear. I can't
be my true self. My mom complains: 'I can see you becoming more detached from us. You're always spending time on the computer.' But the
Internet is my refuge" (Egan 2000, 113). Jeffrey's life online was in sharp
opposition to his face-to-face world. Yet he was able to sustain his emotional life for some time through the relations he was able to have on the
Internet. Jennifer Egan draws the implications from the case of Jeffrey:
"For homosexual teenagers with computer access, the Internet has, quite
simply, revolutionized the experience of growing up gay. Isolation and
shame persist among gay teenagers, of course, but now, along with the in-
hospitable families and towns in which many find themselves marooned,
there exists a parallel online community—real people like them in cyberspace with whom they can chat, exchange messages and even engage in
(online) sex" (113). In Egan's view, information technology provides young
people with connections to subcultures that are absent from their environment and scorned by their parents. One might compare this situation
with the efforts, dating back to the 1960s, of parents in such communities
to censor books in school libraries, like J. D. Salinger's *The Catcher in the
Rye*, for representing youth rebellion with only the suggestion of homosexual content. Today the Internet offers considerably more than Salinger:
interacting with communities of youth rebels, gays, and other cultures
shunned by many parents. Children are now able to participate in cultures

of their own choosing, regardless of parental values. And this is so for young people at a surprisingly early age.[7]

Cultural contacts available to children through information technologies are not always in direct opposition to parental views. My argument is not so much about resistance to parental authority in these situations. Rather, I maintain that the child's world is now composed of media as well as adults. The child learns about the world through machines as well as people. If the content of the child's experience is broader than the objects the parents might select, the more important issue is that media play a central role in constituting the child as a cultural, embodied self. The child is now formed through a media technology of power, a set of discourses, images, and sounds that arrive at the child's awareness through stereos, televisions, telephones, game consoles, and networked computers. The child's body is libidinized in more ways than exclusively through object choices and identifications made with parents. In fact, object choice and identification, ego functions that shape desire, do not grasp well the relation of the child to the information machine.

Young children watching television are not in a mirror stage. The mirror reflects. It brings about a logic of self and other. As Lacan (1968) claims, the small child enters an imaginary misrecognition with others (especially the mother) in which mirrors reflect back to the child an image the child takes as itself. Screens on televisions and computers are technologies more complex than mirrors, however metaphorically they are understood. The logic of the screen is one of incorporation: of the child by the screen and the screen by the child. This is its fusion effect, which is captured in films like Gary Ross's *Pleasantville* (1998), where characters jump into the screen and partake of the diegesis of television from the 1960s, and David Cronenberg's *Videodrome* (1983), where Max Renn, the James Woods character, incorporates a television into his stomach. In both cases, the relation of viewer to screen is one of fusion. The screen is thus a liminal object, an interface between the human and the machine that invites penetration of each by the other.

The machine mediation sets up desire in immediate and indirect paths that, I suggest, follow the logic of fusion and distraction specific to information machines. First, an oneiric consciousness relaxes the ego, blurring its intentionality while focusing the eyes on the screen and the ears to the speakers. The child's televisual gaze changes the body and prepares for a form of desiring unmatched in relations with parents and other children. This state of consciousness is different from the child's response to adults in the room. Next the simulated reality of the small screen's diegesis draws the child into the object, forming a bond of desire in an imaginary register. On the television there may be humans, animations, natural landscapes, animals, or advertisements. In each case the character solicits attention in a mediascape of desire that inscribes the child differently from the domain of face-to-face relations. Television discourse is a one-way flow of images, sounds, and symbols to which the child responds in an imaginary without feedback. The world on the screen is constructed always differently from the world outside the screen, with cultural forms combined in ways impossible in real life. The child comes to desire mediated events and, in the case of television, is on his or her way to becoming what is called in the vernacular "a couch potato." Desire has to be diffracted through the screen and an unconscious constructed in an imaginary register of the body that is outside the oral, anal, and genital phases of libidinal organization.

Take the example of *Teletubbies*, a show broadcast for young children daily on public television beginning in April 1998 in the United States. The show, originally created by the BBC in 1997, is highly successful, with an estimated 500,000 viewers in more than fifty countries. It is considered the first program televised in the United States specifically produced for one-year-olds. The teletubbies are four friendly figures with the names Tinky Winky, Dipsy, Laa-Laa, and Po (see figure 17). They are furry, colorful, round in the middle, and speak with voices of young children. Some might consider them aliens with antennae. The mood of the show is thoroughly warm and cuddly. Teletubbieland, where they reside, is a pastoral of rolling hills, flowers, and bunnies. The teletubbies play with balls and the like, laughing frequently in a continuous state of mild enjoyment.

The show begins with a sunrise. The sun has a face of a baby in its middle, one who is smiling and laughing, inviting the child-viewer into the show in a pre-ego fantasy of identification (see figure 18). *Teletubbies* offers a nonthreatening, gentle visual environment that is pleasant in every way. (The only exception to this pastoral is the vacuum cleaner that frightens the teletubbies and speaks to the fears of the young audience. Interestingly enough, the scary character in the show is a mechanical machine.)

This apparently benign program has nonetheless been the source of much controversy.[8] Reverend Jerry Falwell, for instance, accused *Teletubbies*

FIGURE 17. Teletubbies at play (www.bbc.co.uk)

of celebrating homosexual lifestyles to infants (Woodson 2000). Other critics argue that the program seduces infants into watching television and initiates them into the world of commodities through spinoff products (see figure 19). Susan E. Linn and Alvin F. Poussaint, in "The Trouble with Teletubbies," write in outrage:

> What's worrisome about *Teletubbies* is that, to date, there is no evidence to support its producers' claims that the program is educational for one-year-olds. There is no research showing that the program helps babies learn to talk. There's none to suggest that it facilitates motor development in 12-month-olds. There is no data to substantiate the claim that young children need to learn to become comfortable with technology. In fact, there is no documented evidence that *Teletubbies* has any educational value at all. When asked about research, people associated with *Teletubbies* respond that studies show how much children and parents like the program. That may be so. The fact that children like something, or parents think they do, does not mean that it is educational, or even good for them. Children like candy, too. Given the lack of research, why would PBS import a television program for one-year-olds that has no proven educational value? (Linn and Poussaint 1999)

Linn and Poussaint suspect that something is amiss in this harmless-looking television series. Just because children like something, they intone, "does not mean that it is . . . good for them." Parents, they advise,

FIGURE 18.
Sunrise
(www.news.
bbc.co.uk)

ought to beware, or else their children will "become comfortable with technology." These warnings are indicative of a new discipline of the body.

One thing that is amiss in the show is the complete absence of adults in Teletubbieland,[9] an absence most unusual for children's television programs or books. Children's culture almost always mirrors the social world, where adults are ubiquitous and prevail. Along with the absence of adults goes the absence of parental demands, rules, and punishments. *Teletubbies* does not warn children to abstain from touching their genitals. In fact, it rarely forbids them anything. The childlike figures play and romp without restraint, except for an adult voice-over that announces when it is time for the teletubbies to return home. Their departure is slow and proceeds with interruptions and returns. An indication that the creators of the program are aware of separation anxiety, teletubbies play a *fort-da* game with the audience, disappearing down a hole only to return once or twice before finally bidding the audience adieu. Objects on the show also behave in a hyperreal manner: appearing and disappearing all of a sudden, in magical performances that defy the rules of the material world. The show obeys no obvious narrative logic but that of a one-year-old's fantasy. When the screen emerges in a teletubbie's stomach and runs a skit, this is likely to be repeated. Here the child's emotional demand for repetition, familiar and perplexing enough to parents, guides the flow of images. *Teletubbies*, as one critic writes, is devoted to the pleasure of infants:

FIGURE 19.
Commercial spinoffs (www. austinchronicle. com)

It is this structure of play and the validation of pleasure that has caused many American critics to label this show "pointless." . . . Parents want more from their children's entertainment than mere pleasure. Gratification that does not advance scholarship or skill can strike parents as hedonistic and escapist, especially when involving the consumption of television—already a low status activity. (Woodson 2000)

Teletubbies presents to infants the structure of their own desire—through the mediation of the machine. A fused machinic desire solicits the child and prepares a body outside the Oedipal paradigm.

In the midriff of each teletubbie is a television screen which the teletubbies view, usually once during each broadcast (see figure 20). On the screen are children who perform various acts like finger painting, greeting and saying goodbye to the teletubbies. This doubling of the screen erects a fantasy world of television within television, information machine within information machine. It suggests that beings and televisions are one assemblage, that the viewing child might be a television. The child's mildly attentive consciousness focuses first on the image of the baby in the sun,

FIGURE 20. Stomachs with TVs
(www.pbs.org)

then on the teletubbies, then on the screen in the teletubbies' stomachs. The imaginary merger between the characters on the screen and the child could not be more complete. The media technology of power structures a scene of fusion between the child and the machine. Within the fused position, the child's body becomes one with mediatized culture. Child and other are constituted in a cyborg assemblage. The family has been complicated by cultural objects from outside its private sphere, and the self of the child has been multiplied and dispersed, cathecting not only to the Oedipal triangle but to the mediascape.

CONCLUSION

Parents, of course, remain central figures in the child's emotional life. The Oedipus complex is not eradicated, just complicated, by information machines, as well as by other practices of contemporary families. Sending children to preschool at very early ages diffuses their desire to a wide variety of people. Transformations in family patterns alter the libidinal inscription of the body: mixed or blended families, single-parent families, same-sex families all have increased dramatically since the 1970s, rendering the classic nuclear family a minority. If we add the entry of mothers into the workforce to this list of changes, the picture that emerges is very different from that of the Victorian middle class. What I call the segmented family of the late twentieth century and the early twenty-first multiplies the cultural forms in the home. Above all, the formation of the body through identifications and object choices has altered by dint of information machines. Oneiric assemblages of child and machine inscribe the body with a structure of desire whose shape may be difficult to characterize but whose difference from the Oedipal child is certain.

PART III.

DIGITAL COMMODITIES IN EVERYDAY LIFE

9

WHO CONTROLS DIGITAL CULTURE?

Sharing data is the beginning of humanity.
—Henry Louis Gates, TV ad for Linux

In the third part of the book, I explore the new relation of humans to information machines in areas that are political and social in nature, peer-to-peer file sharing, the organization of space, the alteration of commodities, and new forms of advertising.[1]

LEGISLATING THE DIGITAL

The Digital Millennium Copyright Act (DMCA) of 1998 is most often approached from the point of view of the contending agents: the Recording Industry Association of America (RIAA), the Motion Picture Association of America (MPAA), the Electronic Frontier Foundation (EFF), peer-to-peer file sharing program developers and users, lawyers on both sides of the question. Each of these social agents perceives the DMCA from the limits of its situated position, and each party has some validity to the arguments it makes from that perspective. For many of these agents, the question of copyright law is about the fate of the culture industries, those corporations that control the production, reproduction, and distribution of texts, sounds, and images. I introduce here what I regard as a broader viewpoint: that of the citizen concerned about the general relation of new technologies and cultural democracy, about the question of transculture in an age of globalization, and more broadly still about the long-term relation of human beings to information machines.[2] As a media studies theorist and historian, I view the question of copyright also in terms of the

FIGURE 21. Neo and Councilor Hamann at the engineering level (still from *Matrix Reloaded*)

changing nature of the producer and the consumer, about the character of our culture, and about the scope of democracy or the basic freedoms of the citizen. Ultimately the question that must be raised in connection with the DMCA is that of who controls cultural objects, a question that goes to the heart of contemporary societies, since they increasingly depend on information in a planetary context.[3]

Popular culture compulsively returns to the theme of the future direction of technology. Film after film depicts machines and humans in various conditions of struggle, cooperation, and symbiosis. Robots, of course, are a staple of Hollywood, especially since *Blade Runner* (1982). The recent and highly popular *Matrix* trilogy problematizes not only machines but in particular the complex of information machines that constitute the Internet. A dialogue in the trilogy's second film, *The Matrix Reloaded* (2003), broaches the question of humans and machines in a particularly exigent manner. The scene occurs at a moment in the film when the machines are about to attack the humans. Neo, the hero of the film, played by Keanu Reeves, and Councilor Hamann, played by Anthony Zerba, emerge from an elevator that has descended into the engine room level of the humans' stronghold (see figure 21). The councilor marvels at the complexity of the machines before them.

COUNCILOR: Almost no one comes down here unless of course there's a problem. That's how it is with people: nobody cares how it works, as long as it works. I like it down here. I like to be reminded that the city survives because of these machines. These machines are keeping us alive while other

machines are coming to kill us. Interesting, isn't it? The power to give life
and the power to end it.

NEO: Don't we have the same power?

COUNCILOR: I suppose we do. Sometimes down here I keep thinking about
all those people still plugged into the matrix. And when I look at these machines, I can't help thinking that in a way we have plugged into them.

NEO: But we control these machines. They don't control us.

COUNCILOR: Of course not. How could they? The idea is pure nonsense, but it
does make one wonder, just what is controlling?

NEO: If we wanted, we could shut these machines down.

COUNCILOR: Of course. That's it. You hit it. That's control isn't it? If we wanted
we could smash them to bits. Although if we did we would have to consider
what would happen to our lights, our heat, our air.

NEO: So we need machines and they need us. Is that your point, Councilor?

COUNCILOR: No. No point. Old men like me don't bother with making points.
There is no point.

NEO: Is that why there are no young men on the council?

COUNCILOR: Good point.

NEO: Why don't you tell me what's on your mind, Councilor?

[Music begins, suggesting the importance of the words that follow.]

COUNCILOR: There is so much in this world that I do not understand. See that
machine? It has something to do with recycling our water supply. I have absolutely no idea how it works. But I do understand the reason for it to work.
I have absolutely no idea how you are able to do some of the things you do.
But I believe there's a reason for that as well. I only hope we understand that
reason before it's too late.

Today one might say we are in the same position as these humans of
the future. We can turn the machines off only at the risk of catastrophe, a
condition that compels a rethinking of our relation to machines as one of
agent to tool. In addition, many of the older generation—the Councilor
Hamanns—have no idea what has become of the younger generation in
its interactions with information machines, the virtual realities proliferating on the Internet. Yet there are clearly alternative approaches to this
emerging digital culture, and the direction we take in relation to it will
most likely greatly affect the human condition for the next decades. The
questions may be put as follows: Who controls digital culture? Who ought

to control digital culture? Is *control* a good term to use in relation to digital culture?

CONTROLLING INFORMATION AND ITS HAZARDS

The case of the Soviet Union is instructive in this regard. This bureaucratic state abhorred the free flow of information and attempted to restrict technologies that promoted it such as photocopy machines, computers, videocassette recorders (VCRs), et cetera. When the Soviet Union began to manufacture VCRs, they excluded the capability of recording, limiting VCRs to playback machines, thereby imagining that the government could control the reproduction and distribution of moving images. In their effort to control information, to keep information in the hands of the bureaucrats at designated levels of the hierarchy of the state apparatus, the Soviet political machine wrestled futilely with the increasing spread of machines throughout society that were capable of reproducing and disseminating texts, images, and sounds. As machine after machine was introduced as a consumer item, the Soviets attempted to control culture in the manner it had been controlled on the eve of socialist society by the Tsarist regime before the Revolution of 1917, from the top down. While the West, especially after World War II, increasingly integrated information machines at all levels of society and in all corners of everyday life—raising productivity with automation, empowering consumers against giant corporations like AT&T with inexpensive telephones, promoting youth cultures with cheap radios, assisting in the proliferation of women's subcultures, ethnic communities, and groups with marginalized sexual orientations with electronic devices that preserve images and sounds—the Soviets resisted, fending off communications from the West as well as the information machines that promote the creation and distribution of culture beyond the control of the government. Some observers go so far as to attribute the collapse of the Soviet Union precisely to its defensive and quixotic policy of information control (Castells 1998).

The music industry (the RIAA, until 2003 represented by Hilary Rosen) and the film industry (with Jack Valenti as president of the MPAA) reacted to the rapid spread of peer-to-peer file sharing of music and films much in the manner of the Soviet bureaucracy, and, as far as one can tell at this point, with much the same effect. The culture industries attempted to destroy the new information machines. They lobbied hard for the passage of the DMCA. And they would have us believe that the DMCA is about the author's rights, the compensation of creative people for their innovations. In their suit of September 2003, the RIAA acted as if downloading music files is *the same thing as* taking a music CD from a retail store without paying for it. This claim of equivalence is a political move that ignores the specificity and differences of each media—CDs and digital files. When the CD is taken from the store, the store no longer has it; when the file is downloaded, the person sharing the file still has it. This crucial difference in media is intentionally overlooked by the RIAA (Hull 2003). But if the argument of the RIAA were correct, then the twelve-year-old girl who was subpoenaed by them and settled the threatened suit out of court was capable of performing the same social functions as the music industry, that is, copying and distributing music. And in that case, clearly, the music industry is superfluous and redundant, far less efficient than the girl, who accomplishes the tasks at almost no cost.

If the case of the Soviet Union's effort to control information technocultures is instructive, so is the case of the copyists' assault on the print guilds in the fifteenth and sixteenth centuries. The resort to political institutions like the legislature and the judiciary by industries threatened by technical progress is not at all new. As Jacques Attali (1985) reports in *Noise*, 150 years after the origin of the printing press in Europe, copyists in France requested aid from the Parlement de Paris and received the right to destroy printing presses. The copyists had good arguments. They produced by hand beautiful illuminated manuscripts and codices. Their works compared very favorably to those of the fledgling print industry. During the period of the production of incunabula in the fifteenth and sixteenth centuries, few of the later conventions of page composition were in practice. Margins, word and line spacing, paragraph demarcations, the use of periods and commas—all of these commonplaces of the printed page that make it so readable were not yet in use. Early products of the print industry are ugly and difficult to scan. True enough, the copyists made many errors, and their work was unreliable because of this. But the early print industry, contrary to modern expectations about the consistency of the printing press in comparison with the scriptoria, also habitually made errors (Newman 1985). Authors had no assurance that their manuscripts would be reproduced faithfully by the stationers' guilds. Hierarchies of status within the print guilds did not give pride of place to authors, who had not yet been elevated to the place of genius they would later enjoy. Instead masters and journeymen ruled the place of production. If journeyman compositors wished, they simply altered the text to suit their sense of quality (Johns 1998). The modern conception of the inviolability of the author's work, and the concomitant cultural fetish for a uniform text, were not yet inscribed in the practice of bookmaking. When the French copyists received the go-ahead to destroy printing presses, they easily identified themselves as the aggrieved parties with rectitude (and no doubt God) on their side, just as the contemporary music industry ascribes to itself the defense of the artists and the rights of private property.

But there is an important distinction in the two cases: the feudal copyists' confrontation with the printing press was based on the preservation and authority of tradition; capitalism's confrontation with peer-to-peer networks is justified by its commitment to technical progress. If the music industry wins its case against Internet technology, capitalism loses its legitimacy as the bearer of progress. The copyists did not have to defend themselves against the charge of holding back progress, since no such ideological prescription prevailed. The music industry, on the contrary, must somehow show that progress is promoted by destroying an innovative and very promising information technology. They face an uphill battle, to put it mildly. In their defense, the music industry points to the fact that more music is available to consumers today than ever before. Their conclusion is that the current system works just fine and that peer-to-peer networks will diminish the amount of music in circulation. The argument from complacency echoes the copyists' plaint too closely. If the status quo ante prevailed in the fifteenth century and the printing presses were somehow destroyed, one cannot imagine the loss. The printers' argument that their machines were more efficient, would produce more books at a cheaper cost, and would benefit more individuals could not be proved in 1470. The same is true today: peer-to-peer file sharers cannot prove that a society without the RIAA will be better served than by the current arrangement. These are counterfactual arguments that do not hold much water. Yet it is plain that a printing press works better than the human hand and that peer-to-peer networks are better means of reproduction and distribution than Time Warner and EMI corporate facilities.[4] And to take the argument beyond economic calculation to political effects, one might also say that printing democratized books by enabling individuals of modest means to purchase them, that it made universal education possible for the same reason, and that, finally, it was a condition of possibility for the democratic citizen, since reading is a prerequisite for independent political judgment. Similarly, one can argue that peer-to-peer networks will loosen the stranglehold of the music industry on the circulation of music, allowing many more musicians to be heard than is presently the case, that it will foster a greater proliferation of music as a result. In addition, peer-to-peer networks promote the transformation and recirculation of music by the consumer, effectively laying the groundwork for the elevation of consumption into creativity, ending the bifurcation of production and consumption, and finally introducing the possibility of a democratic culture.

THE POLITICS OF CONTROL, OR POLITICS AS CONTROL

The *Oxford English Dictionary* provides several instructive definitions of *control*. As a noun, its primary definition is "The fact of controlling, or of checking and directing action; the function or power of directing and regulating; domination, command, sway." As a verb, its definition is "To check or verify, and hence to regulate." The *OED* also has updates to the definition of the noun *control* as follows: "*control freak* orig. U.S., a person who demonstrates a need to exercise tight control over his or her surroundings, behavior, or appearance, esp. by assuming command of any situation or exerting authority over others." The *OED* does not, of course, explore the question of the subject of control (what kind of agent has or seeks control?), nor that of the culture of control (to what extent is control by agents important to a culture, and, more significantly, what is the nature of the subjects and objects in the culture that do the controlling or are regulated by such agents?). These questions animate my analysis of the music industry's relation to the innovation of digital technology. The numerous studies that raise the question of control in relation to digital media tend to assume that individual or collective agents are in positions of control or lack of control. They define the question as one of who ought to control the technology, never asking the more basic questions "Is control by agents the best way critically to understand the general relation of digital technoculture to control? Do digital media support, enhance, or undermine practices of control?"[5]

In the case of the DMCA, the music industry attempts to maintain control over their product in the face of the new technology of digital reproduction. The main issue in the enactment of the DMCA is the control of cultural objects. Digitalization has radically altered the conditions of culture. In response, the RIAA has exerted enormous influence on politicians to pass laws, including the DMCA, to extend copyright to cover digital products. In this way, the RIAA hopes to maintain control over cultural objects. It is often argued that the introduction of new technologies is accompanied by disruptions to the existing order of control, eliciting great expectations that democracy, peace, and freedom will thereby be enhanced (Marvin 1988). Most historians of technology, however, point out that as the new technology is disseminated throughout society and is assimilated into it, controlling agents that preexisted the innovation soon regain their dominance (McCourt and Burkart 2003, 342). This view, I argue, is blind to the manner in which information technologies alter both culture and society. Even if dominant institutions are not directly overthrown by new technologies, fundamental aspects of culture are transformed by them. This argument cannot be developed here, although it has been posited by many leading media theorists and historians (McLuhan 1964; Adorno 1972; Heidegger 1977; Kittler 1986; Baudrillard 1994; Manovich 2001; Poster 2001). What I want to avoid, however, is the premature conclusion that peer-to-peer file sharing will quickly be either eliminated or adapted by the RIAA.

Two observations about the introduction of new technologies are pertinent at this point. First, the relation of a technology to social practice is a complex, changing phenomenon that is not reducible to the goals of its developer. The inventors of audio recording (Edison's phonograph), for instance, intended the device for the preservation of voice (Sterne 2003), yet the technology eventually became a means of mass-producing copies of music (Attali 1985). The conclusion one must draw from this case is that new technologies lead to disruptions of old ways of doing things—disruptions that are unanticipated and unpredictable—and so it has been and will continue to be with networked computing. The intended uses of the computer were to further social controls by the elite (to ensure communications under conditions of nuclear war) (Attali 1985); the outcome may be the overturning of certain systems of social control, that is, the culture industry.

The second observation is that digitization has thus far produced strong tendencies in two opposite directions concerning the question of the control of culture.[6]

First, digital culture enhances the ability of large institutions, such as the state and the corporation, to extend the reach of their information and management of the population. In the case of music, the culture industry has responded to digitalization by attempting to extend its control over culture, attempting to sharply limit the ability of consumers to use cultural objects as they wish.

Second, digital culture at the same time empowers individuals to have positions of speech that are difficult to monitor, to act on cultural objects in ways not possible when these objects were available only in analog form, to transform, reproduce, and disseminate information in a manner previously restricted to expensive central apparatuses such as broadcast facilities. Because of the ease and cheapness of the creation, reproduction, and distribution of cultural objects, users have extended their control over cultural objects by methods such as sharing files on peer-to-peer networks.

Networked computing confronts humanity with a dramatic choice of opposing possibilities: an Orwellian extension of governmental and corporate controls or a serious deepening of the democratization of culture. In this context, the most important question to ask about the DMCA is how society will establish practices around the digitalization of cultural objects. Will it follow the wishes of the culture industry, or the practices exemplified in peer-to-peer networks, or some combination of the two, or the impulses of some other set of agents who emerge through the implementation and use of the new technoculture?

FIXED VERSUS VARIABLE CULTURAL OBJECTS

On February 10, 2004, the Los Angeles Times reported that EMI blocked Brian Burton (also known as DJ Danger Mouse) from distributing The Grey Album, a composite blend (a "mash-up" or sampling) of the Beatles' The White Album and vocals from Jay-Z's The Black Album. EMI's attempt to prevent the distribution of the album failed, actually increasing its dissemination. Fred Goldring, a music-industry lawyer, opines that EMI "created their own hell." The Grey Album, the reporters continued, "became probably the most widely downloaded underground indie record, without radio or TV coverage, ever. I think it's a watershed event" (Healey and Cromelin 2004, E43). The protest against EMI included "Grey Tuesday" (February 24), when more than 150 Web sites offered downloadable versions of the album, and an estimated 100,000 copies were downloaded on that day alone. Copyright experts observe that "artists can't use a recognizable sample from someone else's recording unless the copyright holder grants permission" (ibid.). Goldring claims that "artists should have the absolute right to control their work. The problem is, how do you control that in the new world? . . . [But] what does [it mean to control one's work] in a world where everything can be digitized and transmitted around the world at the push of a button?" (ibid.).

EMI's action continues the effort of the music industry to repress sampling, an art form begun in the 1980s with hip-hop. Many artists advocate, contra EMI, "open content" in digital culture, and some even elaborate an aesthetic based on the principle of variable cultural objects (Miller 2004). Artists who have authorized the downloading, altering, and redistributing of their work include Bjork, Moby, Radiohead (posting loops on their Web site for downloading and using in other works), and Public Enemy, "allowing access to original master tracks of the vocals for open remixing" (Vibe 2004).

Modern society developed in the context of fixed cultural objects like books. These objects may be owned, but they cannot be changed once they are produced. If they are altered, the user can alter only his or her copy. All previous and future copies are not affected by the alterations of the user. This is a limitation of analog cultural objects. They can be mass-produced, but only from fixed points of production, points that require great amounts of resources. The user cannot copy these objects in a mass form. This feature of cultural objects, their fixity, has had the further consequence of structuring society into two sharply divided groups, producers and consumers, each with their own capacities and limitations. Consumers were in a relatively passive position in relation to the objects.

Another feature of modern media culture is that, since reproduction required considerable resources, copies became commodities, that is to say, they were distributed through market mechanisms and acquired exchange values or prices. Analog reproduction of cultural objects thus requires a type of material base that falls under the economics of scarcity. Air does not require a market because it is not scarce, at least not yet. Scarcity means that a group of people are willing to pay for an object or service because that is the only way they can obtain it. They go to a market to find these objects, and the price of the objects will reflect the ratio of the number of these objects available and the number of buyers who can pay for them. The economics of scarcity also mean that if I sell you an object, I no longer possess it. Only one person may own a given object at any time.

Fixed cultural objects like books afforded certain advantages to consumers. The consumer, having bought the book, could read it anywhere he or she chose. The consumer could lend the book to a friend or resell it. The consumer could copy the book by handwriting and later by photocopying machines, practices that, though illegal, are impossible to police. The consumer could burn the book or throw it in the trash.

Digital cultural objects do not fall under the laws of scarcity and the market because they require almost no cost to produce, copy, and distribute, and like ideas they do not diminish when they are given away. They are "nonrivalrous," as copyright lawyers say. There is no need for a capitalist market in the area of digital cultural objects, and these objects need not become commodities. Their reproduction and distribution need not fall under the constraints of scarcity economics, and indeed, digital cultural objects *resist* market mechanisms.

Digitization of cultural objects changes each of these limitations or practices and expands the possible practices of analog cultural objects concerning their production, reproduction, distribution, and use. It enables the inexpensive production of cultural objects such as sound recordings or moving images. It places in the hands of the consumer the ability to reproduce these objects very cheaply. And digital networks enable consumers to cheaply distribute cultural objects. They also enable the consumer of cultural objects to change them into new objects and to reproduce and to distribute them. Digitization also means the object is more difficult to destroy, since it exists on the Internet. In short, digitization changes the nature of the producer and the consumer, blurring the boundary between them. The consumer can now be a producer, reproducer, distributor, and creator of cultural objects. Thereby digital technology undermines the systems of controls that were associated with fixed cultural objects and brings control of culture itself into question by opening cultural objects to an unlimited process of alterations.

COPYRIGHT LAW

The Digital Millennium Copyright Act of 1998 extends the copyright law over analog cultural objects to cover digital cultural objects, defined as texts, sounds, and images. The act's main provision is to outlaw the "circumvention of technological measures used by copyright owners to protect their works and . . . tampering with copyright management information" (Digital Millennium Copyright Act of 1998, U.S. Copyright Office Summary, 1). Thus programs designed to defeat copy protection (such as DeCSS and software that cancels the regional limitation of DVD players are now illegal both to create and to distribute in the United States.

The 1998 law also aligns U.S. copyright law with recent agreements of the World Intellectual Property Organization. In addition it establishes ISPs as "safe harbors" in the sense that ISPs cannot be held liable for users' infringements, but the ISP must enforce the rules against infringement, and the RIAA is permitted to subpoena users.

One provision of the law (section 512[h] of the DMCA [17 U.S.C. 512]) gives copyright claimants the right to subpoena ISPs for the identities (name, address, e-mail address, phone) of users they allege are infringing their copyrights. It does not, however, let claimants of infringement get other information about user activity. The RIAA had until March 2004 used these subpoenas (almost three thousand to sue 382 individuals) to force ISPs to turn over the names of alleged file sharers, so the record labels could turn around and sue their fans.[7]

A U.S. court of appeals, however, ruled in December 2003 that the RIAA cannot use subpoenas to compel ISPs to reveal the names of alleged music file swappers. The RIAA may obtain a subpoena from a U.S. district court clerk's office only after proving to a judge that it has sufficient evidence of infringement.[8] Finally the DMCA provides for some exceptions to its mandates, such as when a computer breaks down.[9]

Copyright laws were enacted in the late seventeenth century and the early eighteenth, first in Britain, then in the United States and western Europe, as a response to the new technology of the printing press, which made possible the mass reproduction of texts (Rose 1993). Copyright law is associated with patent law and trademark law but is somewhat different from them. Copyright law covered the *medium* in which inventions or acts of genius were embedded for reproduction. The medium of print required advanced technology, and copyright law forbade anyone not authorized to use that technology for reproducing books and selling them.

Until the mid-twentieth century, copyright gave "authors" a monopoly over their innovations for about seventeen years, but numerous changes in the law extended this to about one hundred years and included the authors' descendants, who are by no means necessarily geniuses. Original copyright law also ensured that "readers" had rights such as "fair use" — the right to quote a work in order to critique it or make fun of it. This provision has been seriously curtailed by the DMCA. Proposals by Microsoft and the culture industries known as Digital Rights Management and Trusted Computing would do away with much of fair use.

Copyright was adapted to new technologies of reproduction as they were invented and distributed in the areas of sound (the music industry, radio) and images (photography, film, and television). In each case, the rights of authors were whittled away in favor of control by media industries (Lury 1993). Each new technology changed the circumstances of reproduction, changed the medium in which the cultural object was embedded and placed on the market, and called for changes in the nature and application of copyright law. For example, copyright law did not explicitly prohibit consumers from making copies (you will not find such a prohibition in early books, and it was printed on LP labels only after the spread of audiotape machines) because consumers did not have the capability of doing this in the media of print, film, early audio recordings, and so forth.

In general, one can say that as reproducers of cultural objects became larger in part because of the need for greater amounts of capital, copyright law increasingly diminished the power of the author or creator and progressively reduced the rights and capacities of the consumer, in both cases in favor of the media corporation (Vaidhyanathan 2001). Copyright law is the chief means by which large corporations in general and music firms in particular attempt to control culture. In the words of Kembrew

McLeod, "Intellectual property law reinforces a condition whereby individuals and corporations with greater access to capital can maintain and increase unequal social relations" (McLeod 2001, 1). Corporations use the threat of legal action systematically to stifle creativity even when the incident in question may fall fully within the "fair use" doctrine. The system of copyright law is so far out of whack that countless examples, such as Time Warner's ownership of the song "Happy Birthday to You," force the conclusion that, with regard to intellectual property, the legal structure no longer provides any semblance of justice. Hence all citizens have an obligation to violate copyright law whenever they can. Since the legislative branch of the U.S. government is under the sway of the media industry, the only alternative available to foster democracy and promote creativity in the realm of culture is Henry David Thoreau's practice of civil disobedience. And digital technology has provided citizens with a practical means to carry out this protest. Digitization threatens the media corporations because one no longer requires great amounts of capital to produce, reproduce, modify, and distribute cultural objects

AUTHORS, ARTISTS, CREATORS, INNOVATORS

Contra the music and film industries, copyright is not about remuneration for artists, authors, creators, and innovators, much less their heirs. Copyright was instituted to promote innovation in society, to improve the quality of life for all. To do so, copyright provides a temporary monopoly for authors to designate firms to reproduce and distribute their work. The argument in copyright law is that the best way to ensure the advance of science and the arts is to create a monopoly and to violate free-market principles of competition by giving authors the exclusive right to receive monetary rewards for their efforts. What benefits society is the innovation or creativity that is contained in the cultural object. Essential to democracy is the maximum dissemination of new ideas, new science, and new art. Original copyright laws foster this aim.

Contemporary copyright law, especially as modified by the DMCA, (mis)uses the privilege given to the artist and instead enables the culture industry to reap large gains. Only as a secondary result of the current arrangements do some artists receive substantial royalties. (Many artists have sued the music industry, claiming systematic underpayment or cheating, and won in the courts.)

The music industry argues against peer-to-peer file sharing that such transmissions violate the artists' royalty benefits. There is no doubt that file sharing bypasses an author's royalties. But the question is how to remunerate innovators in a digital network system. And the answer is by no means that the network must be crippled so that the music industry continues to perform functions of reproduction and distribution that are no longer wanted or needed. There are three problems to highlight concerning the question of author royalties in the age of file sharing.

First, it is by no means to be taken as a natural fact or a universal truth that artists and innovators receive compensation for the reproduction of their works. Each medium and art form is different in this regard. Musicians, for instance, certainly ought to be paid for their performances. Musicians' unions, as a consequence, have in some instances opposed recordings of music, especially when used in public locations like dance halls.[10] But who should be compensated for music in the case of reproduction technologies? Perhaps the engineers, the inventors of these technologies, ought to be paid royalties. The case of library collections of music remains apposite: borrowers of music CDs do not pay royalties to anyone, so that no one is compensated yet the public good is served.

By way of contrast with the music industry, it is worth noting that in the case of film, cinemas provide a value added to the moving images and sound by displaying them in convenient locations, in comfortable circumstances, and on very large screens, often with elaborate sound systems. Such enhancements to the film experience are worth compensation (although the advent of HDTV and large-screen TV monitors in home entertainment systems may challenge cinemas on this score, at least for those who can afford them). The film industry has to some extent learned a lesson from the experience of the music industry. The MPAA complained that downloading films on the Internet sharply cut the sales of DVDs and tapes. It hired Kenneth Jacobson, a former FBI agent, to head its antipiracy efforts. Yet the more prevalent aspect of film piracy involves the unauthorized copying and selling of DVDs, according to Jacobson, amounting to more than 35 million worldwide in 2001. Moreover, he contended, "Film piracy has become so rampant in countries such as China, Russia and Pakistan that the legal markets there have all but evaporated" (Muñoz and Healey 2001, A28).

Second, file sharing, unlike some forms of so-called piracy, does not entail the sale of commodities. File sharing is a nonmarket exchange. It is not similar to early piracy in print, where shops would reproduce books and sell them without authorization from, or compensation to, the author. Nor is it similar to Asian factories that copy CDs and DVDs and sell them cheaply in local markets. In fact, digitization enables costless sharing of cultural objects. It resembles not a violation of copyright but the act of playing music in one's home with friends in attendance, friends who themselves did not necessarily buy the cultural object. One must account for the specificity of the medium of reproduction: digital reproduction, I would argue, does not fall within copyright at all because the kind of materiality of digital files is not characterized by the economics of scarcity. Unlike books, films, and broadcasts, with digital media, unless commodified, there is nothing to pay for.

Third, artists have always incurred debts to others. They are not the complete originators of works of art as copyright law pretends but, at least partially, parasites that rely on previous cultural creations, collaborators, and workers in related fields. Artworks are as much or more the product of collective labor as they are the output of individual agents. No other culture in human history save the modern Western one has detached artists from their context and elevated them in sanctified celebrity. But this cultural practice defies the history of art, with its figures like Rubens, who painted only with a large staff of specialists, and filmmaking with its casts of numerous participants. The collective nature of the creative process is nowhere more evident than in music, from the borrowing practices of Handel and Vivaldi, to the "coverings" of popular music as in Bob Dylan's reliance on Woody Guthrie, to the outright montage-like pasting of bits of works in hip-hop and the practices of DJs (Hebdige 1987; Poschardt 1998, 373–83). Art requires a cultural context of other art, numerous collaborators, and media producers. It also, let us not forget, requires audiences.

The figure of the artist as lone creator is today little more than a fiction serving the music industry as an alibi to abet its control of culture. With the increasing shift to digital culture, artworks, as we have seen, more and more take the form of variable cultural objects, in short, open content. The culture industries, as they have come to be institutionalized, cannot exist if cultural forms are developed as variable objects. Peer-to-peer file sharing is an important step in the articulation and elaboration of culture as open content.

For these reasons, the question of file sharing is not as simple as the music industry would have us believe. A full understanding of the question requires some knowledge of the current practices of file sharing.

PEER-TO-PEER NETWORKS

Most discussions of the current condition of music distribution and file sharing begin and end with Napster (Lessig 1999). Observers presume that the fate of file sharing on the Net rests with Napster. Since Napster was forced to shut down as a free network only to reemerge reborn, like the phoenix, as a dot.com venture, these writers close the curtain on file sharing.[11] Of late, some writers throw KaZaA into the mix but again conclude that since shared files have decreased recently from a high of 900 million to 550 million, the era of the free distribution of music on the Internet is over.[12] But such is hardly the case. A robust, heterogeneous matrix of file sharing continues and evolves.

The circumstances of my own knowledge of file sharing are germane to this discussion. I first became aware of file sharing in the spring of 1999 when I taught a class on Internet culture and learned of file sharing from my undergraduate students. Students were asked to present brief reports on their favorite Web sites. One student spoke about Scour.net, a Web site that contained links to downloadable MP3 music files. Even before Scour, file swapping was rampant on Internet Relay Chat and Usenet. But it is true that Napster vastly expanded the frequency of file sharing by its peer-to-peer architecture and ease of use. Shawn Fanning's program was vulnerable to legal attack because a central location maintained a database of files, acting as a server for clients who used the program to find music to download. Thus if Napster's Web site was closed, the network would disappear. Newer "killer applications" do not suffer this weakness. Programs like KaZaA and Justin Frankel's Gnutella, for instance, enable each user to make his or her own connections with other peers, coming much closer to a true peer-to-peer connection. One can find an overview of the many types of file-sharing programs and networks on sites like Slyck (http://www.slyck.com).

The most basic network for file sharing remains Internet Relay Chat (IRC). Here, after invoking a client program, one makes direct connections with others and exchanges files while both parties remain online. There are also more elaborate subnetworks within the IRC domain. As long as the Internet functions as a decentralized system of networked computers, IRC will be difficult to police, since there are no centralized sites to shut down. IRC, however, does suffer the limitation of scale: it does not provide the kind of networked information that facilitates mass interchange of information.

The next type of file sharing occurs on Usenet, also known as newsgroups. The original purpose of Usenet was the exchange of textual information, which was also true of IRC. Users developed methods of dividing up large music and even film files into chunks small enough to meet the size limitations of the Usenet system. These files are known as binaries and are bundled into groups. One downloads all the parts and then reassembles them on one's computer, resulting in an MP3 file for music, a JPEG file for images, or an AVI file for moving images. Users then developed downloading programs that automatically assemble the parts into complete files. One difficulty with Usenet is the problem of finding the cultural object one is looking for amid the profusion of thousands of groups. Faced with this limitation, users developed Web sites where other users upload reports on each group, indicating the available content. This is done continuously, day after day. As with IRC, it is hard to imagine how Usenet might be policed. Usenet services contain the files, but downloaders simply indicate their choices, as one would do at a File Transfer Protocol (FTP) site. No record is kept of who downloads what files. The shortcoming of Usenet is that the files are available for a limited time only, since the content of the groups changes every couple of days.

More popular than Usenet or IRC are the numerous networks like KaZaA that deploy genuine peer-to-peer programs. Among these are the eDonkey and eMule networks. In these cases, each cultural object is assigned a "hash" number, a long string of letters and numerals that identifies the film, game, e-book, program, or music album to all users connected to the network. The hash numbers are posted, under the file name, at numerous sites on the Web. The user goes to the site and clicks on the file name, and the client program pops up on the user's computer and searches the network for peer locations where the file exists. The program then downloads the file in small parts from several sites at the same time, something Napster could not do. Nor could Napster resume downloading if the site in question went off-line or the user went off-line, a feat the newer programs perform flawlessly. Finally the program assembles the parts into a complete file when it is finished with the download. While you are downloading a file or several files with eMule, others on the network are uploading the same file(s) from your computer. These complex, interlocking Web sites and programs are all free and developed (and continuously improved) by individual file sharers.

Another, somewhat different system is Bram Cohen's BitTorrent. This program also uses identifiers for files, so that the location that contains information about the file does not contain the file itself. Like the KaZaA and eDonkey systems, BitTorrent allows multiple, simultaneous downloading of parts of a file. With BitTorrent, a separate window opens for each download, and uploads are limited to the file being downloaded. File transfers on BitTorrent are particularly fast, making it effective for downloading large files like films. Hence it drew the wrath of the MPAA, which threatened lawsuits against many BitTorrent sites in early 2005.

In sum, thousands of individuals create programs, maintain Web sites, and upload hash numbers of "releases" (cultural content they have digitized and put on their hard disks); and hundreds of thousands, more likely millions, download and share files. Participants in peer-to-peer networks are found across the globe, although numbers of users are no doubt distributed in direct proportion to general Internet use. The peer-to-peer landscape is maintained as a public sphere outside the commodity system. Some sites do request voluntary donations. A distribution system for cultural objects thus subsists without the support of any large institution and with the strong opposition of those corporations that have controlled cultural objects since the development of technologies for the reproduction of information. Despite the moral and legal threats and actions of the MPAA and RIAA, peer-to-peer file sharing continues to flourish and even to expand. It seems that publicity about each new attack by the culture industries only makes more people aware of the peer-to-peer network and increases the number of participants. As one says in the movie business, no publicity is bad publicity for peer-to-peer networks.[13]

Even as one may marvel at the accomplishments of the peer-to-peer system, one may question the moral value of sharing cultural content. Surely downloading files is not a great creative act. Nor, however, is buying a CD in a retail outlet, it must be admitted. One question at stake in the peer-to-peer phenomenon is the value one attributes to commodity exchange in comparison to sharing. But a deeper question still is the potential of peer-to-peer to become a dominant system of cultural exchange. An infrastructure is being set into place for a day when cultural objects will become variable and users will become creators as well. Such an outcome is not just around the corner, since for generations the population has been accustomed to fixed cultural objects. But as we pass beyond the limits of modern culture, with its standardized, mass-produced consumer culture, we can anticipate more and more individuals and groups taking advantage of the facility with which digital cultural objects are changed, stored, and distributed in the network. A different sort of public space from that of modernity is emerging, a heterotopia, to use Foucault's term (Foucault 1986), and peer-to-peer networks constitute an important ingredient in that development, one worthy of safeguarding and promoting for that reason alone. If copyright laws need to be changed and media corporations need to disappear or transform themselves, this result must be evaluated in relation to a new regime of culture that is now possible. In considering the alternatives, let us take the example of the music industry and examine its claim to foster cultural innovation and democracy.

THE MUSIC INDUSTRY

This sector of the culture industry has been exceptionally destructive in its appropriation of copyright law. One can surmise, referring back to the OED definitions of control, that the RIAA qualifies as a "control freak." Here are just some of the ways the RIAA has worked to redefine copyright law (and the law in general in relation to the music industry) to maintain and extend its control over popular music:

1. The RIAA influenced legislatures through campaign contributions to make exceptions to laws governing labor contracts so that it could require artists to sign long-term contracts for five to seven albums. When these statutes are not as favorable as the RIAA wishes, it manipulates the contract to extend its control over artists. Typically, the contract specifies that the music corporation has exclusive rights to the artists' future work. The corporation lengthens this contract for a number of years by spacing out the production of albums, arguing that this is the best marketing strategy. The music corporations habitually delay the production of albums to suit their marketing

interests, thereby, in fact, holding the artists under their contract for as long as the corporation wishes. This practice constitutes one of the few legal examples of indentured servitude in modern society (professional sports being another) (Shemel and Krasilovsky 1990, 10).

2. The contracts with artists require artists to pay for the production of the music media (studio time, etc.), the design and packaging of CDs (about 25 percent of the retail price), and returns (about 10 percent of gross receipts). All these costs are treated either as advances on royalties or deductions from royalties. The corporations are essentially limited to marketing the product, and the Internet represents a form of distribution they do not control. The vast majority of artists never see a penny from the sale of their music. In fact, James Willcox reports, "The record industry acknowledges that less than 10% of its artists will 'recoup,' or make back, the advances they're given when they sign a recording contract" (Wilcox 2003, 89).

3. The music industry has corrupted the system of music distribution in several ways, some of which are:

   a. It paid off radio disc jockeys to play its music, a practice known as payola, now a general term for bribery. The practice of paying for the performance of music began as early as the 1880s, but only after World War II did the payments go to radio DJs, with the "scandal" of exposure occurring in the late 1950s. Payola continues to be practiced today, although on an informal, under-the-table basis (Segrave 1994).

   b. It successfully destroyed the Digital Audio Tape format for home consumption in the 1990s. The RIAA pressured Congress to pass the Audio Home Recording Act of 1992, which mandated the inclusion of copy controls that prevented making more than one copy of a tape. DAT also recorded at frequencies incompatible with those of standard compact discs, 48 kHz instead of 44 kHz. A superior consumer technology was thus destroyed by the music industry, indicating once again the incompatibility of technical advances with corporate controls.

   c. It forced retail stores to maintain high prices for CDs, a practice that in May 2000 was ruled illegal by the Federal Trade Commission and subsequently by the courts (in an out-of-court settlement in 2002). In this case the music industry's monopolistic practice was aborted by the political system.

4. The concentration of the music industry to five major labels (Bertelsmann, EMI, Sony, Time Warner, and Universal) has facilitated its control over artists,

distributors, and consumers. In parallel with trends in other media industries, the music industry has consolidated into an oligopoly structure that re-
strains innovation and stifles diversity in culture.[14] These companies have ac-
counted for over 80 percent of the worldwide sales of recorded music (Negus
1999, 35).

5. The music industry has not given royalties to artists from the sale of work distributed through the Internet. At the height of the controversy over the Napster file-sharing program, Hilary Rosen, speaking for the RIAA, proclaimed
   the moral superiority of the music industry over online "pirates" in protecting
   artists' rights while at the same time denying artists payment for the copies
   of music enabled by networked computing.

6. The music industry's response to file sharing has been "lawsuits, draconian
   legislative initiatives that trample on people's fair-use rights, and threats
   of invasive actions against the very people who buy their products" (Wilcox 2003, 89). In 2003 a computer company (Apple) began experimenting
   with the distribution of music over the Internet. Although costs of reproduction approach zero, Apple charges an exorbitant one dollar for each song
   downloaded. It remains an open question if the music industry can develop
   a viable business model in the age of digital reproduction and peer-to-peer
   distribution.

7. Most methods developed or imagined by the music industry to regain control of what they think of as "their product" involve crippling the technologies of networked computing: introducing watermarks in files, threatening
   ISPs with lawsuits, defeating digital reproduction, including terminal dates
   or number of uses into music files, preventing audio CDs from playing on
   computers, sending out review copies in locked CD players, and so on. Here
   capitalism is directly opposed to promoting progress in technology, a situation that is the reverse of its history during the Industrial Revolution and its
   legitimation by economic theorists like Adam Smith as the economic system
   most conducive to the progress of humanity and its material well-being. The
   music industry has no compunction in trampling on the rights of consumers
   to save its petty profits and refuses even to consider alternatives to its business
   model created by networked technology.

The conclusion is clear that the music industry has corrupted the democratic process of legislatures, the artistic process of music making, the
distribution system of radio, CD and DAT sales, and the new technology

FIGURE 22. German ad against file sharing (www.kino.de/pix/ newspics)

of peer-to-peer file sharing on computer networks. If anyone has a high moral ground in the area of cultural objects, it is not the music industry. When they speak of piracy, we must add that property in the case of the music industry, to quote Pierre-Joseph Proudhon, is theft (see figure 22).

THE POLITICS OF DIGITAL MUSIC

I prefer to analyze the contemporary situation not as an ethical problem but as a political one: who will benefit from the technical advances afforded by digitalization? What limitations have to be imposed on the rest of society in order for the culture industry to maintain its predigital controls over cultural objects? Is this sacrifice worth it? Can capitalism continue to be legitimized in the area of cultural objects if the technological advances of networked computing are held back in order to preserve the music industry in its current form?

In addition to corrupting our political process, the artist, and the distribution media, retarding technical advances, and delegitimizing capitalism in general, the music industry, to maintain its present degree of control over culture, would require new levels of surveillance over individuals that would seriously impinge on privacy (compelling ISPs to monitor their customer's downloads), reduce the scope of civil rights, and generally debase the basic freedoms of citizens. How is this so?

The beginnings of this process date back at least to the Bangermann white paper on copyright prepared for the World Intellectual Property Organization meeting in the mid-1990s. At the time, the music industry was clueless about the implications of networked computing for their industry. The Clinton administration, however, was one degree less clueless. The Bangermann report attempted to impose U.S. copyright standards on the world and to extend those standards to include digital technology. It seriously proposed that every copy of every cultural object fall under copyright law, meaning that if you copy an e-mail from RAM to your hard disk, that qualifies as a copy; if you copy a file from your hard disk to a floppy disk, this act also constitutes copying. If you send a copy of a file to someone else, that also falls under the law. Each of these is a violation of copyright when the content has been copyrighted.

Why did the Clinton administration propose such an impossible expansion of intellectual property? For one, they made the proposal because cultural objects are second only to defense in export value to the United States. A second reason is that the politicians were not aware that networked computing integrates copying within its functions and structures. Copying is automatic and continuous on the Internet. When you direct your browser to a Web site, what you see on your screen are copies made by your computer of files on the Web site you "went to." File Transfer Protocol is also a basic function of digital networks. Copying is essential to the institutions of higher learning that developed networked computers. It represents a basic condition for intellectual freedom, scientific advance, and critical thinking. The Clinton administration easily trampled these hallmarks of a free society simply for the economic gain of some wealthy groups. The music industry, when it finally woke up and recognized the powers of peer-to-peer programs, was even more eager to destroy these features of our institutions.

Institutions of higher learning, have been, I am sorry to say, intimidated by the music industry's threats of legal action. They have far too often put serious restrictions on the free flow of digital information. Some universities have resisted. The best example is MIT, which until 2003 imposed no restrictions. The worst example is Columbia University, which, according to *Wired*, "monitors Internet use and kicks students off the network if they download more than 1 M[ega]bit per second for 10 minutes or longer" (*Wired*, June 2003, 36). In the fall of 2003, many universities were adopting pay-for-use music services and charging students for this (Harmon 2003). A joint committee has been formed (the Joint Committee of Higher Education and the Entertainment Industries) to develop a compromise on downloading music files through university servers, although the RIAA continues to seek legal remedies that would violate such agreements, such as lobbying for a bill in Congress, HR 2517, the Piracy Deterrence and Education Act, while simultaneously negotiating with universities. Universities are committed to the free and open exchange of information, while the RIAA is determined to survive regardless of the cost to the rest of society.

CONCLUSION: ALTERNATIVES TO FILE SHARING?

By 2004 commercial alternatives to file sharing had emerged. The music industry's efforts in this regard, however, were weak and relatively unsuccessful. The Apple Corporation's iTunes provided the first viable downloading Web site for music, charging at first one dollar per song, then, as competition arose, less than eighty cents. But a Russian site, allofmp3 .com, charged only 3.5 cents per song or .01 cent per megabyte.[15] Sites also appeared that allowed musicians to bypass the music industry completely, selling albums directly to consumers.[16] These are examples of commercial applications of music downloading that have successfully adapted the network to ideas developed in peer-to-peer networks. It remains to be seen to what extent they displace file sharing or become the new means of acquiring music.

We are clearly at a crossroads with regard to culture under the legal regime of intellectual property law. It behooves the university, users or consumers, and others to resist the efforts of the culture industry in restricting the development of the digital domain. I argue that we must frame this resistance not in terms of copyright law but in terms of media of culture. We must invent an entirely new copyright law that rewards cultural creation but also fosters new forms of use or consumption and does not inhibit the development of new forms of digital cultural exchange that explore the new fluidity of texts, images, and sounds. The issue of the control of culture must be framed in relation to the kinds of subjects and identities it promotes. Digital cultural objects enable the constitution of subjects in broader and more heterogeneous forms than modern culture with its fixed objects and delimited identities. At stake in the evolution of file sharing and other features of networked computing is a new culture of mobile and fluid selves, ones less beholden to the constraints of modern and even postmodern subject positions. Such a culture of the self is well adapted to encounter in a propitious manner the two great historical tendencies of the twenty-first century: the emergence of intensified global exchanges of a transnational kind and the appearance of a new integration of humans and machines. These developments should be understood not as utopian dreams but as the actuality we face. The salient question is "What will be our cultural resources in the confrontation of this fateful event?"

10

EVERYDAY (VIRTUAL) LIFE

The concept of everyday life has been central to the discourse of critical theory at least since the early 1960s when Henri Lefebvre devoted several volumes to elaborating the idea.[1] In this chapter I review the category of the everyday, testing its critical capacities in the current context when information machines or media have been disseminated widely in places like the home and the street, perhaps undermining the boundary between the quotidian and the extraordinary, the private and the public. I argue that the media transform place and space in such a way that what had been regarded as the locus of the everyday can no longer be distinguished as separate from its opposite. This change operates to revise earlier notions of the everyday but also opens the possibility for a reconfigured concept of daily life that might yet contain critical potentials.[2]

HUMANISM AND EVERYDAY LIFE

A review of Lefebvre's concept of the everyday provides insight into the distance that separates us from critical positions of the immediate postwar period. Lefebvre's intervention in that discourse upset the prevailing conceptual registers. To be critical of domination in the early postwar years, for Lefebvre, meant to call into question the freedom offered by representative democracy, capitalism, or the state socialism of the Soviet Union and the Eastern European bloc of nations. Freedom, in his view, could not be realized in these institutional frames of practice. In the first instance, the everyday was the region outside official politics and large economic organizations. The locus of an "other" to public life was the first step in redefining human freedom. In 1947 he wrote in *Critique of Everyday Life*: "The critique of everyday life involves a critique of political life, in that everyday life already contains and constitutes such a critique: in that it is that critique" (Lefebvre 1991, 94). The issue at stake in the concept of daily life therefore was the recognition of the failure of national politics to offer anything like an adequate domain for human life.

To define the everyday, Lefebvre took over from phenomenology and existentialism the notion of "lived experience," le vécu, erlebnis. The category of lived experience functioned in Edmund Husserl's *Phenomenology and the Crisis of the European Sciences*, in Martin Heidegger's early existentialism of *Being and Time*, and in French translations and adaptations of these works such as Jean-Paul Sartre's *Being and Nothingness* and Maurice Merleau-Ponty's *Phenomenology of Perception* as a critique of rationalist metaphysics deriving from Cartesian, Kantian, and Hegelian traditions. These newer philosophies of the 1920s to the 1950s rejected the ordering of the world through the category of reflected reason, opening the understanding of the human condition precisely to everyday experience. One might say that these critiques of reason-centered reality were the first steps toward positions that inspire much of critical thinking today, from poststructuralist theory to the various cultural studies traditions. The crucial leap was to get outside the Western worldview in which reality moved toward and was moved by reason, not to assert an opposite to reason, as in the writings of romantic philosophy and literature, but to test the limits of what we now call logocentrism, to demote it in status as simply one, however important, regime of rationality. Lived experience could serve Lefebvre as a critical notion only because it was not defined completely within something known as reason.

Lefebvre is aware of the dangers of turning to everyday life as a critical category. Heidegger's treatment of the everyday in *Being and Time*, for instance, was that of the realm of alienation, of the forgetfulness of Being. Lefebvre acknowledged Heidegger's view when he defined the everyday as the "concrete," as "lived experience," but also as "alienation." He points to "a problem which is fundamental for the critique of everyday life. . . . Many men . . . do not know their own lives very well. . . . Men have no knowledge of their own lives: they see them and act them out via ideological themes and ethical values" (Lefebvre 1991, 92). Lack of self-reflection does not automatically lead to critique or to a space of liberation. Quite the opposite: the normal life is one of ideological distortion, of absorption into the language of domination, of the internalization of the false prescriptions and ideals of the hegemonic institutions.

Notwithstanding its dangers, the everyday still offers a point of resistance. This is so because it has no status within the dominant regimes of politics and economics. If modern society is constituted by the separation of distinct spheres into organized practices known as institutions, as Max Weber (1978) argues, then whatever is informal, unorganized, serendipitous, and chaotic may be considered the everyday. True enough, the everyday is subject to a distracted participation in ideology. Nonetheless it escapes institutional appropriation by the massive powers of the state and the economy. And for this reason, Lefebvre finds much in the everyday to offer hope and optimism. Here is his most articulated definition of everyday life:

> Everyday life, in a sense residual, defined by "what is left over after all distinct, superior, specialized, structured activities have been singled out by analysis, must be defined as a totality. . . . Everyday life is profoundly related to all activities, and encompasses them with all their differences and their conflicts; it is their meeting place, their bond, their common ground. And it is in everyday life that the sum total of relations which make the human *and every human being* a whole takes its shape and its form. In it are expressed and fulfilled those relations which bring into play the totality of the real, albeit in a certain manner which is always partial and incomplete: friendship, comradeship, love, the need to communicate, play, etc. . . . The critique of everyday life studies human nature in its concreteness. (Lefebvre 1991, 97)

If there is a center to Lefebvre's use of the term "everyday life," this passage provides the best representation of it.

There is one other effort Lefebvre made to develop a concept of the everyday that is worth noting. In an encyclopedia article entitled "The Everyday and Everydayness," he condensed several volumes devoted to the topic into a few pages. Here he underscores what was to become one of the central aspects of the discussion of the everyday in the discourse of cultural studies: its constructedness. "The everyday," Lefebvre proclaims, "is a *product*" (1987, 9). The everyday is created through the destruction of premodernity and the erection of modern society. In this process, material shortages, he argues, disappeared, and the older referents for history, religion and space itself, became disconnected from practices. Out of this wreckage emerged the everyday, the remainder, so to speak, the last refuge of meaning. In its modern form, Lefebvre continues, the everyday is a domain of "passivity," of "organized passivity" in "work, family, private life, leisure." For him, the passivity of the everyday is most acute in the domain of consumption, where "the needs of the consumer [are] created by advertising and market studies" (10). Only if a revolution transforms this passivity into a festival will humanity escape the banality of the everyday, he concludes.

As I define the problems with this concept of the everyday, it is worth bearing in mind that Lefebvre wrote neither with Kant's systematicity nor with Nietzsche's aphoristic style, his refusal of linear logic. Lefebvre's books are compendiums of thoughts that, from a negative light, threaten to disperse into incoherence or, more favorably, are charming, conversational explorations of themes.[3] The intention of the rest of my remarks concerning his work is not to diminish his image in the eyes of social theorists, nor to disparage his acumen. Instead I regard it as the task of critical theory to define a new frame for understanding the everyday in the context of digital culture. Lefebvre's definition in this passage reveals the limits of the utility of his work for this effort.

In Lefebvre's characterization of the everyday, we find the terms "residual," "total," and "human concreteness." We have seen that "residual" refers to a domain that is outside politics and economics, the great public spheres of modernity. The residual is an opposite that preserves opposition; it is the locus of resistance to what it is not. Thereby Lefebvre confirms the project of modernity, as Habermas (1983) would say, even as he shifts its site from politics and economics to the vague place of the residual. Within the residual, one salient feature of modernity—resistance to oppression—is preserved, redefined, and perhaps expanded. With the residual, Lefebvre initiates a sharp turn of direction in the metanarrative of modernity: the democratic state and the capitalist organization of industry are no longer directly the spaces in which resistance to freedom may develop. The citizen and the worker are no longer the figures in whom are registered the hopes of modernity for greater autonomy. True enough: a successful radical movement would have to confront the practices of the state and the economy, opening them and transforming them in the spirit of collective responsibility. Lefebvre's concept of the everyday as the residual, in this sense, may be said to have anticipated what came to be called in the 1970s "the new social movements" — feminism, ecology, consumer rights, human rights, antinuclear and antiracist politics — which might be extended to include postcolonialism, queer theory, transgender groups, and, today, antiglobalization protest. While each of these groups might have some connection with the critique of the liberal state and market ideology, they may arguably be said to emerge from the everyday. Each of them, in different ways, expands and redefines what came down from the nineteenth century as the scope of human freedom. While this is not the place to specify those expansions, Lefebvre's notion of the everyday holds its place as a move in the direction of postmodern politics, discovering areas of trouble beyond the rights of the citizen and the worker.

If the idea of the residual opens the project of modernity to new interests, the other terms in Lefebvre's definition of the everyday, "totality" and "human concreteness," draw the lines of critique back within the modern, reproducing in the realm of the everyday the criteria of opposition that characterized the fields of the political and the economic. Everyday life for him is residual, to be sure, but also and paradoxically all-encompassing. It is a region in which the human is most fully expressed in its totality. The human is now figured as love, play, friendship, communication, not the eradication of poverty and the dissolution of tyranny that were its earlier referents. Although Lefebvre has altered the traits of the human, it is still the human, and it is still the human in its totality that is at issue. Abandoning the shop floor and the statehouse, Lefebvre attaches to the everyday the utopian space of the truly free individual. The terms, one will notice, remain the same in both cases. Lefebvre's concept of everyday life reproduces the quest for the subject of freedom, however displaced it may be from its historical locations. "Total" and "human concreteness" are thus excessive terms, attempting to do too much (to find more than any term reasonably can) and also achieve too little (they obscure the difficulties of any position in fulfilling their criteria). His terms are mythic and ontological, wanting to insert into the everyday the prefigured telos of freedom.

Given these difficulties, it should not be surprising to find Lefebvre deeply disappointed when he turns to the actual features of the contemporary everyday. Far from the total realization of human concreteness, the everyday looks more to him like Heidegger's realm of inauthenticity. Lefebvre writes in the 1958 foreword to the second edition of *Critique of Everyday Life: Volume 1*:

> We are now entering the vast domain of the *illusory reverse image*. What we find is a false world: firstly because it is not a world, and because it presents itself as true, and because it mimics real life closely in order to replace the real by its opposite; by replacing real unhappiness by fictions of happiness, for example *by offering a fiction in response to the real need for happiness* and so on. This is the world of most films, most of the press, the theatre, the music hall: of a large sector of leisure activities.
>
> How strange the split between the real world and its reverse image is. For in the end it is not strange at all, but a false strangeness, a cheap-and-nasty, all-pervasive mystery. (35)

Far from a domain of unfettered play, love, and friendship, the everyday world of leisure in the arts and the media presents reality as an "illusory reverse image," a camera obscura effect that sounds very much like Marx's classic definition of ideology. Lefebvre is disconsolate in finding the "human concreteness" of the everyday distorted systematically in those places where it might be furthered, enhanced, represented, and advocated. Apparently frustrated by what he sees, Lefebvre casts about for an evil agent responsible for the mess and finds one in "bourgeois decadence" (127). Perhaps the wicked bourgeoisie is only playing its familiar role in the drama of the everyday whose director is Lefebvre himself, or at least his theory of the everyday as the residue of totality and human concreteness. Because the reality of the everyday proves less than expected, Lefebvre scapegoats the bourgeoisie. He also, we must note, gives a large measure of blame to the media—cinema and the press—for the appalling conditions of everyday life.

If things turned sour in 1958, they became bitter in 1968. Just as the historic May events were unfolding, Lefebvre's *Everyday Life in the Modern World*, a one-volume revision of *Critique of Everyday Life*, appeared. If the earlier volume denounced the arts and the media, along with the vile bourgeoisie, for the corruption of everyday life, the new volume discerned a level of organized control over everyday life that was not noticed earlier.

One is reminded of Norman Angell's prediction of perpetual peace as a consequence of international trade appearing just on the eve of World War I (Angell 1914). In the week that France erupted into the largest strike and protest movement in modern history, witnessing a comprehensive rejection of authority at every social level, Lefebvre's book announced the collapse of freedom into the totally administered society:

> In the modern world everyday life had ceased to be a *subject* rich in potential subjectivity; it had become an *object* of social organization. . . . Everyday life has become an object of consideration and is the province of organization; the space-time of voluntary programmed self-regulation, because when properly organized it provides a closed circuit (production-consumption-production), where demands are foreseen because they are induced and desires are run to earth; this method replaces the spontaneous self-regulation of the competitive era. Thus everyday life must shortly become the one perfect system obscured by the other systems that aim at systematizing thought and structuralizing action. (Lefebvre 1971b, 59, 72)

Perhaps I am unfair in juxtaposing the events of May 1968 with the appearance of Lefebvre's book. After all, he wrote a celebration of these events shortly thereafter in which he found new hope in everyday life (Lefebvre 1969). And the achievements of May 1968 were as fleeting as the disasters of World War I were permanent. The passage is also of interest in anticipating a Foucauldian critique of neoliberal individualism in which the control of the population (Foucault's "governmentality") is integrated with the individual's self-regulation or normalization under the sign of freedom.[4]

Lefebvre's analysis of everyday life in 1968, however, is the other side of the coin of his presentation of the concept in 1956: instead of the fulfillment of total human concreteness from the earlier book, we now have the subject being lost and becoming an object. This sharp inversion in the condition of everyday life is produced by a problem with Lefebvre's understanding of everyday life, that is, its reliance on the figures of the human and the subject. Lefebvre's humanism, his turn to the everyday as the place of complete humanity, limits his ability to discern crucial qualities of the everyday, and, for our purposes, leads to a blindness concerning the media or information machines. His contention that everyday life in 1968 is a "closed circuit of production-consumption-production" neither prepares him for the surprise of May 1968 nor points to a heuristic analysis of the place of the media and changes in the media in relation to culture. The discussion of Lefebvre's move to the everyday points us to the conceptual need for a theory of the quotidian that enables a grasp of the specific cultural mechanisms through which the subject is constituted and by which the subject constitutes its world. There are three analytic keys to this understanding: language, consumption, and media.

Lefebvre's understanding of language was shaped by his response to the emergence of structuralism and poststructuralism in the 1960s. He devoted several volumes to this issue, notably *Le language et la société* and *Au-delà du structuralisme* (Lefebvre 1966, 1971a). In both volumes he dismissed the new intellectual trends as vacuous and politically inept, developing in response a critical and social theory of language, one that proved influential to his student Jean Baudrillard. Lumping together structuralists, semioticians, and poststructuralists, Lefebvre rejected what he saw as their ahistorical theory of language, misconstruing it as determinist. The new theories of language for him failed to account for the element of domination in the social system. To that end, he proposed a revision of the Saussurean concept of the sign in which the distinction between signifier and signified was not a quality of language as such but a consequence of the manipulation of culture by the capitalist media. In an important formulation, Lefebvre denounced the splitting of signifiers and signifieds as resulting in a "floating stock of *meaningless signifiers* (stray images either conscious or unconscious)" (Lefebvre 1971b). The term "floating signifiers" would prove useful in the critique of the culture of language and media by Baudrillard. Lefebvre himself did not advance beyond his condemnation of the phenomenon to analyze the cultural mechanisms through which floating signifiers appeared in everyday life, how these constituted new subject positions, and how the new language pattern might be the locus of a critique, pointing to possible cultural formations that might not realize human concreteness and the total subject.

If Lefebvre's critique of language in everyday life failed to articulate positions beyond familiar left humanism, his view of consumerism also was seriously limited. Again one finds that Lefebvre is sensitive to a change in the nature of consumption, a new concern with the cultural aspects of an activity previously associated with material exhaustion of objects. In the following passage from *Everyday Life in the Modern World*, Lefebvre complains that consumption has become a mystified embrace of symbols:

> Consuming of displays, displays of consuming. Consuming of displays of consuming, consuming of signs and signs of consuming; each subsystem, as it tries to close the circuit, gives another self-destructive twist, at the level of everyday life. . . . Thus every object and product acquires a dual existence, perceptible and make-believe; all that can be consumed becomes a symbol of consumption and the consumer is fed on symbols, symbols of dexterity and wealth, of happiness and of love; sign and significance replace reality, there is a vast substitution, a massive transfer, that is nothing but an illusion created by the swivel's giddy twists. (108)

The shift to the consumption of symbols, a crucial aspect of postmodern consumer practices (Firat and Dholakia 1998), is registered by Lefebvre as a fall from "reality." One cannot begin to explore everyday life since the mid-twentieth century with such a humanist metaphysic.

The third central feature of an analytic of everyday life, the media, is barely touched on by Lefebvre. A shift to the media requires an understanding of language and consumption such that the role of the media becomes a question, not a simple negative instance of alienation. Once everyday life is extracted from the humanist frame of Lefebvre, it becomes available for a cultural study of the position of specific media, of how particular media participate in constructing cultural forms in the domains of language and consumption. This proves to be a highly complex task for the cultural analyst, in part because of the agency of information machines. The framework of subject-object that so profoundly shapes modernist cultural analysis cannot serve as a guide in a domain of everyday life where machines are a central feature of the landscape. The emergence of new media since the 1990s has raised this issue to a new level of urgency, stimulating important initiatives that are too numerous to list here.[5] In the next section, I examine some of the questions that arise for an understanding of everyday life when attention is paid to media, and I offer an analysis of my own experiences of media to highlight some of the dangers and opportunities that the media instigate.

The study of the place of media in everyday life is plagued with difficulties. Media mediate. They go between established social and cultural positions and between the categories deployed to comprehend these positions. They are machines—neither subjects nor objects, neither minds nor bodies, neither persons nor things, but both at the same time and yet different from each. They enter our lives in funny ways, obliquely, behind the back of our cultural self-understanding. The standard Western notion of machines as tools, with users as subjects and machines as objects, with a utilitarian ethic presumed for the subject and a privilege given to the subject's intentionality or consciousness—this long-standing framework for fitting tools into culture does not do justice to the complexity of the practice of humans with information machines. Since the introduction of print, each generation has confronted the issue of media, taking as a given the media existing in its youth, and responding variously with anxiety or joy to the placement of new media in society. In what follows, I analyze my relation to several media in the order I encountered them, attempting to understand how each medium altered my subject position, extrapolating from there to the experience of some others. I include only a few of the media I encountered, since a comprehensive discussion is beyond the scope of this work.

My purpose differs from standard autobiography. I am not attempting to illuminate my singular life or to confess moral events. I am not even trying to contextualize my life, indicating its contingencies and historical determinations. Instead I hope to use my experience as a case study of the historic synergy of human and information machine. By demonstrating how profound and extensive has been the role of media in my life, I offer a model to further the conceptualization of everyday life.[6]

Radio

The example of radio illustrates a fundamental feature of all media: they bring diverse cultures into close contact, a degree of proximity not possible without them. In this way, media greatly accentuate the tendency of daily city life to mix populations from different ethnic or racial origins. Media enact this mixing in ways different from the urban topography. Juxtaposing cultures in media is often haphazard and instantaneous, whereas cities are known for neighborhoods with particular ethnic groupings. Media tend in this respect to destabilize local customs, to extend awareness of other ways of life, and to add complexity to the process of socialization.

A boy of six or seven in the late 1940s, living in the Flatbush area of Brooklyn, I was introduced to new cultures through the radio. I remember clearly being in bed with a cold and turning the radio dial in boredom until I tuned in a country and western music station, music I had never heard before and was foreign to the culture of my upbringing. The whining, plaintive sounds from throats and violins that emanated from the small speaker were a revelation to me. I had never heard anything like it and could not imagine the cultural context from which it sprang (I had not yet seen Western movies or television shows). There I was, alone in the bedroom, listening to the strange sounds and being fascinated by them. The radio brought me a new culture. At the same time, it opened my sensorium to music: I would continue to love music to this day. Later I studied the saxophone and clarinet, playing in high school bands and an ROTC band. I also love recorded music—but more of that later.

Perhaps of greater import than my experience of the radio was that of my schoolmate Paul Simon a few years later in Queens, New York. He reported in a TV interview in the late 1990s hearing rhythm and blues, rock-and-roll, and other black music on the radio in Kew Garden Hills, an area where he lived that had few African Americans. In both his case and mine, the radio allowed the introduction of other cultures in a manner outside the control of parents, although admittedly the consequences of his listening were far greater than mine. Children could discover cultures through music that otherwise would remain unavailable to them. The youth culture and popular music of the 1960s were deeply affected by radio listening, contributing significantly to forms of popular culture that would take by storm not only the United States but much of the world.

During the years of my youth, the radio was a fixture in my family's home. I did not regard it as special in any way. When I listened to country and western music that day in the 1940s, I did not appreciate the radio itself, had no sense of its ability to overcome geographic and social distance. My focus was totally on the music. Yet I had made a bond with the radio. Mark-radio could now enjoy this music at any time. Unlike Radio Raheem in Spike Lee's film *Do the Right Thing* (1989), I could not take the radio with me through the streets. But I could come back to it after a day at school, to its fixed place in my home, and turn the dials to connect with a culture remote from the familiar middle-class Jewish world. In fact, when I began to hear Jewish music, mostly at summer camps, I regarded it as exotic and strange compared with radio music.

The radio I heard in Brooklyn came from the culture industry, the media corporations that controlled the airwaves since the onset of broadcasting in the 1920s. In Britain in the 1970s, Anglo-Africans customized radio to suit the needs of their community (Hebdige 1987). Pirate radio, as it was known in mainstream media, enabled the local community to hear music unavailable on the commercial and public stations. In addition, disc jockeys employed the newer cassette technology to compose music with bits and pieces from the culture and politics of the day. Inexpensive radio transmitters along with cheap cassette recorders formed an assemblage that empowered the Anglo-African community and enriched their daily lives with the music of their choice. The question of control in everyday life arises from the examples of British pirate radio and my listening. Shall we understand the dissemination of information machines in everyday life under the sign of democratization?

Television

My experience of radio was isolated. I listened usually alone in a room to a station of my choice. Radio did not intercede between me and my family but substituted for other activities I might do without any company. Not so with television. Television was watched by the family as a whole, displacing conversation, parlor games, and other forms of conviviality. Television introduced into the home a collective popular culture, one bringing to the family a culture from outside (Spigel 1992). Since there were few stations in the 1950s, everyone with televisions tended to watch the same programs.[7] In my experience, radio simply brought to my attention alternatives to my immediate cultural surroundings; television introduced into the home a new national culture, one with which the family could not compete.[8]

My father, I later realized, was an early adopter of information technologies. He was an accountant whose busy season was tax time. He insisted I help him at these times, and I recall the early versions of copy machines and primitive adding machines he used. The copy machines were messy affairs with specially coated paper and liquids of all sorts. The world of work, I learned, was also saturated with information machines.

But in 1949, shortly after the introduction of nationally broadcast television shows, he purchased a TV. Aside from images of Howdy Doody and Milton Berle, my clearest memory is of neighbors filling our modest-sized living room to watch and listen in awe to our nine-inch Admiral television set, a large, free-standing object with lots of polished wood encasing the tube. In those early days, television created a community of sorts. My family and neighbors all marveled at the technical feat of broadcast moving images and sound. Here was something new and important. Yet to my young eyes, television was interesting but not astonishing. It was easy to accept its novelty, but it did not seem extraordinary. I suppose this is a basic difference between adults and children in the reception of new media.

Television's greatest emotional effect on me came in sporting events. I remember distinctly my profound disappointment and frustration when in September 1951 Bobby Thompson hit a home run against the Brooklyn Dodgers to give the New York Giants the pennant. I was alone in front of the television with no one to share this depressing event, just the tube, which disgusted me deeply.

These media—radio and television—impacted my life in important ways. I recall that the technical feats they accomplished did not surprise me in the least. I simply accepted that text, images, and sound could appear from outside my small world. While the wonders of these media affected me deeply at times, my life was concentrated mostly on sports and friends. Playing baseball, stickball, basketball, and football were the really important occasions of my life. The rest was supplementary (broadcast sports events) or marginal (country and western music, sci-fi films, and novels). For my youth, activities with others took priority over mediated experience. Nonetheless radio and television entered into my life and significantly altered the contours of everyday experience.[9] I learned skills of shifting registers from face-to-face relations to information machines and back. Growing up in the 1940s and 1950s, I was moving increasingly toward a culture of multiplicity. If the ethnic mix I encountered in these early years was limited, the ontological mix of human and machine was rich and diverse. Multiculturalism began for me through the mediation of information machines and only later extended to street life.

Typewriter

In junior high school in 1953, students were required to take a course in typing. I had little interest in the machine at the time, but learning to touch-type has proved to be an invaluable skill. When I went off to college in 1958, a few years later, I received a gift of a Royal portable electric typewriter, which I used for years, eventually writing my dissertation on it. Even though typing was considered a menial skill beneath the dignity of a future "professional," I accepted it and grew to enjoy using the machine. When I arrived in California, having never traveled west of Philadelphia, on September 2, 1969, to take an assistant professorship at UC Irvine, my office equipment consisted of a dictionary and a typewriter, a meager setup cost by today's standards.

A good portion of my work life has consisted since then in using a keyboard. For any reader of my generation, I need not belabor the difference between an electromechanical keyboard and a computer keyboard. The former, notwithstanding Friedrich Kittler (1990) and William Burroughs (1959), was a miserable affair. Changing text required messy liquids and powders. Multiple copies, with carbon papers that inevitably left stains on clothing and hands, were truly bothersome. On these machines, the transfer of the life of the mind into material form was painstaking and tedious. Often this work was subcontracted (as we now say) to full-time typists. Because of the limits of the typewriter, writers did not produce texts in an edited form, leaving manuscripts to professionals for final polishing, or typescripts almost unreadable with erasures, crossed-out passages, marginal revisions, scribbling of all kinds.

The electromechanical typewriter was truly a tool of an older kind. It required skill. It was a machine that resisted the operator's intentionality, demanding some physical force to produce markings on paper. The object that emerged from it bore the traces of labor—of the imperfections in the keys, the uneven spread of ink on the ribbon, and the variable force of the typist's fingers across the qwerty. Computer keyboards, by contrast, elide these markings of the body. Word-processed files appear to inscribe the intellect of the writer directly, obeying with precision the author's intentions, even correcting them on the fly. There are indeed experiments with disabled computer users in which the brain directly transposes its thoughts to the screen, bypassing entirely the activity of writing.[10] Information machines have clearly transformed the domain of work, constructing symbiotic human-machines or cyborgs in the process (Zuboff 1988).

The shift from the typewriter keyboard to the computer keyboard is ontological: the former instantiates and reinforces a subject-object relation. The paper page receives the mechanical blows of the keys as the writer pounds on the machine to produce the inked page. The typewriter merely improves the legibility of the page over the hand-manipulated quill, ink pen, or ballpoint, where one formerly scratched inscriptions into the paper. The computer keyboard, by contrast, sends digital signals to the central processing chip through the word-processing program, producing an output of letters on the screen that lack the material properties of the typed paper page. The letters on the screen are fluid, easily changeable and movable. No more scratching out and brushing of white liquids. The words appear on the screen almost as quickly as they are thought or revised. Spelling and grammar are instantly checked. A thesaurus is only a few keystrokes away. Other files on one's machine are also ready to be marked, copied, and pasted into the text. Bibliographical annotations are just as available, not only from information existing in one's database but from other databases at remote locations anywhere in the world. The same keyboard serves many functions, not only word processing. Switching between programs magically transforms the keyboard into a calculator, an input system for a database, a music selector, a telegraph-like communication system, and so forth.

The keyboard is a liminal apparatus. It sutures the consciousness of the writer to the vast stores of information on the Net and the versatile facilities of programs on one's hard disk. There is no opposition of creative mind to dumb (typewriting) machine, but instead interaction between writer, keyboard, computer program, and network, each having considerable cognitive abilities. The mind moves with the aid of the keyboard into the screen, merging with global information systems through the interface. Writing is no longer an isolated activity but one that affords simultaneous connections to others through chat rooms, e-mail, and instant messaging. And the keyboard, perhaps a collapsible one, moves with the user through everyday life far more easily than a portable typewriter, accompanying the user wherever he or she happens to be. The keyboard user is thus always, for better or worse, ready to write.

Videocassette Recorders

Copyright became an issue again with the suit of the motion picture industry against Sony Corporation for the sale of VCRs. Sony won the case, and the consumer was able to gain some control over the video signal.

I bought my first VCR, a Betamax machine, in 1981 for the explicit purpose of recording a broadcast on public television of the Pierre Boulez–Patrice Chereau performance of Richard Wagner's *The Ring of the Nibelungen*. This recording enabled me to teach a course on *The Ring* to undergraduates in Southern California, all eighteen or so hours of Wagner's music to elevate their spirit, or so I hoped. Since commercial VHS or Beta tapes of the performance were not available, the videorecorder was a condition for my pedagogy.

What I recall most vividly about the VCR was the first time I pressed the fast-forward button. The image moved at my command. The image was no longer something that came into my home at its own pace, at its own time, at the behest of the broadcaster's programming. Only seeing the blurred image in fast-forward mode did I realize how, until then, I had experienced the television image-sound as a fixed cultural object, one that I could only receive in the same way that I watched a movie in the cinema. With the aid of the videorecorder, cultural objects need not appear for the consumer at the whim of some company, from the outside, but can be transformed by the consumer in the very process of consumption. Again the question of control in everyday life emerges.

THE WALKMAN

As a hi-fi snob, I was uninterested in portable cassette players introduced by Sony as the Walkman. My children were not so constrained, quickly adopting the medium. In the early 1980s, in a mall in Mission Viejo, California, with my wife and daughters, I was bored by shopping. My younger

daughter offered me her Walkman with a U2 cassette in it. I was astonished. Standing in the same position in the midst of clothing stores and
the like, I was enveloped by the gorgeous, bleating sounds of The Joshua
Tree, literally displacing me from my surroundings. A simple audio device
transported my consciousness to the musical space. If radio commingles
cultures, shifting spatial arrangements, the Walkman blends in the same
body different senses from divergent locations, in this case the visuality
of the mall with sound from U2's recording studio. Such alterations in
the spatial and temporal configuration of the everyday urge us finally to
consider the question that has been at the horizon of these analyses: the
control of daily culture.[11]

Michael Bull, in Sounding Out the City, studied this question in relation
to what he calls (to avoid litigation by Sony Corporation) the personal
stereo. Based on ethnographic interviews with users of Walkmans, Bull
frames the diversity of their views using the theory of the culture industry
developed by the Frankfurt school. Bull pleads for recognition of the importance of information machines in daily life, arguing that they afford
individuals new levels of control over their daily lives: "The use of personal
stereos greatly expands the possibilities for users to aesthetically recreate
their daily experience" (Bull 2000, 86). For Bull, the Walkman alleviates
the boredom of daily routine but in the end accommodates the individual
to the exigencies of late capitalism. The individual as agent escapes the
ugliness and grind of the city only to accommodate herself to the offerings
of the culture industry, in the form of both technology (the Walkman) and
the music. The enhanced control rendered by the machine proves illusory
to the analyst informed by Frankfurt school theory (156). Walkman users
select music but lose the opportunity of mutual recognition that is the
hallmark of the Western city: "Personal-stereo use demonstrates a structural negation of reciprocal forms of recognition as lying at the heart of
everyday urban relations" (182).

UBIQUITOUS COMPUTING

A final example of technoculture might shed new light on Bull's ambivalent conclusion, this one, alas, not from my personal experience, because
it is an emerging development. In this case I refer to the imminent integration of computing with the body through miniaturization. Walkmans,

personal digital assistants, cellphones with online capability, geographic positioning systems — these new appendages to the mobile body in everyday life are being enhanced with greatly increased computing power. As that occurs, all the power of information technology will be harnessed by, and coupled with, the body.

The distribution of information machines throughout the space of the everyday proceeds apace. Major research laboratories devoted to digital technology, the MIT Media Lab in Cambridge and the former Xerox PARC in Palo Alto in particular, report on projects to bring computing power to urban places inhabited hitherto only by humans and mechanical machines (with due recognition to cockroaches, rats, and the occasional plant). Streetlights, roads, fire hydrants, and building facades are designated or already colonized by computer chips, video cameras, audio devices, and the like. Appliances inside and outside the home already bear digital commanders. From cars to humble toasters, computing power is everywhere. If industrial society has destroyed thousands of plant and animal species, it has replaced them with silicon in equally impressive variations. If the physical plant of the city and the mechanical devices inside buildings and vehicles harbor digital technology, so do the human populations. Walkmans, mobile phones, beepers, and personal digital assistants accompany the peripatetic urbanite from Singapore and Tokyo to Helsinki and Los Angeles. It is increasingly unusual to encounter a person in public who does not pack such devices.

Mark Weiser, a longtime chief technologist at Xerox PARC who died in 1999, frames this dispersion of information machines as the culmination of the history of computing. He argues that digital computing develops in three stages: an early phase of mainframe machines, a second era of desktop computing, and finally a third stage of ubiquitous computing.[12] Weiser regards computers as tools and argues that their best disposition is to become invisible. We need not be confronted by huge mainframes or have our desks cluttered by monitors, keyboards, and pointing devices. Instead, he predicts, computers will disappear into our notepads, eyeglasses, and clothing. He advocates the complete normalization of computing such that people "cease to be aware of it." Like road signs and billboards that we view without awareness of reading, computing should fade into the background of our lives. Weiser's understanding of ubiquitous computing is flawed with the same difficulty as Lefebvre's concept of the everyday: it is thoroughly humanist. Information machines, for Weiser, enhance human activity in the same manner as hammers.

Weiser's research on new information technologies promotes the disappearance and simultaneously the spread of computing. He develops surfaces, large and small, like notepads and blackboards, that are actually computers. Primitive versions of these devices exist as smart badges, or "tabs," that identify the bearer to doors and buildings, inform others of one's whereabouts, and inform other computers of the identity of the user. Thus doors open automatically, receptionists know the location of visitors, and "computer terminals retrieve the preferences of whoever is sitting at them" (Weiser 1991). The newer devices, "pads" and "boards," would substitute for the conventional desktop. "Scrap computers," as Weiser calls them, they would function like Post-It notes or pads of paper, except that, as computers, they would have all the powers of a digital machine—memory, storage, communication. Unlike "inert" pads, these "computers" cannot become lost, since they have the ability to beep their location to their owner. While the "pads" and "boards" are not to my knowledge in use, they certainly afford conveniences. What Weiser does not acknowledge is the disruption they bring to the familiar picture of everyday life in industrial society. For that reason, it behooves us to pause a while before information machines become invisible, and reconsider the world where information machines are everywhere.

Ubiquitous computing disturbs the sense of physical location, extending and multiplying the body throughout the globe. Profound risks and possibilities accompany ubiquitous computing. The dangers are already becoming apparent, with permanent surveillance as its outcome. Global positioning systems are perhaps convenient for the traveler, but information machines, considered in totality, present a vision in which any individual can be located by anyone at any time. In a world where democracy is not at all assured or fully developed, dominant institutions may avail themselves of such surveillance for dubious or malevolent purposes. Reliance on the familiar distinction between the public and the private becomes no longer possible, fundamentally upsetting the markers of freedom in each domain. Information machines fold into prevailing systems of domination, threatening the hard-won liberties of the past few centuries. The nightmare of Gilles Deleuze's "control society" (Deleuze 1992a) and George Orwell's 1984 come readily to mind and are even surpassed by futuristic information technologies already extant.

If the risks of everyday life in the brave new world of information technology are extreme, so equally are the possibilities not simply of conveniences in Weiser's sense but of globalizing democracy in a new configuration of humans and machines. As anyone may be located by anyone, so anyone can communicate with anyone else. This novelty makes practical for the first time the term "human." But it does so, as I have indicated, only through the symbiosis with machines. Humachines are able to connect to others out of mutual interest, no longer limited by the vagaries and shortcomings of territorial specificity—blood, race, ethnicity, proximity, scourges of the past millennia that some prefer to dignify by the term "community." Marx's invocation to the workers of the world to unite is now armed with the communications network that makes it possible, albeit by no means guaranteed. If the nation-state and the corporation scurry to bend this network to their brandings with identities (social security numbers, credit card numbers, etc.), the Internet also resists this distortion by opening new paths of multiple identity, anonymity, temporary identity, fluid identity.

The everyday life emerging in information society is a battleground over the nature of human identity. If the old order has its way, identities will be stabilized, and information machines will become as invisible as they will be ubiquitous. But if alternatives are developed, a global space of humachines may emerge whose life task becomes precisely the exploration of identity, the discovery of genders, ethnicities, sexual identities, personality types that may be enjoyed, experienced, and also transgressed. Henri Lefebvre, with his humanist vision, celebrated a possible everyday of a permanent festival. In a vision of the "city as play," he dreamed of an everyday life that became "a creation of which each citizen and each community would be capable" (Lefebvre 1971b, 13). Paradoxically, only as we leave the human behind, and with it all the detritus of progress so dismaying to Walter Benjamin's angel of history (Benjamin 1969a, 257–58), and enter the posthuman epoch does this vision take on the force of political possibility.

11

CONSUMERS, USERS, AND DIGITAL COMMODITIES

Every technology . . . requires the inculcation of a form of life, the reshaping of various roles for the humans, the little body techniques required to use the devices, new inscription practices, the mental techniques required to think in terms of certain practices of communication, the practices of the self oriented around the mobile telephone, the word processor, the World Wide Web and so forth.

—Nikolas Rose, *Powers of Freedom*

In the United States and in most industrialized countries, individuals in their everyday lives are bombarded continuously by advertisements. Walking in the street or driving through it, one's eyes are assaulted by billboards, store signs, huge electronic monitors, brand names visible on the clothing of others, promotional information on buses, benches, and company cars. The visual space of contemporary urbanity is a mosaic of images and texts all selling something, all competing for the attention of the passersby with bright colors, tempting imagery, all displayed in the largest possible size. Entry inside buildings offers no respite from the assault. Department stores feature monitors urging the shopper to buy the products on the screen (McCarthy 2001). The purchase itself is no mere acquisition but a submission to the publicity departments of untold corporations of one's preferences as the information flits at electronic speeds from one's credit card through the computers networked around the globe and finally into the omnivorous databases of the insatiable transnational behemoths. In the space of the city, the individual is labeled and branded into the category of the consumer with a consistency that would be admirable were it not so deplorable.

Imagine my surprise, then, when I visited Ljubljana, Slovenia, in June 1987, a couple of years before everything collapsed in degrees of chaos on the other side of the Cold War's Iron Curtain. Hollywood programmed my mind to expect a depressing urban landscape dominated by a monotony of grays. John Urry notes this phenomenon as "the tourist gaze" that is prefigured in "film, TV, literature, magazines, records and videos, which construct and reinforce the gaze" (Urry 1990, 3). Nothing could be farther from the truth in the mixed economy of Yugoslavia under Marshal Tito. A hiatus in the conference I was attending afforded me a chance to stroll in the city. Even in my jet-lagged state of mind, I was truly astonished, upon perambulating through some main streets, to find an almost complete absence of billboards, signs, images, the repertoire of the marketer's imagination. So bereft of advertising were the streets that the only way to discover what a retail shop was selling was for the visitor to the city to walk right up to the store window and peer inside. The relief from advertising, for this New Yorker cum Southern Californian, was in turn disconcerting, arresting, and fascinating. I was charmed by the lack of information as my eyes relished the buildings, trees, shrubs, and, yes, people. How different was an urban experience of the everyday without the relentless appeals of the market! Ljubljana taught me to look differently at the visual spectacle of Los Angeles, with strip mall sandwiched next to strip mall in an appalling homage to free enterprise in its postmodern mode.

The alternative to the street as the space of everyday life is the home. Here one is no more secure than when outside from the constant hawking of wares and services. An array of media facilitates the intrusion of marketers into the home. Least annoying for most of us are the ads that arrive every morning with the daily newspaper. Soft pornography strewn across the pages of the most respected dailies is a privilege of the marketing departments of corporations that somehow eludes the moralists who decry its presence in other media such as the World Wide Web or cable television. Erotic images are acceptable, for this logic, when they are part of a commercial. Radio and television commercials are bothersome too, but by now they merge almost into invisibility and inaudibility inside the shows themselves as our minds filter out their blaring solicitations. Movies on videotape or DVD enjoyed in living rooms and dens increasingly feature promotional material at the beginning of the cassette or disc, forcing one to fast-forward to avoid them. Most objectionable, perhaps, are the calls from telemarketers, interrupting us at dinner or whenever their statistical predictions of our availability indicate they are most likely to reach us. Even fax machines attached to private telephone lines are not immune to the wiles of the solicitor, at least not until some recent rulings by the U.S. courts may impose a modicum of restraint. Advertisers offer free Internet service providers, free e-mail accounts, even free computers, if only the individual would act like a consumer and permit the tracking of purchasing activity. In every room of the home except the toilet, the private individual is hailed, by means of the media, as a consumer. In public and in private, publicity finds us and renders us, consciously or not, willingly or not, and above all else, as consumers.

MARKETS AND MEDIA

Once upon a time, people shopped in markets. They went to designated locations at designated times to find an array of stalls or a row of shops, each staffed with salespeople. As soon as one entered such a place or even happened to be in the vicinity, one opened oneself to the cries of the sellers. In the tiny, crooked streets of the Arab and Jewish sections of old Jerusalem, or in the world's oldest continuous market in Cairo, markets like this still exist. In prosperous yuppie communities throughout the West— from the Winterfeldt Markt in Berlin on Wednesdays and Saturdays, to the farmers' market in tiny Laguna Beach, California, from 7 A.M. to noon on Saturdays, merchants offer their fresh produce to the public. Because the shoppers must place themselves at the market, they engage in a process of self-construction as consumers. When one leaves such markets, one is no longer a consumer but a worker, friend, family member, and so forth. The market in these anachronisms of premodern social life is a contained domain, one sustained by local knowledge, by word of mouth, by numerous social practices, but, in any case, without the assistance of the media.[1]

However important such market practices were (and are) to participants, they did not constitute anything like a consumer society. For that configuration to arise, numerous and fundamental changes would have to take place in the social fabric. Prominent among these is the rise and dissemination of information machines known as media. I will explore the relation of media to consumption in the everyday, pursuing in particular the significance of the change from mass media to new media; from newspaper, radio, and television to the Internet; and from the analog reproduction of cultural objects to their digital formation and dissemination. My chief question is this: Is a new form of relation to goods and services possible in the new media context outside the model of the consumer?

Media themselves are not necessarily linked with consumption. In the print revolution of the sixteenth and seventeenth centuries, with the development of a book industry, media were implicated in the first place with the world of religion and also to a lesser extent with the classics, literature, science, and popular culture. Studies of the early craft of printing underscore its relation to religion (de Certeau 1984; Saenger 1989). Books provided individuals with alternative practices of prayer. Because a book was portable in size, one could carry it to church and read silently, reversing the practice of the collective reading of large scrolls. The nascent printing industry produced individual volumes that were themselves sold as commodities on a market but yet folded into existing practices of literacy connected with religion, humanism, politics, science, and various dimensions of popular culture, not least of which was erotica. This industry was also regulated by guild practices that controlled production rates, managed labor conditions, and oversaw the entire process of manufacturing. Until the eighteenth century, according to historians of print, the figure of the author was restricted to a relatively minor role in book commodity production (Johns 1998). The purchaser of a book was interested in knowing the guild that produced it, as well, of course, as the book's content. The buyer, these scholars tell us, was not focused on the celebrity of the author. One of the conditions of the emergence of contemporary consumer society is a shift in awareness toward recognizing the prominence of authors' names, figures that circulate through society with fetishistic force, eventually to include actors, singers, brand names, and even corporate logos, attached to the commodity, to be sure, but also hovering over it as a desirable value.

By the later decades of the nineteenth century, print production methods had advanced to the point where the publication of daily newspapers was possible. A condition for the possibility of the penny press in industrial society included, in addition to technical advances in papermaking and the printing press, the introduction of advertising copy. Unlike books, newspapers, as we know, included promotions for the full variety of commodities and services. Income from these advertisements permitted publishers to reduce the price of the newspaper to the point at which it could be purchased by the ordinary laborer. The number of potential consumers of newspapers expanded exponentially, so that one could begin to speak of a mass market. Historians of the press in the United States trace the birth of the penny press to the 1830s, when the price of an issue came down from annual subscriptions of six or eight dollars to a daily price of one cent. Sales rose accordingly from several to tens of thousands of copies (Shudson 1978, 18). Mass circulation, properly speaking, did not arrive until the 1890s, when figures rose to the hundreds of thousands. The largest newspaper in New York City, for instance, sold some 600,000 copies on a day in 1896 (111). With such a mass market was born the potential for what we have come to call mass culture, portending an enormous change in consumption practices. One can say that what we now call "broadcast media" emerged with the mass production of newspapers: it entailed the dissemination from a relatively small number of points or producers or addressers of the same information or cultural object, in principle, to the entire society.

My argument is that without media the activity of consumption and the figure of the consumer do not take on their current status as major aspects of social life. A very different inflection characterized consumption before the advent of contemporary media. My nostalgic descriptions of the streets of Ljubljana and the Berlin Winterfeldt Markt notwithstanding, I do not argue that the earlier conditions were somehow better, more moral, or closer to democracy. Far from it. Rather, consumption in the era of mechanical reproduction was a different regime of practices, a different technology of power, to use Michel Foucault's term, from what currently prevails (Foucault and Gordon 1980a). The analysis of consumption in the recent period must take into account the role of the media in supporting this difference. For each type of media, the analysis must also determine the specific relation to activities of consumption, and with the concomitant construction of the consumer subject. Before turning to the question of media regimes and consumption, I consider the understanding of this question by prominent theorists of consumption, in particular Michel de Certeau, testing the extent to which their contribution to the analysis of consumption includes a recognition of the place of the media.

CONSUMER THEORY AND THE MEDIA

Social and cultural theory in the modern era was preoccupied with two main questions: the democratic nation-state and the industrial economy. The values of freedom and equality were calibrated to the understanding of politics and economics. Issues of family life, gender relations, sexual preference, consumer patterns, and emotional dynamics were decidedly subordinate to the world-historical concerns of determining the most appropriate institutional forms for the realization of human freedom. With great subtlety, intellectuals and scholars investigated the variations of state formation, industrial development, and market cycles. In these areas, the essence of human nature was actualized. A promethean vision of human progress accompanied arguments over the organization of modern life. In this theoretical context, the consumer was a secondary, marginal figure. Consumption was considered necessary for the reproduction of labor and the satisfaction of needs. Yet it was not connected directly to the great drama of human betterment. A domain of "passivity," consumption was outside history, a sideshow to the main event of political economy. Fuat Firat and Nikhilesh Dholakia put it well: "The 'passivation' of consumption came to be the prevalent mode of consumption in modernity" (Firat and Dholakia 1998, 65). The free citizen and the free laborer were modernity's achievements, not the free consumer. What could not be thought during the heyday of modernity was consumption as a regime of practices, one that varied significantly from period to period, was intelligible as an activity, and was central to the cultural process of constructing a symbolic order.

A salient feature of postmodernity is the recognition of the complexity and importance of consumption. Michel de Certeau is a leading theorist of this change. His works, especially The Practice of Everyday Life, Heterologies, and Culture in the Plural (de Certeau 1984, 1986, 1997), constitute a thorough rethinking of the question of consumption in everyday life. Of course, he is not alone in this endeavor, as many of the important discussions of consumption in daily life attest (Gardiner 2000). I will review de Certeau's discussion of consumption with an eye to the question of the media. While recognizing the invaluable contribution he makes to a reconceptualization of consumption, I raise the question of its incompleteness or inadequacy with regard to the role of media, a problem that plagues much of the social and cultural theory of everyday life.[2] I also take de Certeau as typical of a group of thinkers who work in a similar direction, from Georg Simmel and Henri Lefebvre to Pierre Bourdieu. The following critical evaluation is intended not as a dismissal of the work of these thinkers but as a plea for recognition of the question of information machines.

De Certeau is certainly cognizant of the way that commercial capitalism transforms the visual landscape of urban daily life. Much like my impression of the difference between communist Ljubljana and capitalist Los Angeles, de Certeau notes:

> The modern city is becoming a labyrinth of images. It is endowed with a graphics of its own, by day and by night that devises a vocabulary of images on a new space of writing. A landscape of posters and billboards organizes our reality. It is a *mural landscape* with the repertory of its immediate objects of happiness. It conceals the buildings in which labor is confined; it covers over the closed universe of everyday life; it sets in place artificial forms that follow the paths of labor in order to juxtapose their passageways to the successive moments of pleasure. A city that is a real "imaginary museum" forms the counterpoint of the city at work. (de Certeau 1997, 34)

Advertising for de Certeau mars the city, pollutes the urban panorama, but, we must ask, how are these images to be understood in the context of the full array of media visuality, including film, television, and the Internet? Does de Certeau's highly influential theory of the everyday account for the relation of media to consumption?

An irony characterizes de Certeau's intervention in the theory of consumption. He turns to language theory to theorize consumption as an active practice. For historians and social scientists, especially of the period of the 1970s in which de Certeau wrote, social agency was an attribute of action. Language theory, especially structuralist linguistics, was considered by these scholars as a threat to agency, as a deterministic system that eviscerated the freedom of the individual and group, as we have seen in the last chapter in the writings of Lefebvre. Their view is a modernist one, as outlined earlier. Action here concerns political and economic practices. De Certeau, on the contrary, revalues consumption as an active practice by turning to the very register of analysis regarded by modernists as forestalling such recognition. De Certeau complains that the quantifying methods of social science reduce the understanding of consumption. Social scientists who use quantitative methods, he complains, see cultural products "merely as data on the basis of which statistical tabulations of their circulation can be drawn up." They do not recognize them "also as parts of the repertory with which users carry out operations of their own" (de Certeau 1984, 31). Statistics, he protests, are limited to grasping "the material used by consumer practices." But "consumers produce . . . indeterminate trajectories." And there is a "*formality* proper to these practices, their surreptitious and guileful 'movement' " (34). De Certeau discovers this "form" through a poststructuralist theory of language.

De Certeau explores the implications of the modernist study of consumption. He finds that this approach not only misses the "form" of consumption but denigrates the position of the consumer. In the hands of modernist social science, "Consumers are transformed into immigrants" (40). "The practices of consumption are the ghosts of the society that carries their name" (35). More generally, de Certeau discloses the problem with modernist analyses: "A society is . . . composed of certain foregrounded practices organizing its normative institutions *and* of innumerable other practices that remain 'minor.' . . . It is in this multifarious and silent 'reserve' of procedures that we should look for 'consumer' practices having the double characteristic . . . of being able to organize both spaces and languages, whether on a minute or a vast scale" (48). This is the crux of the matter for de Certeau: the "form" of consumption missed by the "technocratic rationality" of social science is its construction of "spaces and languages." With this argument goes a sea change in the understanding of consumption. From the passive, quantifiable action of individuals, consumption becomes a cultural creation, a poiesis, as he terms it, a making and a using, a signifying constellation. Here is the sense in which de Certeau deploys a language theory: consumption is a type of "enunciation," a production of meaning, a sort of speech act. Consumption is not simply a purchase of an object fixed in its meaning but a resignification of that object. Commodities move from factories to stores to homes and are transformed in the process. The last move into the home includes a remaking of the object, not physically but culturally. In the practices of food preparation, in the decoration of appliances like refrigerators with children's artwork, notices, and memorandums; in every one of the acts of consumption, meanings are constructed and life is thereby organized and configured. Those who find social agency in work and politics systematically ignore the creativity of consumption.

Upgrading the value of the practice of consumption, de Certeau also presented a reconsideration of everyday life. His influential discussion of the rhetoric of walking in the city is only one aspect of his complete rethinking of the everyday. Significantly, he introduced terms associated with warfare (strategies and tactics) to theorize the productive side of everyday practices. Strategies are the instrumental actions of large institutions; tactics are the resisting practices of individuals and groups. The difficulty with these categories for the current discussion is that they occlude the mediation of information machines. They do not allow for a differential understanding of the material constraints and openings afforded by each medium. Instead de Certeau introduces a binary of determinist, institutional strategies and creative, countervailing tactics. The only agents for de Certeau are strategists and tacticians, not assemblages of humans with information machines. But let us look first at what de Certeau writes about the media.

Explicit discussions of the media are few in de Certeau's chief theoretical works. The Practice of Everyday Life barely mentions media. Here, in a rare exception, he speculates on the impact of computers: today "the scriptural system moves forward on its own; it is becoming self-moving and technocratic; it transforms the subjects that controlled it into operators of the writing machine that orders and uses them. A cybernetic society" (de Certeau 1984, 136). These words were written in the late 1970s before IBM's personal computer appeared, so it is understandable that de Certeau thinks of the machine as little different from mechanical technologies. For him the computer controls the user just as machines in the factory dictate the movements of workers. In a slightly earlier work, de Certeau discerns a salient problem with other information machines, broadcast media: "Information, especially the press, television, video, etc., reserves to a smaller and smaller circle of producers the possession or use of increasingly expensive equipment" (de Certeau 1997, 109). He fails to see that computers would vastly expand positions of speech and counter the centralization of points of enunciation inherent in earlier electronic media. In the end, de Certeau worries about the fate of speech in daily life as a consequence of the spread of broadcast media. His prognosis is not good: "The press and the radio deceive or satisfy this 'solitary crowd' with celestial magic, the exoticism of easy love, or the terrors of drugs. What spreads is the feeling of fatality. Humans are *spoken* by the language of socioeconomic determinism long before they can speak it. . . . Will it be possible for humans to create spaces for themselves in which their own speech can be proffered?" (de Certeau 1997, 111). In this analysis, the advantages of "tactics" appear insufficient to combat the alienations of mediated consumption.

Even with this brief and overly schematic review of de Certeau's theory of the everyday, it is clear that we need to move on to a framework that more directly addresses the relation of media to everyday consumption.

VARIETIES OF CONSUMERS AND MEDIA

Before turning to the media's role in daily acts of consumption, we must first explore further the issue of consumption. Various theorists have deconstructed the binary of production and consumption to indicate the importance of the latter (Lefebvre 1971b; Baudrillard 1998). These efforts succeed in decoupling consumption from production and demonstrate the way consumption brings forth its unique type of human action. Consumption, in the hands of these theorists, has its own semiotics and its own logic of practice. But consumption here remains too singular, monolithic, and ahistorical. If we are to connect consumption with media, it is necessary first to understand the varieties of consumption, the expanse of practices that characterize consumption in different times and places. Certainly different groups consume differently: age, sex, class, gender, ethnicity, race, and region—each of these variables significantly affects patterns of consumption. I am not, however, interested in a totalizing taxonomy of consumption or a comprehensive matrix that would locate globally and throughout the ages each act of consumption. To open the question of media and consumption at the most general level, it is necessary only to outline the broad historical configurations of consumption.

One must ask how consumption has changed over the centuries and look for links with media.

To define these historical configurations, one must develop a sort of combinatory in the manner of Louis Althusser (Althusser and Balibar 1970), or a technology of power as in Foucault (Foucault and Gordon 1980a). One must suggest the common features of consumption that may vary over time in their combination, inflection, and emphasis. The analyst would then be able to comprehend consumption as a cultural construction and each pattern of consumption as a delimited practice. Fuat Firat and Nikhilesh Dholakia (1998) have offered a combinatory with four variables: the social relationships entailed in consumption, the degree of the public nature of the act and the object consumed, the participation of the consumer in the development or production of the product, and the intensity of activity in consumption. These criteria afford a complex understanding of consumption patterns, as the authors show, in early modern, modern, and postmodern contexts in the West. The four criteria enable and encourage the analysis of many of the aspects of consumption.[3] Although these categories are rich at the social level of consumption, they are limited with respect to cultural issues. They do not adequately point to language, identity, imagination, and desire as aspects of consumption. When examining the relation of media to consumption, these cultural issues will be particularly exigent.

Nonetheless Firat and Dholakia present a historical picture of consumption patterns that draws attention to many of the important issues. They indicate how consumption has become in the modern period of industrial capitalism and representative democracy more and more individual, private, passive, and alienated from production. This classic view of the modern consumer as couch potato contrasts sharply with that of the period before modernity and to the recent years that Firat and Dholakia are content to designate as postmodern. In quantitative terms, modern consumer activity increased dramatically with the invention of so many appliances, small and large, and the advance of fashion to promote rapid changes in clothing. Yet in qualitative terms the consumer became increasingly marginalized as a social actor, increasingly denigrated as passive, frivolous, boring, unimportant, and "feminine" (Huyssen 1986). These characteristics apply most fully to the United States and to a lesser extent other industrialized societies in Western Europe and Asia; they are least adequate in reference to societies less affected by urban, industrial patterns.

When they move on to consider the consumer pattern of postmodern society, Firat and Dholakia prove the worth of their combinatory. As they show, each of the characteristics of the modern consumer begins to diminish in the closing decades of the twentieth century. A shift in the pattern of consumption occurs away from privacy, individualism, passivity, and alienation from the workplace toward other directions. Yet the main feature of postmodern consumption, in their account, is not the collapse of modern traits but the emergence of multiplicity in consuming patterns. What held together as a stable hierarchy of patterns of consumption in modern society has simply dispersed into heterogeneity. To "keep up with the Joneses," one had to have a clear idea of what and how the Joneses consumed. A fixed idea of consumption for wealthy, middle-class and poorer folk was generally known and accepted at least as somewhat legitimate. The only problem was what one could afford, how much money one needed to scurry after the lifestyle of the Joneses. Postmodernity, by contrast, entails the vast expansion and fragmentation of consumer patterns. One sees this clearly in the burgeoning of clothing styles that originated among the young, the poor, and minority groups. These patterns of consumption shift first to wealthier youth in majority ethnicities and then, surprisingly, to adults. Consumer culture no longer trickles down from the leisure class but climbs up from society's lower reaches of age, wealth, and status. Cultural capital (Bourdieu 1984) emanates from the lifestyle, language, and self-presentation of benighted groups.

Everyday consumption in postmodernity also differs from the modern in the relation of individual identity to the object consumed. "In modernity, the subject (the consumer being) encounters the objects (products) as distinct and distanced from her/himself. In postmodern consumption, the consumer renders products part of her/himself, becoming part of the experience of being with products" (Firat and Dholakia 1998, 96–97). In modern society, consumer objects represented social status; in postmodernity they express one's identity. Along with this change emerges the sense that consumption is part of self-construction. Identity becomes more mobile and fractured, subject to alterations in what and how one feels at the moment. Further complicating the pattern of consumption is globalization. In the modern condition, consumption patterns were defined nationally or regionally. Increasingly consumer products flow across national boundaries, grafting onto the local cultures in patterns of hybridity (Bhabha 1993). In Southern California in the early 1990s, I witnessed an exhibition of African art that depicted black African hairstyles as imitations of Afro-American styles. These in turn originated in Afro-American communities as imitations of African practices, part of the return-to-roots phenomenon. In the postmodern condition, consumption patterns mirror and transform one another across the globe in an endless feedback loop.

Much can be said about the political implications of postmodern consumer patterns. One can question the complicity of capitalism in furthering or benefiting from the new consumption combinatory. Critics like Evan Watkins (1993) make strong arguments that the dispersed, multiple, flexible self of postmodernity is highly desirable for the market and production conditions of late capitalism. The attractions and promises of postmodern consumption are here little more than alibis for the exploitation and alienation of labor. When the consequences of consumption are examined in a global perspective, the results are more discouraging in terms of widespread poverty, pandemic dislocation, and endemic warfare (Castells 1993; Hardt and Negri 2000). But for my purposes here, it is necessary to defer such discussion and turn our attention to the media. What role do digital media as compared with analog media play in the emergence of post-postmodern consumer culture?

GENERAL ARGUMENT: MEDIA AND MEANING

Media play a decisive role in the consumption of cultural objects. Narratives, songs, drawings, dramatic performances, rituals—these cultural objects that date from the distant past, well before the development of technical means of cultural reproduction, required the mediation of language, sound, image, and other material methods of objectifying culture. In the millennia before industrial society, the theater was perhaps the most elaborate of these technical systems (Weber 2002). As we examine the impressive technical feats of new media and their bearing on consumption, it is important to bear in mind that media are as old as culture, influencing, constraining, enhancing, and generally making possible from the beginnings of human society the practices of culture. Media are neither new nor supplementary but essential to human culture, profoundly influencing what and how symbols, sounds, and images are produced, distributed, and received.

DIGITAL MEDIA AND CONSUMPTION

Digital media radically transform both the cultural object and the subject position of the consumer. When cultural objects are digitized, they take on certain characteristics of spoken language. Like an oral sentence or a song, digitized voice is easily and with little cost reproduced by the networked computer user. We do not say of someone who repeats a sentence out loud that he or she is a consumer of that sentence. The model of consumption does not fit practices of speech or singing. Similarly, players of digitized sound are not consumers but, in accepted parlance, users. Both the cultural object and the "consumer" switch registers with digitization into that of speech on the one hand and that of user on the other.

Digitized cultural objects, however, also take on characteristics of analog or mechanical reproduction. In the case of sound, digital reproduction affords an exact replica of the original song or spoken words. Even better than analog media, digital media clone aural and other cultural objects. In addition, digital sounds, like long-playing records and audiotape, but even more efficiently than them, permit massive reproduction and worldwide distribution of copies. Digital cultural objects conform to the protocols of the Internet and flow through it like fish in water. "Consumers" become "producers" as the functions of reproduction and distribution are structured in the Internet as automatic operations.

Unlike either oral speech or analog or graphic media of reproduction, digital cultural objects add new operations that obliterate the conditions of the position of consumer. Digital cultural objects may be transformed by the "consumer" in their reception. Segments may easily be added or subtracted from the cultural object. Bits and pieces of *any other* cultural object may be inserted into, or blended with, the one in question. Sampling, the musical practice of merging sounds from several locations, becomes a general feature of all cultural objects. The cultural object thereby loses its fixity, and the "consumer" becomes not a user but a creator. It is true that voice performance alters music at each iteration. It is also true that ingenious methods have been devised to mix sounds from several sources in media like audiotape, as in hip-hop music. Film too is essentially a montage medium that encourages the rearranging of moving images from the original shooting. But these operations require learned skills and are difficult to accomplish. Digital objects, by contrast, are inherently open to transformation.

The proof of the power of these changes may be seen in the challenges that digital media pose to the labyrinthine corporate structures that control cultural objects: the media industries. In the past decade, each major industry has faced a threat to its existence from the digitization of cultural objects and the transformation of consumer into creator/user. At the same time, these corporations have responded by attempting to strip from the "consumer" the rights he or she had in the period of analog cultural objects. The culture industry has attempted to prevent copying of music, print, and films, an endeavor that is most ineffective in the digital domain. The history of copy-protected software indicates the futility of this project. The culture industry has further attempted to restrict the use of the cultural object; with DVD video by introducing regional limits and "broadcast flags" for television, with audio by crippling playback on computers, embedding watermarks in the digital data to discourage copying, restricting the time or the number of plays the user may have, bringing legal action against file-sharing programs, and so forth. In the eyes of the culture industry, the only way to maintain power is to dissolve the materiality of the cultural object completely, eliminating all use practices of consumers with books, long-playing records, video- and audiotapes, DVDs, and the rest. Instead the culture industry hopes to make cultural objects accessible to consumers only on a pay-per-use basis. Consumers will have, in this view, no object at all, only access. What this desperate gesture by the culture industry forgets is that the cultural object, at some point, must become accessible to the consumer, and at that point it becomes available for recording in digital formats. However complex the methods of copy protection embedded in cultural objects by the media industries, hackers are able to defeat them.

Some examples from the history of the struggle between the culture industry and "consumers" over the past decade will suffice to convince the reader that digital cultural objects are a new breed, one whose implementation offers a wide range of political choices with great consequences for the future of society.

In the 1980s, the music industry trumpeted the coming of digital long-playing records and later compact discs as "perfect music forever." They were eager to sell albums at vastly inflated prices in the new formats and to encourage music lovers to replace their "obsolete" collections of analog records with "jewel"-cased, shiny CDs. The greed of the music industry was as unrestrained as their enthusiasm for the "digital" domain. In addition to highly exploitative, exceptional labor contract conditions that stripped from musicians ordinary workers' rights, the music industry squeezed the retail outlets to hike prices, threatening them with severe retributions for failure of compliance. I have told this story in chapter 9, but it is worth underscoring in the context of an analysis of the consumer. In the mid-1990s, young people with computers started converting .cda files on CDs into MP3 files and trading, sharing, and even selling them in IRC sites and through programs like Scour. Napster, coming along in the late 1990s, was simply the best program that facilitated these exchanges. After the music industry successfully sued Napster, peer-to-peer programs like Gnutella picked up the slack and even amplified the base of user-creators upward of fifty million (by 2002) worldwide. Enjoying the wide bandwidth connections of DSL and cable modems, user-creators exchanged not only MP3 files but entire digitally encoded movies. Jack Valenti, then president of the Motion Picture Association of America, saw this coming and called an extraordinary meeting in 2000 of corporate leaders of all media to combat "piracy," in other words to enforce legally protected control of culture by a motley and decidedly unartistic coterie of entrepreneurs. It is worth noting that no other sector of U.S. capitalist enterprise has been so challenged since the labor strikes of the 1930s.

If the economic base of the music and film industries is threatened by the humble file transfer protocols of digital cultural objects as practiced by consumers cum user-creators, the heart of postmodern capitalist culture, television advertising, faces the same fate with the advent of new digital recording technologies for televised programs. Scholars in television studies have given some attention to the relation of this cultural medium to everyday life. Generally, however, these studies have focused on the patterns of use of TV watchers in the context of the home and family relations. Researchers typically employ qualitative methods (ethnographies) to discover how television watching is integrated into daily life.[4] They have not yet adopted the perspective that emerges after the introduction of new media (i.e., globally networked computing) in which television might be understood as an information machine.

For example, Ien Ang (2000), a noted television scholar, discusses most informatively the efforts of the advertising industry to maintain its economic interest in television as changing technologies enable the consumer progressively to bypass commercials. Ang reformulates de Certeau's theory of tactics, resistive consumer practices, for the media domain. "The very corporate foundation of commercial television," she argues, "rests on the idea of 'delivering audiences to advertisers'; that is, economically speaking, television programming is first and foremost a vehicle to attract audiences for the 'real' messages transmitted by television: the advertising spots inserted within and between the programs. The television business, in other words, is basically a 'consumer delivery enterprise' for advertisers" (Ang 2000, 184). Faced with the automatic skipping of thirty-second segments in early TiVo and ReplayTV recording machines, television executives even assert that there is an implicit "contract" between advertisers and viewers that the program may only be viewed so long as the commercials are received.[5] As de Certeau might have predicted and as Ang demonstrates, television watchers have always resisted the intrusion of commercials. Zapping (changing channels during ads), muting the sound with the remote, and zipping (fast-forwarding through promotions after time-shifting the program onto tape) are time-honored methods whereby consumers use techno-tactics to circumvent advertising. (The introduction of cable and satellite technologies, vastly expanding available programming, also deeply challenged the networks' control of television.) Thus consumer society was always fraught with strife against imposed forms of control. Ang continues: "The development of the consumer society has implied the hypothetical construction of an ideal consuming subject through a whole range of strategic and ideological practices, resulting in very specific constraints, structural and cultural, within which people can indulge in the pleasures of leisurely consumption" (Ang 2000, 185). The evidence of zapping, muting, and zipping controverts the happy ideology of consumer capitalism. Not only is the TV watcher far from a passive couch potato, but consumption, especially in its mediated forms, is a zone of continual social and economic conflict, perhaps of greater significance in the postmodern era than the classic regions of strife: politics and economics.

The latest round of the struggle over television commercials began with the introduction of digital television recorders in 2000 (Harmon 2002). These devices (TiVo and ReplayTV) record programs on a hard disk and, among their many features, allow the viewer *automatically* to skip commercials. Clicking a simple menu option eliminates all commercials, delivering the prerecorded program without interruption. Although little more than three million of these devices were in place by mid-2002, their potential to alter the future of television reception incited worried outcries from television producers and advertisers alike. Repeating the scenario of the music and film industries, television finds itself fundamentally at risk simply because the cultural object has been digitized and the "consumer" has chosen to deploy the new medium to ends other than those of capitalism. Using their influence in Congress and the pressure of their huge resources, they succeeded in compelling TiVo and ReplayTV to eliminate these functions at least from the obvious menu of options of the machines.

But if the new technologies offer consumers the means to mitigate or even bypass the commodification of cultural objects through advertising, capitalism retains numerous techniques to sustain market culture in general and its products in particular. It is enough in this context to mention briefly just one of these: the brand. Consumer objects under capitalism appear in the market with iconic designations known as brands. Names, images, colors, designs, packaging styles — all are produced to associate the object (a loaf of bread, a pair of shoes, a toaster) in the purchaser's mind with a manufacturer. As Celia Lury observes, the design effort is to constitute the brand as "the objective properties of things" (Lury 1999, 499). Brands function to fix in our minds the fact that commodities come from companies. In the domain of cultural objects, brands have not worked well. Consumers identify cultural objects not with corporations (Universal, Warner Brothers, Random House) but with stars, directors, musicians, and authors. If brands are the basis of the intellectual property of material consumer objects, celebrity creators play that role in the cultural domain. With the changes I have outlined in the nature of the digital cultural object and the consumer-user-creator, what must now be put in question is precisely the intellectual property of authors.[6]

The functions of the producer and consumer remain relatively stable in markets for noncultural objects. While new technologies do enable producers to modify commodities to particular consumer preferences in what is termed a postmodern economy, no one argues that consumers are thereby producers, distributors, or reproducers of the commodity. The world of material commodities adheres to the brand and divides agents accordingly into producers and consumers. Not so in the domain of culture. Here the older legal and economic structures that ensure commodification on the basis of authorship are disintegrating before our eyes. Copyright law, designed for an age when cultural objects were material commodities like cars and cereals, is now an obstacle to the development of a post-postmodern culture, one no longer characterized by fixed cultural objects and positions of creator and consumer, but by fluid text, sounds, and images, costless reproduction and distribution, and potentially collective creation. In blogs, massively multiple online games, and peer-to-peer file-sharing programs, consumers are transformed into users, creating content as they download it. In these contexts, the passive individual consumer of mediated industrial capitalism evaporates, and new figures of mediated practices are born. An important task of cultural theory is to account for this change and articulate concepts that capture this transformation, discerning new modes of resistance in the process that go beyond the logics outlined by de Certeau to help clarify the politics of digital culture.

12

FUTURE ADVERTISING: DICK'S *UBIK* AND THE DIGITAL AD

Consumption changes significantly in the age of digital information. Acts of consumption — buying, window shopping, browsing — are routinely recorded, stored, and made available for advertisers. Profiles of the lifestyles of consumers are now so finely granulated and accurate that retailers are likely to know better than the consumer what he or she will buy and when the purchase will take place. Automated programs on one's computer, known as "bots," have better memories of consumer preferences than does the consumer. Information machines such as TiVo gather data of viewing habits and on that basis anticipate consumer desires for entertainment. The individual finds himself or herself in a brave new world of consumption, prefigured only in the imagination of science fiction writers. Here I investigate the current condition of consumption by closely reading one such work of science fiction, Philip K. Dick's Ubik, a work that presciently depicts the future of advertising.

It can be argued that the genre of science fiction is no longer possible. This is so for the simple reason that what some call the overdeveloped nations have so integrated into their social processes scientific achievements, technological novelties, and, above all, the system for the continued, indefinite development of science and technology that the distance has collapsed between what can be imagined in science fiction and what has been realized or can be foreseen to be realized in society. Science fiction requires the sense of a future as separate from the present. But this future is now part of the present expectations of everyday life. We anticipate that nanotechnology will make obsolete industrial labor; that cloning of human beings will initiate ethical dilemmas; that worldwide communication systems will bring about the demise of the nation-state. These expectations are the lifeworld of the present and as such cannot be regarded solely as a future "other." With the proliferation of cyborgs, robots, clones, and androids, the age of the humachine has arrived. The future tense will have to be reimagined, probably outside the genre of science fiction. The social imaginary has integrated the research agendas of science and technology to such an extent that the future is imploded into the present. In a sense, there can be no more aliens.

In this spirit, I explore the relation between Philip K. Dick's *Ubik* and the mediascape that we call the hyperreal. In particular, I examine the culture of advertising by comparing the representation of commodities in print and digital media. More specifically, I compare, in the context of *Ubik*, the cultural role of the representation of commodities in print with that in various forms of digital ads. At issue is the difference of print and visual forms, analog and digital formats. As a genre, science fiction has the advantage of exploring the relation of humans to machines,[1] a relation that has become a general aspect of the human condition. For quite some time, science fiction has been exploring what we now accept as the posthuman. With the multiplication and dissemination of increasingly advanced information machines, the earth has entered a posthuman era. Our society has done so under the general regime of the commodity, which, at the cultural level, disseminates itself in the discourse of advertising.[2] Dick's novel explores the Ubikquity of the ad and its relation to the formation of a humanity that is synthesized with information machines. In this chapter, I examine Dick's representation of the culture of the ad, with an eye to the light it sheds on the current state of advertising in new media. Does the digital form of the ad change anything with respect to the construction of the subject? Does it matter that cyberspace is filled with ads, that ads on television are more and more produced with computer technology? Are we heading toward the world of Dick's *Ubik*?

In a strange confluence of events, *Ubik* was published in 1969,[3] the year of the first transmissions of information across telephone lines between computers, a technology now known as the Internet. Perhaps stranger still, Dick's novel is set in June 1992, some eight months before Mosaic, the first Web browser, was distributed on the Internet, signaling a transformation of the Net into graphic format and foreshadowing its mass adoption. In these coincidences, print media and digital media, separated by centuries of technical development, met, crossed, and went their separate ways.

My reading of Ubik has a limited purpose. I am not attempting to provide a decisive interpretation of the novel as a whole, but rather examining one aspect of it. I do not situate the novel systematically in relation to Dick's other works,[4] science fiction writing of the period, or in general, although I do discuss some of Dick's other works and the works of some scholars in relation to certain questions. I focus neither on the author's relation to the text nor on reviewing the corpus of scholarly treatment of the text. The specific theme I wish to consider is the way the novel depicts a world in which culture is shaped by mediated information. In this sense, Dick's portrayal of such a world may assist us in understanding more about our own circumstances. The question of the media is central to this culture of information, and I examine the issue of media in the work at three levels: the printed form of the novel itself, the role of mediated information in the imaginary world of Ubik, and the relation of this world to the digital culture of the present.

UBIK'S STORY

For readers familiar with Dick's work and with science fiction writing in general, the plot of Ubik will not come as a big surprise, but to those not conversant with the conventions of the genre, a plot summary of Ubik might appear as preposterous as that of most nineteenth-century operas. With this warning to the reader, I proceed with my summary.

Set in the near future, Ubik opens with a crisis in a security company, Runciter Associates, which is having difficulty tracking individuals whose extraordinary psychic powers make them dangerous information thieves. The band of these "psis" is headed by Ray Hollis, an antagonist who never appears in the novel. Glen Runciter, president of the company, and his chief tester for psionic fields, Joe Chip, attempt to account for the strange, sudden invisibility of the telepathic individuals. In Ubik's world, information is central, and it is made fragile by "teeps, parakineticists, precogs, resurrectors and animators" (17)—an assortment of abilities to act at a distance through brain power, abilities that today, we might note, are simulated by a variety of information technologies. Runciter Associates is solicited by companies to counter the effects of the telepaths. It employs "inertials," individuals who, for example, make it impossible for those who see the future to decide which future is most likely to occur. In these unusual encounters, to understate the matter, Ubik anticipates the collapse of privacy that today is achieved through machines. No one is safe from the prying minds of the psis. There is no interior space that provides a safe haven for information, desire, anything one might rather not make available to others.

In addition to telepaths, society is composed of another group who act through brain power alone, the half-lifers. These are individuals who have, in our sense of the term, died, but whose brains are kept in a minimal state of activity, enough so that they are able to communicate, in a manner of speaking, with living humans. Again the novel presents a group whose bodies, like those of the psis, have little importance. Like Hans Moravec (1988), who would have us cast off our meat and upload our consciousness to the Internet, Dick explores states of being that minimize the importance of the body. Glen Runciter's wife, Ella, exists in such a state in what Dick calls a "Moratorium" in, of all places, Switzerland.

The action continues when Runciter is approached by a woman who wants to hire his firm to counter an alleged breach of security in a company located on the moon. Runciter believes the psis that are missing from his intelligence maps are engaged in this information attack. He takes his inertials to the moon. But the job is actually a trap set by archenemy Hollis, and Runciter's people are killed, or more accurately reduced to cryogenic half-life.

From the social world of information security issues, the novel at this point shifts focus to the world of the half-lifers and to the communication between them and those who are alive in the normal sense of the word. It must be emphasized here that Dick makes undecidable who is in half-life and who is not. I will return to this issue later. Among the nominally half-life individuals is a teenage boy, Jory, who sustains himself by "eating" the brain activity of the others in the Moratorium, the storage facility for half-lifers. Earlier, when Glen Runciter visited his wife, his communications with her were blocked by Jory, who displaced her weak brain activity with his own. Jory's prey have only one defense against him, a "product" known as Ubik, a "reality support" that protects the half-lifers by emitting substances into the atmosphere that interfere with Jory's predations. Since the half-lifers sustain only mental activity, I find it difficult to understand how the reader is expected to accept that a material effect from Ubik can intervene in their communications. Such are the imponderables of Dick's novel, however.

The last third of the novel concerns the efforts of the half-lifers, Joe Chip in particular, to defend themselves against Jory. They are assisted by Glen Runciter, who manages to communicate to the half-lifers across reality systems about the great powers of Ubik.

There is another subplot that is essential to understanding the book. As in many Dick stories, Ubik includes a beautiful young woman, a "dark-haired girl," who attracts the protagonist, in this case Joe Chip, and appears to threaten him at the same time. In Ubik this character is Pat Conley, a person who has the extrasensory ability to move time backward and thereby change the future. After the attack on Runciter's employees on the moon, the world appears to be in a state of regression. The inertials appear at once to age very quickly, suggesting that time is flowing rapidly into the future, and to experience external reality as moving into the past, suggesting a process of entropy so dear to Dick's understanding of physical reality. The reader and some of the characters think that Pat Conley is responsible for these disastrous happenings, but that turns out not to be the case. Jory is the villain. The aging and regression are effects of the condition of half-life. They do not affect external reality. They are only the perception of the half-life population as they undergo death at the hands of Jory.

Ubik is, even for science fiction, a strange work, combining the exotica of science fiction such as telepaths and half-lifers with the mundane objects of commodity culture. I suggest that it offers a picture of the hyperreal world of mediated information through the rhetorical techniques of science fiction.

MEDIA IN UBIK

Dick is sensitive to changes in media, to new media, to the role of media in people's lives. For example, in a passage of no particular importance to the plot, he takes the trouble to describe an electronic newspaper (a "homeopape") much like what currently exists on the Internet. One can format the homeopape to deliver one's personally designed newspaper. Here is Dick's description: "Joe Chip . . . twiddled the dial of his recently rented 'pape machine. . . . he dialed off *interplan news*, hovered momentarily at *domestic news* and then selected *gossip*." In Dick's world, the 'pape can speak: " 'Yes sir,' the 'pape machine said heartily." And it is able to print out one's selections in color and chosen fonts: "A scroll of printed matter crept from its slot; the ejected roll, a document in four colors, niftily incised with bold type." It also has the capability of voice recognition: " 'This isn't gossip,' Joe Chip said to the 'pape machine." In response to the character's dissatisfaction with the news delivered to him, the machine gives instructions regarding its proper use. "The 'pape machine said, 'Set the dial for *low gossip*.' " Like today's intelligent agent programs and help menus, the machine provides users with feedback on its best use (Dick 1969, 19–20). Although Dick does not explain how the machine obtains newspaper information, the reader must assume some electronic connection between the machine and a database of current news, in principle much like the Internet's ability to store and distribute information to any computer.

Ubik is not different in this respect from much of Dick's other work in its sensitivity to, and prescience about, information machines. In one novel, *The Penultimate Truth*, the spiritual leader of the nation is literally constructed by media, the person having died years before. Protector Talbot Yancy, his image broadcast on "giant television screens," urges the Western Democracies on to battle in their interminable and disastrous war with the Soviet Union. Humans live underground because of radiation, in a miserable, bellicose existence. Set in the early part of the twenty-first century, this novel, published in 1964, explores in remarkable detail the simulation effects possible with information machines. In the following passage, a character observes the simulation of Yancy with awe:

> "I take off my hat to you. You're good." He had almost been captured himself, as he had stood watching the simulacrum of the Protector Talbot Yancy deliver absolutely the proper intonation, in the exact and correct manner, the text modified and augmented — meddled with — by Megavac 6-V . . . even though he could see the Megavac 6-V and although this was not visible could sense the emanation of the reading matter directed by the 'vac toward the simulacrum. Could in fact witness the true source which

animated the purely artificial construct seated at the oak desk with the American flag behind it. Eerie, he thought. (Dick 1984, 59)

The Penultimate Truth sets out with precision the emergence and logical conclusion of televisual politics. In Dick's hands, information media transform political reality into a web of images and sounds that are impossible to refer back to a referent. Politics, for him, have already, by dint of the media, transcended agora-like community and representational logics, moving into the constructed effects perhaps best realized in the Gulf War of 1991.[5] We can recall that, thanks to such media, Jean Baudrillard quipped that "the war did not take place" (Baudrillard 1995a). Dick understood that media change reality, an insight that became central to New Left politics a few years after the publication of The Penultimate Truth. As the United States entered the colonial conflict with Vietnam in 1964, leading to the televisual politics of phony consensus by Lyndon Johnson and to the televised films of combat that catalyzed antiwar sentiment, Dick presented Cold War political leadership as bound with mediated propaganda images.

In The Ganymede Takeover, another novel from the same period as The Penultimate Truth and Ubik, Dick manifests a sharp recognition of the importance of advertisements, especially those disseminated on television. He writes concerning the views of one of his characters: "How much he had learned from TV commercials! While others turned down the TV set when the commercials came on, Balkani turned them up. The programs had nothing to sell but middle-class morality, a dreary product at best, but the commercial offered a world where dreams were for sale, where youth and health came in a box, and all pain and suffering were smoothed over with long, beautiful, slow-motion hair. Avant-garde films? Balkani jeered at them. Nothing lay in the most surrealistic of them to compare with the charisma of TV commercials" (Dick and Nelson 1967, 132). The culture of advertising and media are central to Dick's sense of the construction of reality. The mediated world of commodities plays a pivotal role for Dick in the functioning of fictional worlds. TV ads are not trivial, obnoxious interference with entertainment; nor are they artless products of pecuniary impulses. They are instead the spiritual center of the world, far more worthy of visual attention, Dick mocks at pretentious high culture, than experimental cinema.

The media, for Dick, are thus significant in their ability to alter culture (and politics), to work miracles on symbolic systems. Let us consider, then, this mixture of commercialism and media within the limits of print.

THE PRINT MEDIA

The novel consists of seventeen chapters, each starting with an epigraph. The first sixteen epigraphs are advertisements for a product called "Ubik." Here is the epigraph to the first chapter: "Friends, this is clean-up time and we're discounting all our silent, electric Ubiks by this much money. Yes, we're throwing away the blue-book. And remember: every Ubik on our lot has been used only as directed" (Dick 1969, 1). Each advertisement is for a different product. They are cars, beer, coffee, salad dressing, headache and stomach medicine, shaving razor, kitchen cleaning aid, bank services, hair conditioner, deodorant spray, sleeping pills, breakfast food, bra, plastic wrap, breath freshener, and cereal, a list of ordinary consumer objects. Each ad contains a warning to the consumer like "Safe when used as directed." None of the ads have any direct relation to the chapter they introduce. The chapter preceded by the ad for beer, for instance, contains no mention of beer or any beverage, for that matter. Rather, the ads appear on the printed page like commercials on radio and television, interrupting the flow of the program, distracting the attention of the reader/viewer from what has come before and what will follow, yet also justifying the text/program, as we shall see. Dick uses the epigraph, a device of the print medium, to emulate electronic broadcast media. In fact, the tone of the epigraphs resembles the audio portion of ads in electronic media. The epigraphic voice is informal, plain, and solicitous, more like television than other print media such as magazines and newspapers. Dick's chapter epigraphs work against the limits and constraints of the conventional print format, in which they serve as emblems or metonymies for the text that ensues, distinguishing themselves by their complete irrelevance to the body of the chapter.

In their discontinuity with the chapters, the ads, however, do inject commodity culture (in its print-mediated form) into the work. They provide a mood of commercialism, a spirit of the commodity that operates outside the story (for the most part) but nonetheless imparts a general cultural character to the work. The ads address the reader as a member of a mediated (capitalist) culture. Further in that direction are the frequent small reminders of a money economy: for example, in apartments, doors and small appliances (such as coffee makers) require coins to operate. Dick leaves nothing to the reader's imagination concerning the capitalist nature of the world of Ubik. Yet this capitalism has a decidedly informational quality. Runciter Associates, once again, is a security firm that provides antidotes to information piracy. True enough, the thieves are not mechanical but psionic, individuals who have extraordinary psychic abilities. The effect, however, is much the same as the security problems in late capitalism or postmodern society, where information machines penetrate protected physical space to retrieve private data. The psis, as Dick calls them, substitute easily for computerized databases hooked into networks, listening devices, global positioning systems, satellite photography, and the rest, culminating in a society where nothing can be hidden or secret.

The epigraphs, then, are an integral part of a general setup in which information is central to the social system, whether as advertising or as security issues. Although not the first writer to offer this insight, Dick senses that culture is becoming political and becoming mediated. It is also becoming vulnerable and at risk.

About two-thirds of the way through the novel, the term "Ubik" enters the story directly, leaving the confines of the epigraph to intrude on the text of the chapter. Ubik appears first in the text as a televised commercial, providing a link with the epigraphs. "Has boiled cabbage taken over your world of food? That same old, stale, flat, Monday-morning odor no matter how many dimes you put into your stove? Ubik changes all that; Ubik wakes up food flavor, puts hearty taste back where it belongs, and restores fine food smell," announces Glen Runciter on his employee Joe Chip's television (127). At this point, Joe thinks Runciter is either dead or in a half-life coma. The reader learns later that the reverse is true, or apparently true, since, in Dick's novels, reality is always in question for the characters and the reader.[6] The commercial goes on to speak of what emerges as Ubik's true function, a "reality support." The world around the half-life of Joe Chip is regressing temporally, and Ubik is Runciter's proposed solution to the problem. In a wider sense, Ubik is the elixir for life's difficulties; commodities offer, as we recall from The Ganymede Takeover, a spiritual antidote to life's misery, the dream of gratification. When

Runciter on the TV ad urges Joe to try Ubik, we are all addressed as users of commodities.

At first the role of Ubik is a mystery to the characters, just as it is to consumers in capitalist society. Gradually its wondrous powers become clear to the protagonists, Joe Chip and the other employees of Runciter Associates. It seems they have died physically and are being sustained in a sort of cryogenic hospital, surviving only in their brain function. They are assailed by Jory and can protect themselves from his predations with the use of Ubik. Thus Ubik, the reality support, functions as an information shield or spiritual shell that maintains the brain activity of half-life. Or at least that is what the narrative suggests at a literal level. From the perspective of understanding Ubik as an allegory of mediated culture, we can say that commodities such as Ubik sustain consumers in their reality as a kind of half-life in capitalist culture. If Joe Chip and the others are metaphors for consumers in information capitalism, then Ubik (a synecdoche for all commodities) sustains cultural life against dangers of all kinds (represented by Jory).

In addition to its epigraphic role as ubiquitous commodity and as reality support in consumer culture, Ubik has a third role in the novel, one that is most difficult to interpret. The last chapter's epigraph reads as follows: "I am Ubik. Before the universe was, I am. I made the suns. I made the worlds. I created the lives and the places they inhabit; I move them here, I put them there. They go as I say, they do as I tell them. I am the word and my name is never spoken, the name which no one knows. I am called Ubik, but that is not my name. I am. I shall always be" (215). The ad for Ubik now sounds much like the voice of God in the book of Genesis.[7] Interpreting this epigraph has been a focus of scholarly attention, and to that I now turn.

GOD UBIK?

Katherine Hayles summarizes the discussion of the final epigraph and offers her own interpretation.[8] Hayles muses, "To my knowledge, no one has attempted to explain why Ubik changes from signifying the worst excesses of capitalism to standing for a ubiquitous God. Many critics even suggest that Ubik has somehow 'really' been God all along. I want to suggest that on the contrary, Ubik undergoes a sudden transformation and that this transformation cannot be understood except in relation to the revelation that behind Pat stands Jory and behind Jory stands his animalistic appetite. Only after acknowledging this appetite (which must be understood as operating on the multiple levels signified by 'consuming') can the author discern, among the trashy surfaces of capitalist excess, the divine within the world—and by implication, within himself" (Hayles 1999, 187). In short, Hayles explains the contrast between the epigraphs of the first sixteen chapters with that of the last chapter as a Gnostic revelation of God within the beast of capitalist culture. But this leads her to a more general argument concerning language itself. For Hayles, Dick's novel explores and deconstructs the boundary of the human individual and the world, the line between the inside and the outside. Language in the form of media draws into permanent instability the ontological demarcation of the human. Hayles concludes her argument: "Ubik's distinctive achievement is to represent simultaneously the performative power of language and the mediated, uncertain relation of language to the material world while also mapping this difference onto an 'inside'-'outside' boundary that hints at the complexity of communication between self and other, conscious and unconscious. The hope Ubik holds out is that although boundary disputes will never disappear, inside and outside can be made to touch each other through the medium of writing that is no less valuable for infecting our world with all manner of epistemological and ontological instabilities" (188). For Hayles, the issue at stake in the final epigraph is neither God nor capitalism but the relation of writing to the self. Her interest in the novel, certainly an important interpretative stance, rests with literature and culture.

I offer a somewhat different interpretation of the last epigraph and of the novel as a whole. It is necessary to consider the combination of the ordinary commercials in the first sixteen epigraphs, the seemingly religious last epigraph, the role of Ubik in the action of the novel as reality support, and the literal meaning of the word ubiquitous as existing everywhere, a meaning that is discussed by the characters in the novel. If we take these four instances of Ubik together, we are confronted with a culture permeated by commercials such that reality is sustained by them. People are steeped in the culture of advertising. They are able to maintain their sense of reality only by imbibing commodity culture. They resist life's threats, such as Jory, by heeding commercials. If the half-lifers are understood to represent the general population of consumer culture, living in the hyper-real world of mediated information, their identities then persist through that culture. Incursions by individuals with strong emotions, like Jory, endanger the continuity of the consumerist world. Even if we accept this argument, the dilemma of the last epigraph is not resolved. To do that, we must find a connection between religion, the ultimate spiritual force, and commodities.

Such a connection was explored by Walter Benjamin in *The Arcades Project* (Benjamin 1999). Fascinated by the panorama of objects of capitalist society and the aesthetics of their presentation, Benjamin extended Marx's analysis of the fetishism of commodities. For Marx, a commodity became invested with more interest than it intrinsically had (and hence became a fetish) because the labor that produced it was secreted from its appearance on the market. The outrage for Marx and the force of his critique focused on the disappearance of the labor act from the activity of consumption. Benjamin looked beyond that perception to the phantasmagoria of the commodities themselves. "With the new manufacturing processes that lead to imitations," he wrote, "an illusory appearance (*Schein*) settles into the commodity" (Buck-Morss 1991, 191). The work of critique for Benjamin subsisted at the level of the appearance of the commodity, supplementing Marx's depth analysis of the commodity in relation to the production process. Benjamin's "dialectics of seeing," as Susan Buck-Morss has termed the method of the Arcades Project, revealed, among its other insights into daily life, the relation of the appearance of the commodity on the capitalist market to religious experience. Walking through the streets of Paris, Benjamin's highly original ethnography of consumerism introduced the eye of the *flâneur*, one whose consciousness retreated from the heights of focused philosophical acumen and systematic self-reflection (let us call it Kantian consciousness) and, with body in motion, loosely regarded the things in the urban environment with the curiosity of a child.[9] In the state of mind of the flâneur, commodities appeared as magical, as invested with spiritual properties of myth, aura, and sublimity. Here was a new sublime of the everyday, one that transported the would-be consumer to a transcendent world of fulfillment, a heavenly redemption from the arduous exigencies of capitalism. The most exquisite supernatural qualities were found not in the cathedrals but in the objects before one's gaze in store windows.

Dick noted the same link of commodity culture with high spiritual values in the passage quoted earlier from *The Ganymede Takeover*, except here the everyday sublime pertained not to the commodity itself but to the solicitation, to the advertisement. Dick recognized more directly than Benjamin that the spirit of capitalism rests not with the commodity as object but with the culture developed to promote it, with, as he says in *Ubik*'s seventeenth epigraph, the word. What enables the final epigraph to work as a link to the earlier ones and to the play of Ubik in the novel is that commercials are cultural objects, strings of words, images, and sounds. And they are so arranged as to fascinate all who encounter them. They constitute the highest promise of happiness and fulfillment of any experience in capitalist society. Dick's novel recognizes the spiritual force of the commercial.[10] When Dick paraphrases the Old Testament with "I am Ubik. . . . I am the word. . . . I am . . ." (215), he perhaps at one level introduces the voice of God; but at another, and in my view far more significant, level he invokes the highest spiritual force, the force that is the ultimate "reality support," as the cultural dimension of the capitalist solicitation, of the ad.

DIGITAL DICK?

If the reader is with me so far, I would like to take one step further in the analysis: to account for the fact that, since at least the second half of the twentieth century, commercials appear primarily in mediated form, specifically transmitted through the airwaves and wires of the electronic media. As we have seen in relation to the 'pape in *Ubik* and the computer simulation in *The Penultimate Truth*, Dick was highly aware of the effectiveness of media and was aware of their specific traits. Visual media achieve certain effects, print others, and audio still others. How, then, was Dick to present the qualities of electronic media through the limitations of print? How could Dick suggest the culture of televised commercials with the specific attributes of the printed page? It is this problem, I believe, that he attempted to solve by the seventeenth epigraph.

Friedrich Kittler reminds us of the limits of print as a storage medium. Without the ability to store sounds and moving images, the printed page cannot achieve the spectacular effects of cinema, television, the World

Wide Web. "Writing can store only writing, no more, no less. The holy books testify to this fact. The second book of Moses, chapter twenty, fixes a copy of what Jaweh originally had written with his own finger on two stone tablets: the law. Of the thunder and lightning, the dense cloud and very powerful trumpet that accompanied the writing-down on the holy mountain of Sinai, The Bible could store nothing but mere words" (Kittler and Johnston 1997, 37). And Dick in Ubik could not store and transmit to the reader the magic of the commercial except by referring back to that volume. Kittler argues that, owing to the limitations of the printed page, words are obliged to stimulate a "hallucination" of the scene in the reader's consciousness, a poetic imaginary that produces in the mind the very absences all too apparent in the page: the sounds of thunder and trumpets, the clouds and the lightning, and so forth. Dick, with his seventeenth epigraph, summons that imaginary with an allusion to the Bible.

If the mediascape of the 1960s, when Ubik was written, was dominated by cinema and television, we have moved on, since the mid-1990s, to the digital transformation of cultural objects—text, sounds, and images— and to their global storage and transmission on the World Wide Web. And if televised commercials were the "reality support," the Ubik, of the 1960s (and the early 1990s, when Ubik is set), so digital technology now increasingly dominates the task of encouraging consumers to buy the effluents of late capitalism. The message of Ubik is a warning about the ontological capacities of the analog advertisement, its seemingly limitless ability to create reality. If that is so, what might be the nature of the reality support of the postanalog world of digital culture?

Dick's insight into the spiritual qualities of contemporary media culture deploys the genre of science fiction to express itself. We might ask if this same genre is capable of translating for us the media effects of digital culture. To some degree, Dick anticipated this development. He certainly included computers in his novels. But more than that, he depicted phenomena that could only be realized with the development of digital technology. I refer to his anticipation of virtual reality systems (the helmet-and-glove variety, or the cave) in the short story "We Can Remember It for You Wholesale" (1966), in which a company is able to provide customers with experiences by implanting information in their brains. Many such novelties are strewn through the pages of Dick's novels and short stories.

The question remains if the genre can sustain its own realization, so to speak, if the digital culture of the Internet has not brought forth a mediated construction of reality so that the premonitions of science fiction now inhabit the earth.

One direction that the genre of science fiction has taken in response to digital culture is cyberpunk. Starting with William Gibson's 1983 novel *Neuromancer*, a spate of work by Gibson, Bruce Sterling, Pat Cadigan, Neal Stephenson, and others has explored the theme of digital culture in future worlds. Writers have addressed many aspects of networked computing, among them the struggle for information security. This is the leitmotif of Neal Stephenson's novel *Cryptonomicon*. Stephenson's fascinating work juxtaposes the work of decoding communications during World War II with a contemporary project to build a "data haven" in a location somewhere near the Philippines. The story's double temporality highlights the historical importance of the question of information security. And, indeed, the potential loss of the privacy of records and other information in the circuits of the Internet threatens the security of the nation-state. In the 1940s, information access was crucial in determining the outcome of the contest between Germany and Japan and the United States, Britain, and the Soviet Union, all nation-states. But by 2000, the nation-state itself was in jeopardy, or at least saw itself as being in jeopardy, as a consequence of the digital network.[11] *Cryptonomicon*'s fictional representation of a possible data haven suggests that information security is the dream of a host of unsavory types: drug dealers, Mafia groups, terrorists, gamblers, dealers in illegal commodities from weapons to body parts, slave traders—you name it. But data privacy is also the desire of countless others. Since the nation-state is the dominant political force, one that claims right of access to all information within its territory, it is the default enemy of the data haven. Stephenson's novel unfortunately gets sidetracked from exploring the ramifications of the data haven, turning instead to a hunt for gold bullion lost in World War II, and thus ironically mirroring those entrepreneurs from the mid- to late-1990s who treated the Internet not as an experiment in communications but as a gold rush. Yet Stephenson's novel does raise the question of information security in the digital age.

In conclusion, I suggest for future exploration that the question of information privacy dovetails nicely with Dick's exploration of the mediated commercial in Ubik, indicating that capitalism's effort to commodify culture runs into difficulty at several levels in the digital domain. A new contradiction of capitalism emerges in digital culture whereby the urge to sell commodities comes into conflict with the need for private information. Since all commercial transactions are digitally recorded and stored in databases, information about acts of consumption is compiled to such an extent that portraits of consumers are available for general commercial exploitation, in other words, for targeted advertising.[12] In the digital age, shopping is no longer private, even when it is done inside one's home. Capitalism, it appears, cannot have its cake of a zone of commodified culture and eat it as well, so to speak, in private. The future of digital advertising will be ubiquitous at the cost of a kind of blowback effect in which corporate databases are open to hacker-consumers. If the world, as in Ubik, is made available for the dissemination of commercials, the sources of that dissemination will be open as well to public scrutiny.

CONCLUSION

Open source and open content are tendencies within new media that build on structural features of digital technologies. The digital transcoding of text, image, and sound, packet switching, speed of data transmission, ease of reproduction, the global reach of networks, relative cheapness of computer technology as a point of media production as compared with broadcast systems—all of this suggests the possibility of success for the "open" movements with great consequences for culture and politics (Galloway 2004). It just may be that the expansive hopes generated by earlier media technologies will come to fruition in the digital domain.

Yet, as we have seen in relation to peer-to-peer file sharing, dominant institutions, in this case the music industry, do not easily give up their privileges or cede their positions to the promises of new technologies. Great resistance is engendered against new media tendencies that offer cultural directions that do not fit the model of the commodity characteristic of modern society. In particular, the nation-state as a political form and the corporation as an economic form already mount serious attacks against networked computing. Fears of terrorism and uncontrolled speech, abhorrence of child pornography, and opposition to unconstrained, costless exchanges of texts, images, and sounds are motive enough for established forces to be wary.

Yet again, these same forces aspire to deploy networked computing to extend their reach and elaborate their existing practices. They adapt the Internet to their own uses, hoping to corral its advantages. Dependence on networked computing by states and corporations is already so advanced that, even if they wished, they could not destroy it. As hegemonic institutions integrate the new media, so they disseminate it and enrich it.

But can they tame and domesticate it, fine-tune it to eliminate properties that either do not suit them or threaten them? This political question
is the salient one for this study. My own view of the matter is not optimistic. The nation-state and the capitalist firm, in the two centuries of
their social dominance, have proved highly adaptive to changed conditions
and challenges of many types. The outlook, especially in today's political
landscape, is certainly not promising.

Firm conclusions about the future of assemblages of networked computing and humans, however, must be considered foolhardy. The technology continues to change dramatically, new users go online from many
different cultures and political regimes, new media combine with other
media and other cultural forms in unpredictable ways. All of which suggest we are in the midst of an event of very large proportions, an emergence that is best studied closely and incorporated into one's political
choices. In this conjuncture, discourses that rhetorically paralyze the spirit
are especially noxious, however realistic and wise they might appear.

One final word of caution: Don't teach your children to share, or they
just might.

NOTES

INTRODUCTION

1. From http://www.iwaynet.net/~ggwiz/f/infoplease.htm, accessed in 2005.
2. For an excellent account of how media transform the relations of humans to machines, see Hayles 2005.

I. PERFECT TRANSMISSIONS

1. For an extensive review of recent technologies that perform this coupling, see Mitchell 2003.
2. For a discussion of information and communications theory in relation to cultural theory, see Taylor 2001, chapter 4.
3. Ignacio, according to one report, denied he included this image on his page, claiming that it appeared only on mirror sites. See the discussion at http://www.fractalcow.com.
4. Rosenzweig informed me of his researches on Ignacio and "Evil Bert" in an e-mail of July 5, 2003. He provided me with the following references: Greg Miller, "Cyberculture: The Scene/The Webby Awards," *Los Angeles Times*, March 9, 1998, D3; Peter Hartlaub, "Bert and bin Laden Poster Tied to S.F. Student," *San Francisco Chronicle*, October 12, 2001, A12; Gina Davidson, "Bert and Bin: How the Joke Went Too Far," *The Scotsman*, October 14, 2001, 3.
5. See the Web page of Nikke Lindqvist (2001) at http://www.lindqvist.com for comprehensive documents relating to the incident.
6. For a discussion of the problem of disappearing Web sites in relation to studying the Evil Bert–bin Laden incident, see Rosenzweig 2003.
7. For those still skeptical about the incident, a similar event might be helpful. A reporter for the BBC in Kabul submitted a story about a document found in a Taliban redoubt left behind by retreating al-Qaeda forces. This document, also downloaded from the Internet, outlined instructions for making a thermonuclear device. To the reporter's chagrin, however, the instructions proved to be a hoax from a humor newsletter entitled *Annals of Improbable Research*, humor that was lost not only on the Taliban and al-Qaeda but also on the BBC reporter. "Taliban Thwarted by Irreproducible Result," http://www.dailyrotten.com/archive.
8. One of these is the noxious intensification of surveillance. See Lyon 2003.
9. The global encounter of cultures has produced some truly bizarre responses in the West. The imposition of the burqa on women in Afghanistan is, in some feminist circles, not the cause for critique of Afghanistan but an indication of the blindness

of Western media and politicians to their own cultural assumptions. Similarly, Akhil Gupta has recently elevated superstitions about reincarnation into the status of critique of Western models of childhood (Gupta 2002). While those models are certainly open to critique, narratives of reincarnation are hardly an appropriate level to enter that door. "Critique" is, after all, a cognitive, in the Kantian tradition, and could hardly bear the weight of modes of credulity suggested by Gupta.

2. POSTCOLONIAL THEORY AND GLOBAL MEDIA

1. Fanon 1967; Memmi 1965; Said 1982; Spivak 1999; Bhabha 1994. Bart Moore-Gilbert (1997) cites Robert Young (1995) as the origin of this triumvirate of postcolonial theory. I am indebted to Vinayak Chaturvedi for leading me to the work of Moore-Gilbert and for giving me thoughtful comments about this chapter.

2. For an example of an analysis that crosses the divide between the analysis of the state and "culture," see Mbembe 2001.

3. The spirit of resentment that so detracts from Ahmad's work is on display in Ahmad 1995b, 1996a, and 1996b, 409–28.

4. Since this study is concerned with communication and media, it is worth noting that the strife between colonizer and colonized included, from early on, systems of information gathering. See Bayly 1996.

5. Partha Chatterjee argues that the binary colonizer-colonized emerged as a political strategy and necessity within the situation of postcolonial discourse. In *The Nation and Its Fragments*, he attempts to overcome the limits of this epistemological constraint by tracing, for the colonizer and the colonized, "their mutually conditioned historicities" to show "the specific forms that have appeared, on the one hand, in the domain defined by the hegemonic project of nationalist modernity, and on the other, in the numerous fragmented resistances to that normalizing project" (Chatterjee 1993, 13). A similar argument is made by Dipesh Chakrabarty in relation to the binary of elite and subaltern (Chakrabarty 1985, 375–76).

6. For an interesting analysis of the role of literature in cross-cultural contacts, see Schwab 1996.

7. For an excellent statement and critique of Spivak's argument, see Al-Kassim 2002. But for a somewhat different view, see Vergès 1999, which discerns in postcolonial Reunion a cultural situation in which "the individual invents herself or himself" (78) in a choice between two "temptations": to find solace in nostalgia for a precolonial past or, existentially, to focus on the present alone.

8. Other observers turn to globalization as a point of critique of postcolonial theory. Often these critics find in the trend of globalization a reason to dismiss the culturalism of the postcolonial theorists. See, for example, Dirlik 2000.

9. Apter (1999, 217) is concerned with new media only as represented in cyberpunk fiction.

10. The first of Appadurai's works to change the way colonization is framed is no doubt his

essay in *Public Culture* (Appadurai 1990). But I will focus on his more recent work *Modernity at Large* (Appadurai 1996), in which the earlier essay is the lead chapter. Also of major importance in understanding the cultural aspects of globalization is Ong 1999.

11. In a more recent piece, Spivak complains that "there is a lack of communication between and among the immense heterogeneity of the subaltern cultures of the world" (2003, 194). Yet her agenda consists in renewing the relation of the West and the rest by suturing "their re-activated cultural axiomatics into the principles of the Enlightenment" (190).

12. For an overview of theories of globalization in relation to the homogenization or hybridization of cultures, see Crane 2002.

13. Foucault frequently uses such language in characterizing the individual's relation to power. For example, he writes of the eighteenth-century *lettres de cachet* that through them power was distributed in "complex circuits" and that "a whole political network became interwoven with the fabric of everyday life" (Foucault 1994, 168).

14. Foucault 1978, 127–30.

15. Foucault and Gordon 1980b, 120.

16. See, for example, Jules-Rosette 1990, and for other responses to the introduction of computers, see Ess and Sudweeks 2001. For Internet use in Australia, see Goggin 2004.

17. See Poster 2002 for a discussion of attempts at exclusivity in a chat room.

18. For an assessment of this phenomenon, see Siochru 2003; and Surman and Reilly 2003.

19. See also Gilroy 2005 on the issue of parochialism and cosmopolitanism.

20. Kalpagam argues that in India during the colonial period, the state, through policies of "governmentality," opened space in which Indian identity could be formed on the model of the rational, economic man (2000, 420). The new mediascape alters this situation by enabling other forms of self-construction. See also Scott 1995 for another Foucauldian analysis of colonial power.

21. For an example of the role of print and television in fanning the flames of extreme Hindu nationalism, see Rajagopal 2001.

22. For an alternative view, see Harpold and Philip 2000.

23. For a comprehensive evaluation of new media in India, see the special issue of *Contemporary South Asia* (2003).

3. THE INFORMATION EMPIRE

1. Arjun Appadurai (1996) makes a fascinating case for such developments in *Modernity at Large*, especially chapters 8 and 9.

2. For another effort to theorize the relation of new media to the subject-object binary, see Stroehl 2002.

3. See, for example, the essays in Ramonet 2002. The authors collected in this volume can do little more than bemoan every aspect of developments within media, old and new.

4. Maturana developed the idea of "structural coupling" to express the relation of humans to machines. A full explication of this idea is found in Mingers 1995. I am indebted to Marianne Constable for this reference.

5. This argument is made by Villalobos-Ruminott (2001, 39).

6. Hardt and Negri affirm the tentative nature of their intervention in a response to critics of *Empire* in Hardt and Negri 2001.

7. See, for example, the compelling work of Douglas Kellner (2003).

8. See, for example, the special double issue of *Rethinking Marxism* (Mustapha and Eken 2001) and the collections of critiques under the title *Debating Empire* (Balakrishnan 2003) and *Empire's New Clothes* (Passavant and Dean 2004).

9. Jodi Dean (2004) has also addressed this question, although from a different framework and with somewhat different conclusions.

10. Also of interest on the question of globalization and culture is Nancy 2002.

11. Abbe Mowshowitz has theorized the virtual in relation to social organization. See, for example, Mowshowitz 1992.

12. In *Multitude* Hardt and Negri do discuss the Napster case in this regard; see pp. 180–81.

13. Marcel Swiboda and Kirt Hirtler, for example, argue that "whilst it is conceivable and even tangible that the technologies of informatics, communications and biopower harness great creative potential and may provide the means for an ontological survey of subjective production . . . Hardt and Negri do not seem to provide any thoroughgoing examples of how this co-operation or collectivity is presently taking shape." They want "accounts of more concrete instances in which 'subjective cooperation' is presently taking shape and how the very practices of technologically enhanced knowledge-production might proceed" (Swiboda and Hirtler 2001, 139).

14. For an analysis of the material structure of the Internet, see Galloway 2001.

15. For more developed explorations of this question, see, for example, Guattari 1993; Hayles 1999.

16. See Resnick and Wolff 2001 and Dyer-Witheford 2001 for discussions of the concept of immaterial labor.

17. Beckett's text reads a bit differently from Foucault's. In this highly cryptic text, Beckett writes: "What matter who's speaking, someone said what matter who's speaking" (Beckett 1974, 16).

18. See, for example, the argument in Beniger 1986.

19. In a recent defense of the concept of multitude, Negri (2002) continues to characterize it as "postmodern." For a critique of the concept of multitude in relation to the question of representation, and therefore of media in general, see Passavant and Dean 2002.

20. Hardt and Negri trace the concept of the multitude back to Spinoza, specifically in his book on politics. See Negri 1997; Hardt and Negri 2000. On the concept of the multitude, see also Montag 1999. I am indebted to Sean Hill for bibliographic suggestions on this question. See also Virno (2004), who argues, like Hardt and Negri,

that "the multitude" is related to the new primacy of language and communication in labor.

4. CITIZENS, DIGITAL MEDIA, GLOBALIZATION

1. See Garcia Canclini 2001.
2. See Étienne Balibar's magnificent essay "Citizen Subject," in *Who Comes after the Subject?* ed. Eduardo Cadava, Peter Connor, and Jean-Luc Nancy (New York: Routledge, 1991), 33–57. Also of great interest is Balibar's "Subjection and Subjectivation," in *Supposing the Subject*, ed. Joan Copjec (New York: Verso, 1994), 1–15.
3. For an excellent discussion of the role of cyberspace in the politics of India, see Sundaram 2000.
4. Charles Ess has been central to this effort. See his recent "themed section" of *New Media and Society*, which collects several interesting essays on the use of information technology outside the West. The issue includes pieces on Borneo, the Philippines, and South Africa (Ess and Sudweeks 2001).
5. I refer to the comments of Katherine Hayles to the panel at which I presented an early version of this chapter during the 2000 MLA Annual Convention in Washington, D.C. It was published as Hayles 2002a.
6. On the novelty of our world situation, see the crucially important book by Michael Hardt and Antonio Negri (Hardt and Negri 2000).

5. IDENTITY THEFT AND MEDIA

1. A summary of the act may be found at http://www.consumer.gov. The crime is defined specifically as the theft of information with the intent to commit an unlawful activity.
2. The *New York Times*, in 2004, reported even larger numbers. See O'Brien 2004.
3. Jennifer Terry indicated to me that identity theft, as an economic act, promotes a type of subject that manages its risks, an actuarial self, as well as the interests of the insurance industry.
4. Copies of the advertisements may be found at a Web site entitled "Upbeat and Downstairs," http://daryld.com/citiads.php.
5. Akira Lippit has pointed out to me that in the movie the characters are entirely taken over by the aliens, constituting a unitary being, not a duality of victim-thief as in the commercial. For more on the movie and its context, see Mann 2004.
6. The artist Gillian Wearing has worked with the representation of gender and race in relation to visual and text media. See her interview at http://www.jca-online.com/wearing.html. I am grateful to Gary Hall and McKenzie Wark for bringing Wearing's work to my attention.
7. The same problem occurs in the Festschrift of Davis (Diefendorf and Hesse 1993), where the anachronistic use of "identity" pervades the editors' introduction to the volume. Normally historians object to such usage, as when Erik Erikson (1958) psychoanalyzed Martin Luther. My objection concerns not the projection by historians of

terms not present in the epoch under study, but the complete absence of any reflection on the meaning of the term and the way it might be deployed in historical analysis.

8. I am indebted to Étienne Balibar for pointing me to the extraordinary chapter in Locke that discusses the question of identity. Balibar himself treats the issue in relation to the question of property and its link to identity as in the following definition of identity he attributes to Locke: (1) that all the actions of the laboring body are accompanied with a conscious representation, or a representation of their meaning and their ends in consciousness—the ultimate site of personal identity; and (2) that this body forms an indestructible whole, that it is not split or broken but expresses a proper life in the continuity and diversity of the actions of what Locke metonymically called "its hands" (Balibar 2002, 304).

9. Locke 1937, 20. I thank my colleague Bill Maurer for pointing out this reference.

10. There are numerous exceptions to this type of identity politics, perhaps best exemplified in, and most often associated with, the work of Judith Butler beginning with *Gender Trouble* (Butler 1990).

6. THE AESTHETICS OF DISTRACTING MEDIA

1. For an early and quite illuminating discussion of this issue, see Nichols 1988.

2. I thank Randy Rutsky for reminding me of Weber's analysis of this term.

3. For an argument that Benjamin does anticipate digital culture, or at least that his theory affords an important avenue to understanding contemporary media, see Schwartz 2001.

4. My argument is in opposition to Lev Manovich (2001), who tends to see an ambivalent relation between analog media like film and digital art.

5. This opposition is not very different from that of Lyotard's collaboration in the 1960s with Cornélius Castoriadis and Claude Lefort, indicated in the title of their journal of that time, *Socialism or Barbarism*.

6. Some works of note that I will not discuss but are central to the debate are Heim 1987; Lanham 1989; Bolter 1990; Delany and Landow 1991; Landow 1994; Ulmer 1994; Aarseth 1997; and Ryan 1999.

7. Hayles's example of a hypertext book is Pavic 1988.

7. THE GOOD, THE BAD, AND THE VIRTUAL

1. Cited in Tebbel 1975, 171. I wish to thank Jon Wiener for calling my attention to this passage.

2. The U.S. gross receipts for the film were $6.1 million.

3. Face-to-face relations should not be understood as unitary but as themselves differentiated in numerous rhetorics. Michael Taussig (1993), for example, provides one such analytics. The problem is that when one draws lines between different media, one inevitably gives the impression of the unity of each medium. This is of course by no means the case.

4. This argument would have to be modified to allow for the variability of practices with each medium, as Judith Yaross Lee pointed out to me at a conference at Ohio University in May 2001. She rightly refers to Paul Saenger's study of the book of hours in the late Middle Ages (Saenger 1989), which shows how the production in manuscript and book form of the small book of hours promoted, through its portability, silent reading and a new ethics of prayer as private contemplation.

5. See Levinas 1985.

6. Raphael Sassower discusses Levinas's ethics in relation to technology and science. See Sassower 1997, 111–14.

7. I am here contrasting Kant and Nietzsche on ethics. For an opposite view, see Smith 1998. Smith, explicating Deleuze, argues for a line of continuity between Kant and Nietzsche, rather than an opposition, that progressively develops an "immanent" ethical position.

8. One might well carry my line of argument about ethics and information further by considering the ethical qualities of machine-to-machine communications, as well as that of human to machine, as opposed to human and machine. For a statement of this problem by a philosopher, see Johnson 1994.

9. After a hung jury, Naughton was convicted of possession of child pornography, a verdict that was thrown out of court on appeal. Before the second trial, he reached an out-of-court settlement in which he pled guilty to a count of interstate travel with intent to have sex with a minor, agreeing as well to develop computer programs for the FBI to assist them in apprehending online pedophiles. In 2002, the Supreme Court decided that only animated digital images of children are permissible.

8. INFORMATION MACHINES

1. There is a growing bibliography on the issue of race in psychoanalysis. I wish to call attention to a small selection of these works. There are the classical works by Du Bois (1999) and Fanon (1967). Also of interest in relation to colonization is Mannoni 1990; and for a Lacanian perspective, see Ortigues and Ortigues 1966. Of special note is Spillers 1996. See also Lane 1998, a collection with essays of mixed quality.

2. On the vexed question of the relation of psychological diagnosis of multiple personality to the postmodern concept of multiple selves, see Layton 1995.

3. Two excellent studies of children and media that form an excellent introduction to what is a vast body of literature are Kinder 1991 and Livingstone 2002. See also Morely 1986.

4. For an analysis of the child's bedroom in the late twentieth century, see Mitchell and Reid-Walsh 2002, chapter 4, "Physical Spaces: Children's Bedrooms as Cultural Texts."

5. On the profound importance of privacy to the bourgeois nuclear family, see Lukacs 1970.

6. Hulbert 2004, 31. Hulbert's piece was based on a Kaiser Family Foundation Report of

November 1999 entitled "Kids and Media @ the New Millennium." In a later study by Rideout et al. (2003), the findings were even higher, especially for computers.

7. For an analysis of Web sites for and by children, see Mitchell and Reid-Walsh 2002, chapter 5, "Virtual Spaces: Children on the Cyber Frontier."

8. For an analysis of the discourse on children viewing television, see Luke 1990.

9. The one exception is the adult voice-over at the beginning and ending of each segment, perhaps reflecting a transition from the "normal," adult world to the exclusively children's world of *Teletubbies*, or covering over the anxiety of this "separation" for the child.

9. WHO CONTROLS DIGITAL CULTURE?

1. I am grateful to Steve Jones and Jonathan Sterne for their bibliographic help with this chapter.

2. Michael Strangelove (2005) places file sharing in the largest context of resistace to capitalism within the Internet.

3. For a similar argument, see Gillespie 2004.

4. The class work on the history of the music industry since its inception is Sanjek 1988.

5. Two studies stand out on the question of control: Beniger 1986 and Kelly 1994, the former taking the position that digital technology furthers control by large corporations, the latter that this same technology undermines it.

6. The dual direction of digital media is argued brilliantly by Wendy Chun (2005) as a dialectic of control and freedom.

7. Personal e-mail from Wendy Seltzer, lawyer for the Electronic Frontier Foundation, December 1, 2003.

8. Op-ed, *Los Angeles Times*, January 3, 2004, B14.

9. A full analysis of the legal aspects of the DMCA is expounded well in Lessig 2001.

10. See Thornton 1996 for a discussion of the resistance of the Musicans' Union in England to the use of recordings in dance halls.

11. For excellent accounts of the Napster affair, see Spitz and Hunter (2005) and Lee (2005).

12. A study by economists in 2004 disputes the claim of the RIAA that sales have been adversely affected by file sharing. Felix Oberholzer-Gee of the Harvard Business School and Koleman S. Strumpf of the University of North Carolina, Chapel Hill, maintain that file sharing has no measurable effect on sales of CDs. They suppose that downloaders would not buy the CD they are obtaining from peer-to-peer networks (Schwartz 2004).

13. For an alternative view, see Jeff Howe (2005), who argues that "piracy" is organized hierarchically and depends not on "democratic" peer-to-peer networks but on an elite of skilled technicians.

14. For a history of this consolidation up through the mid-1970s and its influence on popular music, see Chapple and Garofalo 1977.

15. I am grateful to Jamie Poster for alerting me to this site.

16. See, for example, http://www.cdbaby.com, where artists sell CDs they make themselves. Garrett Wolfe informed me of this site.

10. EVERYDAY (VIRTUAL) LIFE

1. For an excellent overview of Lefebvre's work on the concept of everyday life, see Lefebvre 2000.

2. One fascinating theory of everyday life in relation to technology is Michael 2000. He treats various technologies (walking boots, cars, TV remote controls, dog leashes) in new combinations of machines and human beings, based on the theoretical perspectives of Bruno Latour, Donna Haraway, and Michel Serres. Michael is interested in the mixing of humans and technologies, forming new social and cultural subjects. His work is highly recommended, but it does not problematize media as such.

3. Kristin Ross (1996) disagrees with this assessment of Lefebvre's concept of everyday life. She argues that it is the most coherent of the several French theories of everyday life, including those of Louis Althusser and Michel de Certeau. I am grateful to Ray Guins for pointing me to the special issue of *Parallax* that includes Ross's essay.

4. See the essays in Bratich and Packer 2003 that attempt to develop this theme.

5. One thinks of the work of Hayles (1999), Turkle (1995), Stone (1995), Bolter and Grusin (1996), and Manovich (2001), to mention only a few pathbreaking works on the question. Above all, one must not forget the person who really initiated work on the media: McLuhan (1964). For a recent summary of the current state of studies of new media, see Marshall 2004.

6. For a discussion of the role of the personal case history or anecdote in social and cultural analysis, see Michael 2000, 14–16; and Michael 2003.

7. Michael (2000) contrasts television with the Internet and other media regarding the ability of each to promote a common culture. This is increasingly characteristic of television studies: that is, finding an advantage to broadcast systems where the same signal is transmitted to millions of receivers.

8. For the change in the public-private relation wrought by television, see Meyrowitz 1985.

9. For an excellent analysis of the impact of television in places outside the home, see McCarthy 2001.

10. This work is still in the formative stages, but there is some progress. See, for example, Kahn 2001.

11. For a subtle investigation of this question, see Guins 2001, 351–65.

12. See Weiser (1998), who writes extensively on this subject. See also Weiser 1997, 1993a, and 1993b. I am grateful to Katherine Hayles for informing me about Weiser's work.

11. CONSUMERS, USERS, DIGITAL COMMODITIES

1. Arjun Appadurai (1996), in a chapter titled "Consumption, Duration and History," proposes a convincing general scheme for the practices of consumption (interdiction,

sumptuary law, and fashion). It would be useful to combine this sort of analysis with attention to the role of media in consumption as I am proposing it.

2. Highmore 2002. Of the thirty-six selections in the reader, only one can be included in the category of media, an excerpt from Spigel 1992.

3. For an interesting collection on ethnicity, daily life, and technology, see Nelson and Tu 2001.

4. See, for example, Ang 1985; Silverstone 1994; and Gauntlett and Hill 1999.

5. "The free television that we've all enjoyed for so many years is based on us watching these commercials," said Jamie C. Kellner, chief executive of Turner Broadcasting. "There's no Santa Claus. If you don't watch the commercials, someone's going to have to pay for television and it's going to be you" (Harmon 2002).

6. Rob Latham illustrates well the difficulty of balancing an appreciation for the new forms of agency in digital technology that militate against the passivity suggested by the term "consumption" in favor of the term "user" against the persistent power of capitalism to reinforce the older figure of the consumer (Latham 2002, 225, 230).

12. FUTURE ADVERTISING

1. For an exploration of this argument, see Mirzoeff 1999, chapter 6. Also helpful for a general approach to the genre of science fiction film is Sobchack 1997.

2. Many scholars and theorists have explored the relation of media to consumer culture. The history of this relation is well developed in Marchand 1985. Also noteworthy are Featherstone 1991 and Firat and Dholakia 1998. On the relation of advertising to the latest developments in consumer technology, see Harmon 2002.

3. For bibliographic information on Philip K. Dick, see Levack 1988.

4. See, for example, Pohl and Kornbluth 1953.

5. Dick had already explored the theme of the virtual political leader in The Simulacra (Dick 1964).

6. At first the reader feels confident that Glen Runciter escaped the bomb explosion on the moon and is alive, whereas Joe Chip and the other employees are in a half-life state. But on the last page of the novel, Runciter gives someone coins that have the profile of Joe Chip on them, and the narrator warns Runciter in the book's final words: "This was just the beginning" (216). Earlier Joe Chip had received funny money with Runciter's image imprinted on it, and this was part of many events that, the reader thought, were Runciter's efforts to communicate to the half-life people. But now the reverse appears to be the case: Runciter is in half-life, and Joe Chip is trying to communicate with him. This ambiguous reality is common to Dick's work and underlines the fact that there is no stable grasp on reality among any of the characters in the novel, and hence no stable grasp on reality as objective anywhere.

7. Although it is from the Gospel according to John 8:58: "Jesus said unto them [the Jews], Verily, verily, I say unto you, Before Abraham was, I am."

8. Carl Freedman (1995), for example, interprets the last epigraph in relation to the

theme of paranoia in Dick's novels. Peter Fitting (1976) presents a Marxist view of the novel as a whole and the epigraph in particular. Both essays were published first in *Science Fiction Studies*, the leading journal in the field. Carl Freedman (2000) also devoted a chapter to Dick, although it does not treat *Ubik*.

9. See also the important work of Anne Friedberg (1993), who suggestively terms this state of consciousness a mobile virtual gaze.

10. I am interested not in Dick's personal views of religion but rather in the way the "religious" epigraph works in the text in question.

11. For an excellent discussion of the effort by the Clinton administration to defeat privacy on the Internet through encryption systems, see Gurak 1997.

12. See Tedeschi 2003 for a report on the use of "interactive ads" in which companies sell information about online browsing to other companies.

REFERENCES

Aarseth, Espen. 1997. *Cybertext: Perspectives on Ergodic Literature*. Baltimore: Johns Hopkins University Press.

Abu-Lughod, Janet. 1989. *Before European Hegemony: The World System, A.D. 1250–1350*. New York: Oxford University Press.

Adas, Michael. 1998. *Machines as the Measure of Men: Science, Technology, and Ideologies of Western Dominance*. Ithaca: Cornell University Press.

Adorno, Theodor. 1972. *Dialectic of Enlightenment*. New York: Continuum.

Ahmad, Aijaz. 1992. *In Theory: Classes, Nations, Literatures*. New York: Verso.

———. 1995a. "The Politics of Literary Postcoloniality." *Race and Class* 36 (3): 1–20.

———. 1995b. "Postcolonialism: What's in a Name?" In *Late Imperial Culture*, ed. Roman de la Campa, E. Ann Kaplan, and Michael Sprinker, 11–32. New York: Verso.

———. 1996a. "Interview." *Radical Philosophy* 76:29–38.

———. 1996b. *Lineages of the Present: Political Essays*. New Delhi: Tulika.

Al-Kassim, Dina. 2002. "The Face of Foreclosure." *Interventions* 4 (2): 168–74.

Althusser, Louis, and Étienne Balibar. 1970. *Reading Capital*. London: New Left Books.

Amin, Samir. 1989. *Eurocentrism*. New York: Monthly Review Press.

Ang, Ien. 1985. *Watching Dallas: Soap Opera and the Melodramatic Imagination*. London: Methuen.

———. 2000. "New Technologies, Audience Measurement, and the Tactics of Television Consumption." In *Electronic Media and Technoculture*, ed. John Thornton Caldwell, 183–96. New York: Routledge.

Angell, Norman. 1914. *The Great Illusion: A Study of the Relation of Military Power to National Advantage*. Toronto: McClelland, Goodchild and Stewart.

Appadurai, Arjun. 1990. "Disjuncture and Difference in the Global Cultural Economy." *Public Culture* 2 (2): 1–24.

———. 1996. *Modernity at Large: Cultural Dimensions of Globalization*. Minneapolis: University of Minnesota Press.

Apter, Emily. 1999. *Continental Drift: From National Characters to Virtual Subjects*. Chicago: University of Chicago Press.

Asadullah, Ali. 2001. "Spice Girls: Exactly the Reason Why Bin Laden Hates the West." *Islam-Online*, September 10, 2001.

Attali, Jacques. 1985. *Noise: The Political Economy of Music*. Minneapolis: University of Minnesota Press.

Bal, Mieke. 1997. *Narratology: Introduction to the Theory of Narrative*. Toronto: University of Toronto Press.

Balakrishnan, Gopal, ed. 2003. *Debating Empire*. New York: Verso.

Balibar, Étienne. 1991. "Citizen Subject." In *Who Comes after the Subject?* ed. Eduardo Cadava, Peter Connor, and Jean-Luc Nancy, 33–57. New York: Routledge.

———. 1994. *Masses, Classes, Ideas: Studies on Politics and Philosophy before and after Marx*. New York: Routledge.

———. 2001. "Une citoyenneté sans communauté?" In *Nous, citoyens d'europe*, 111–50. Paris: Editions de La Découverte.

———. 2002. " 'Possessive Individualism' Reversed: From Locke to Derrida." *Constellations* 9 (3): 299–317.

Barthes, Roland. 1977. *Image, Music, Text*. New York: Hill and Wang.

Baudrillard, Jean. 1983. *In the Shadow of the Silent Majorities, or the End of the Social and Other Essays*. New York: Semiotext(e).

———. 1994. *Simulacra and Simulation*. Ann Arbor: University of Michigan Press.

———. 1995a. *The Gulf War Did Not Take Place*. Bloomington: Indiana University Press.

———. 1995b. *Le crime parfait*. Paris: Galilée.

———. 1998. *The Consumer Society: Myths and Structures*. Thousand Oaks, Calif.: Sage.

Bayly, C. A. 1996. *Empire and Information: Intelligence Gathering and Social Communication in India, 1780–1870*. New York: Cambridge University Press.

Beckett, Samuel. 1974. *Texts for Nothing*. London, Calder and Boyars.

Beniger, James. 1986. *The Control Revolution: Technological and Economic Origins of the Information Society*. Cambridge: Harvard University Press.

Benjamin, Walter. 1969a. "Theses on the Philosophy of History." In *Illuminations*, ed. Hannah Arendt, 253–64. New York: Schocken.

———. 1969b. "The Work of Art in the Age of Mechanical Reproduction." In *Illuminations*, ed. Hannah Arendt, 217–51. New York: Schocken.

———. 1999. *The Arcades Project*. Cambridge: Belknap Press.

Bernauer, James, and David Rasmussen, eds. 1988. *The Final Foucault*. Cambridge: MIT Press.

Bhabha, Homi. 1993. *Local Cultures*. New York: Routledge.

———. 1994. *The Location of Culture*. New York: Routledge.

Bianco, Katalina. 2001. *Identity Theft: What You Need to Know*. Chicago: CCH.

Bolter, Jay David. 1990. *Writing Space: The Computer, Hypertext, and the History of Writing*. Cambridge, Mass.: Eastgate Systems.

Bolter, Jay David, and Richard Grusin. 1996. "Remediation." *Configurations* 4 (3): 311–58.

Bourdieu, Pierre. 1984. *Distinction: A Social Critique of the Judgment of Taste*. Cambridge: Harvard University Press.

Bradner, Scot. 2003. "I Don't Want You to Be Me." *Network World*.

Bratich, Jack, Jeremy Packer, and Cameron McCarthy, eds. 2003. *Foucault, Cultural Studies, and Governmentality*. Stony Brook: SUNY Press.

Brigham, Linda. 1997. "Cinema and the Paralysis of Perception: Robbe-Grillet, Condillac, Virilio." In *Reading Matters: Narratives in the New Media Ecology*, ed. Joseph Tabbi and Michael Wutz, 119–35. Ithaca: Cornell University Press.

Buck-Morss, Susan. 1991. *The Dialectics of Seeing: Walter Benjamin and the Arcades Project*. Cambridge: MIT Press.

Bull, Michael. 2000. *Sounding Out the City: Personal Stereos and the Management of Everyday Life*. New York: Berg.

Burroughs, William. 1959. *Naked Lunch*. New York: Grove Press.

———. 1993. *Naked Lunch*. London: Flamingo Modern Classics.

Butler, Judith. 1990. *Gender Trouble: Feminism and the Subversion of Identity*. New York: Routledge.

———. 1993. *Bodies That Matter*. New York: Routledge.

———. 1997a. *Excitable Speech: A Politics of the Performative*. New York: Routledge.

———. 1997b. *The Psychic Life of Power: Theories of Subjection*. Stanford: Stanford University Press.

Castells, Manuel. 1993. "The Informational Economy and the New International Division of Labor." In *The New Global Economy*, ed. Martin Carnoy, 15–43. University Park: Pennsylvania State University Press.

———. 1996. *The Rise of the Network Society*. Cambridge, Mass.: Blackwell Publishers.

———. 1998. *End of Millennium*. Malden, Mass.: Blackwell Publishers.

———. 2001. *The Internet Galaxy: Reflections on the Internet, Business, and Society*. New York: Oxford University Press.

Chakrabarty, Dipesh. 1985. "Invitation to a Dialogue." *Subaltern Studies* 4:364–76.

Chapple, Steve, and Reebee Garofalo. 1977. *Rock 'n' Roll Is Here to Pay*. Chicago: Nelson-Hall.

Chatman, Seymour. 1978. *Story and Discourse: Narrative Structure in Fiction and Film*. Ithaca: Cornell University Press.

Chatterjee, Partha. 1993. *The Nation and Its Fragments: Colonial and Postcolonial Histories*. Princeton, N.J.: Princeton University Press.

Cheah, Pheng. 1999. "Spectral Nationality: The Living On of the Postcolonial Nation in Neocolonial Globalization." *Boundary 2* 26 (3): 225–52.

Cherry, Sheila. 2002. "Al-Qaeda May Be Stealing Your ID." *Insight on the News* 18:18.

Chow, Rey. 1996. *Primitive Passions: Visuality, Sexuality, Ethnography, and Contemporary Chinese Cinema*. New York: Columbia University Press.

Chun, Wendy Hui Kyong. 2006. *Control and Freedom: Power and Paranoia in the Age of Fiber Optics*. Cambridge: MIT Press.

CNN. 2001. " 'Muppet' Producers Miffed over Bert–bin Laden Image."

Cole, Simon. 2003. *Suspect Identities: A History of Fingerprinting and Criminal Identification*. Cambridge: Harvard University Press.

Collins, Patricia Hill. 2000. *Black Feminist Thought: Knowledge, Consciousness, and the Politics of Empowerment*. New York: Routledge.

Colwell, C. 1996. "Discipline and Control: Butler and Deleuze on Individuality and Dividuality." *Philosophy Today* 40 (1): 211–16.

Contemporary South Asia. 2003. Special issue, *Contemporary South Asia* 12 (1).

Crane, Diana. 2002. "Culture and Globalization: Theoretical Models and Emerging

Trends." In *Global Culture: Media, Arts, Policy, and Globalization*, ed. Diana Crane, Nobuko Kawashima, and Ken'ichi Kawasaki, 1–25. New York: Routledge.

Daniel, Sharon. 2000. "Collaborative Systems: Evolving Databases and the 'Conditions of Possibility' — Artificial Life Models of Agency in On-Line Interactive Art." *AI and Society* 14 (2): 196–213.

Darley, Andrew. 2000. *Visual Digital Culture: Surface Play and Spectacle in New Media Genres*. New York: Routledge.

Davis, Kristin. 1998. "Making Identity Theft a Crime." *Kiplinger's Personal Finance Magazine* 52:16.

Davis, Natalie. 1983. *The Return of Martin Guerre*. Cambridge: Harvard University Press.

de Certeau, Michel. 1984. *The Practice of Everyday Life*. Berkeley: University of California Press.

———. 1986. *Heterologies: Discourse on the Other*. Minneapolis: University of Minnesota Press.

———. 1997. *Culture in the Plural*. Minneapolis: University of Minnesota Press.

Dean, Jodi. 2001. "Cybersalons and Civil Society: Rethinking the Public Sphere in Transnational Technoculture." *Public Culture* 13 (2): 243–65.

———. 2004. "The Networked Empire: Communicative Capitalism and the Hope for Politics." In *Empire's New Clothes: Reading Hardt and Negri*, ed. Paul Passavant and Jodi Dean, 265–88. New York: Routledge.

Delany, Paul, and George Landow, eds. 1991. *Hypermedia and Literary Studies*. Cambridge: MIT Press.

de Lauretis, Teresa. 1984. *Alice Doesn't: Feminism, Semiotics, Cinema*. Bloomington: University of Indiana Press.

Deleuze, Gilles. 1992a. "Postscript on the Societies of Control." *October* 59 (winter): 3–7.

———. 1992b. "What Is a *Dispositif*?" In *Michel Foucault: Philosopher*, ed. François Ewald, 159–68. New York: Routledge.

———. 1995. *Negotiations, 1972–1990*. New York: Columbia University Press.

———. 1998. "Having an Idea in Cinema." In *Deleuze and Guattari: New Mappings in Politics, Philosophy, and Culture*, ed. Eleanor Kaufman and Kevin Heller, 14–19. Minneapolis: University of Minnesota Press.

Deleuze, Gilles, and Félix Guattari. 1987. *A Thousand Plateaus: Capitalism and Schizophrenia*. Minneapolis: University of Minnesota Press.

Derrida, Jacques. 1978. *Writing and Difference*. Chicago: University of Chicago Press.

———. 1986. "Declarations of Independence." *New Political Science* 15:7–15.

———. 1987. *The Post Card: From Socrates to Freud and Beyond*. Chicago: University of Chicago Press.

———. 1994. *Specters of Marx: The State of the Debt, the Work of Mourning and the New International*. New York: Routledge.

Dery, Mark, ed. 1993. *Flame Wars: The Discourse of Cyberculture*. South Atlantic Quarterly.

Dewitte, Philippe. 2002. "Homo Cybernatus." *Hommes & Migrations* 1240:1–79.

Dibbell, Julian. 1993. "A Rape in Cyberspace." *Village Voice*, 36–42.

Dick, Philip K. 1964. *The Simulacra*. New York: Ace.

———. 1969. *Ubik*. New York: Vintage.

———. 1984. *The Penultimate Truth*. New York: Carroll and Graf.

Dick, Philip K., and Ray Nelson. 1967. *The Ganymede Takeover*. London: Legend.

Diefendorf, Barbara, and Carla Hesse, eds. 1993. *Culture and Identity in Early Modern Europe (1500–1800): Essays in Honor of Natalie Zemon Davis*. Ann Arbor: University of Michigan Press.

Dirlik, Arif. 2000. *Postmodernity's Histories: The Past as Legacy and Project*. New York: Rowman and Littlefield.

Donath, Judith. 1999. "Identity and Deception in the Virtual Community." In *Communities in Cyberspace*, ed. Marc Smith and Peter Kollock, 29–59. New York: Routledge.

Dreyfus, Hubert. 1999. "Anonymity versus Commitment: The Dangers of Education on the Internet." *Ethics and Information Technology* 1 (1): 15–21.

Du Bois, W. E. B. 1999. "The Souls of Black Folk." In *W. E. B. Du Bois: The Souls of Black Folk, Authoritative Text, Contexts, Criticism*, ed. Henry Louis Gates Jr. and Terri Hume Oliver. New York: Norton.

Duhamel, Georges. 1930. *Scènes de la vie future*. Paris: Mercury.

Dyer-Witheford, Nick. 2001. "Empire, Immaterial Labor, the New Combinations, and the Global Worker." *Rethinking Marxism* 13 (3–4): 70–80.

Ebnet, Matthew. 1999. "Sex-Change Webcast Stirs E-thics Debate." *Los Angeles Times*, December 9, E1, E4.

Egan, Jennifer. 2000. "Lonely Gay Teen Seeking Same." *New York Times Magazine*, December 10, 110–32.

Erikson, Erik. 1958. *Young Man Luther: A Study in Psychoanalysis and History*. New York: Norton.

———. 1963. *Childhood and Society*. New York: Norton.

———. 1968. *Identity: Youth and Crisis*. New York: Norton.

Ess, Charles. 2001. "Introduction: What's Culture Got to Do with It?" In *Culture, Technology, Communication: Towards an Intercultural Global Village*, ed. Charles Ess, 1–50. Stony Brook: SUNY Press.

Ess, Charles, and Fay Sudweeks. 2001. "On the Edge: Cultural Barriers and Catalysts to IT Diffusion among Remote and Marginalized Communities." *New Media and Society* 3 (3): 259–69.

Fanon, Frantz. 1963. *The Wretched of the Earth*. New York: Grove.

———. 1967. *Black Skin, White Masks*. New York: Grove.

Featherstone, Mike. 1991. *Consumer Culture and Postmodernism*. London: Sage.

Febvre, Lucien. 1982. *The Problem of Unbelief in the Sixteenth Century: The Religion of Rabelais*. Cambridge: Harvard University Press.

Fernandez, Maria. 1999. "Postcolonial Media Theory." *Art Journal*, 59–73.

Firat, Fuat, and Nikhilesh Dholakia. 1998. *Consuming People: From Political Economy to Theaters of Consumption*. New York: Routledge.

Fisher, Kevin. 2000. "Tracing the Tesseract: A Conceptual Prehistory of the Morph." In

Meta-morphing: Visual Transformations in the Culture of Quick Change, ed. Vivian Sobchack, 103–30. Minneapolis: University of Minnesota Press.

Fiske, John, and John Hartley. 1978. *Reading Television*. London: Methuen.

Fitting, Peter. 1976. "Ubik: The Deconstruction of Bourgeois SF." In *Science-Fiction Studies: Selected Articles on Science Fiction, 1973–1975*, ed. R. D. Mullen and Darko Suvin, 203–9. Boston: Gregg Press.

Flitterman-Lewis, Sandy. 1992. "Psychoanalysis, Film and Television." In *Channels of Discourse, Reassembled*, ed. Robert Allen, 203–46. Chapel Hill: University of North Carolina Press.

Foucault, Michel. 1977. *Discipline and Punish: The Birth of the Prison*. New York: Pantheon Books.

———. 1978. *The History of Sexuality: An Introduction*. New York: Pantheon.

———. 1983. *This Is Not a Pipe*. Berkeley: University of California Press.

———. 1986. "Of Other Spaces." *Diacritics* (spring): 22–27.

———. 1991. "Governmentality." In *The Foucault Effect*, ed. Graham Burchell, 87–104. Chicago: University of Chicago Press.

———. 1994. "Lives of Infamous Men." In *Power: Essential Works of Foucault, 1954–1984*, ed. James Faubion, 157–75. New York: New Press.

———. 2002. *"Society Must Be Defended": Lectures at the Collège de France, 1975–1976*. New York: Picador.

Foucault, Michel, and Colin Gordon. 1980a. *Power/Knowledge: Selected Interviews and Other Writings, 1972–1977*. New York: Pantheon Books.

———. 1980b. *Power/Knowledge: Selected Interviews and Other Writings, 1972–1977*. New York: Pantheon Books.

Freedman, Carl. 1995. "Towards a Theory of Paranoia: The Science Fiction of Philip K. Dick." In *Philip K. Dick: Contemporary Critical Interpretations*, ed. Samuel Umland, 7–17. Westport, Conn.: Greenwood Press.

———. 2000. *Critical Theory and Science Fiction*. Hanover, N.H.: Wesleyan University Press.

Freud, Sigmund. 1949. *An Outline of Psychoanalysis*. New York: Norton.

———. 1960a. *The Ego and the Id*. New York: Norton.

———. 1960b. *Jokes and Their Relation to the Unconscious*. New York: Norton.

———. 1965. *New Introductory Lectures*. New York: Norton.

Friedberg, Anne. 1993. *Window Shopping: Cinema and the Postmodern*. Berkeley: University of California Press.

Galloway, Alexander. 2001. "Protocol, or How Control Exists after Decentralization." *Rethinking Marxism* 13 (3–4): 81–88.

———. 2004. *Protocol: How Control Exists after Decentralization*. Cambridge: MIT Press.

Garcia Canclini, Nestor. 2001. *Consumers and Citizens: Globalization and Multicultural Conflicts*. Minneapolis: University of Minnesota Press.

Gardiner, Michael. 2000. *Critiques of Everyday Life*. New York: Routledge.

Gauntlett, David, and Annette Hill. 1999. *TV Living: Television, Culture and Everyday Life*. New York: Routledge.

Genette, Gérard. 1980. *Narrative Discourse: An Essay in Method*. Ithaca: Cornell University Press.

Gillespie, Tarleton. 2004. "Copyright and Commerce: The DMCA, Trusted Systems, and the Stabilization of Distribution." *Information Society* 20 (4): 239–54.

Gilroy, Paul. 2005. *Postcolonial Melancholia*. New York: Columbia University Press.

Gitlin, Todd. 2001. *Media Unlimited: How the Torrent of Images and Sounds Overwhelms Our Lives*. New York: Metropolitan.

Goggin, Gerard, ed. 2004. *Virtual Nation: The Internet in Australia*. Sydney: University of New South Wales Press.

Grewal, Inderpal, and Caren Kaplan. 2001. "Global Identities: Theorizing Transnational Studies in Sexuality." *GLQ: A Journal of Lesbian and Gay Studies* 7 (4): 663–79.

Guattari, Félix. 1993. "Machinic Heterogenesis." In *Rethinking Technologies*, ed. Verena Conley. Minneapolis: University of Minnesota Press.

Guins, Rayford. 2001. " 'Now You're Living': The Promise of Home Theater and Deleuze's 'New Freedoms.' " *Television and New Media* 2 (4): 351–65.

Gunning, Tom. 1995. "Tracing the Individual Body: Photography, Detectives, and Early Cinema." In *Cinema and the Invention of Modern Life*, ed. Leo Charney and Vanessa Schwartz, 15–45. Los Angeles: University of California Press.

Gupta, Akhil. 2002. "Reliving Childhood? The Temporality of Childhood and Narratives of Reincarnation." *Ethnos* 67 (1): 1–23.

Gurak, Laura. 1997. *Persuasion and Privacy in Cyberspace: The Online Protests over Lotus Marketplace and the Clipper Chip*. New Haven: Yale University Press.

Habermas, Jürgen. 1983. "Modernity, an Incomplete Project." In *The Anti-Aesthetic: Essays in Postmodern Culture*, ed. Hal Foster, 3–15. Port Townsend, Wash.: Bay Press.

———. 1989. *The Structural Transformation of the Public Sphere*. Cambridge: MIT Press.

———. 1990. *Moral Consciousness and Communicative Action*. Cambridge: MIT Press.

Hacking, Ian. 1995. *Rewriting the Soul: Multiple Personality and the Sciences of Memory*. Princeton, N.J.: Princeton University Press.

Hall, Stuart. 1996. "The West and the Rest: Discourse and Power." In *Modernity: An Introduction to Modern Societies*, ed. Stuart Hall, David Held, Don Hubert, and Kenneth Thompson, 184–227. London: Blackwell.

Haraway, Donna. 1985. "A Manifesto for Cyborgs: Science, Technology, and Socialist Feminism in the 1980s." *Socialist Review* 80 (March–April): 65–107.

Hardt, Michael. 1998. "The Withering of Civil Society." In *Deleuze and Guattari: New Mappings in Politics, Philosophy, and Culture*, ed. Eleanor Kaufman and Kevin Heller, 23–39. Minneapolis: University of Minnesota Press.

Hardt, Michael, and Antonio Negri. 2000. *Empire*. Cambridge: Harvard University Press.

———. 2001. "Adventures of the Multitude: Response of the Authors." *Rethinking Marxism* 13 (3–4): 236–43.

———. 2004. *Multitude: War and Democracy in the Age of Empire*. New York: Penguin.

Harmon, Amy. 2002. "Digital Video Recorders Give Advertisers Pause." *New York Times*, May 23.

————. 2003. "Penn State Will Pay to Allow Students to Download Music." *New York Times*, November 7.

Harpold, Terry, and Kavita Philip. 2000. "Of Bugs and Rats: Cyber-cleanliness, Cyber-squalor, and the Fantasy-Spaces of Informational Globalization." *PMC* 11 (1).

Hartmann, Heinz. 1964. *Essays on Ego Psychology: Selected Problems in Psychoanalytic Theory.* New York: International Universities Press.

Hartsock, Nancy. 1997. "The Feminist Standpoint: Developing the Ground for a Specifically Feminist Historical Materialism." In *The Second Wave: A Reader in Feminist Theory*, ed. Linda Nicholson, 216–40. New York: Routledge.

Hay, James. 1992. "Afterword." In *Channels of Discourse, Reassembled*, ed. Robert Allen, 354–85. Chapel Hill: University of North Carolina Press.

Hayles, N. Katherine. 1999. *How We Became Posthuman: Virtual Bodies in Cybernetics, Literature, and Informatics.* Chicago: University of Chicago Press.

————. 2000. "The Invention of Copyright and the Birth of Monsters: Flickering Connectivities in Shelley Jackson's *Patchwork Girl*." *Journal of Postmodern Culture* 10 (2).

————. 2002a. "The Complexities of Seriation." *PMLA* 117 (1): 117–21.

————. 2002b. *Writing Machines.* Cambridge: MIT Press.

————. 2005. *My Mother Was a Computer: Digital Subjects and Literary Texts.* Chicago: University of Chicago Press.

Healey, Jon, and Richard Cromelin. 2004. "When Copyright Law Meets the 'Mash-up.' " *Los Angeles Times*, March 21, E1, E43.

Hebdige, Dick. 1987. *Cut 'n' Mix: Culture, Identity and Caribbean Music.* New York: Methuen.

Heidegger, Martin. 1977. *The Question concerning Technology and Other Essays.* New York: Harper and Row.

Heim, Michael. 1987. *Electric Language: A Philosophical Study of Word Processing.* New Haven: Yale University Press.

Highmore, Ben, ed. 2002. *The Everyday Life Reader.* New York: Routledge.

Ho, K. C. 2000. " 'Sites' of Resistance: Charting the Alternative and Marginal Websites in Singapore." AIOR Conference, Lawrence, Kansas.

Hongladarom, Soraj. 2001. "Global Culture, Local Cultures, and the Internet: The Thai Example." In *Culture, Technology, Communication: Towards an Intercultural Global Village*, ed. Charles Ess, 307–24. Stony Brook: SUNY Press.

Howe, Jeff. 2005. "The Shadow Internet." *Wired* 13:154–59.

Hrachovec, Herbert. 2001. "New Kids on the Net: Deutschsprachige Philosophie Elektronisch." In *Culture, Technology, Communication: Towards an Intercultural Global Village*, ed. Charles Ess, 131–50. Stony Brook: SUNY Press.

Hulbert, Ann. 2004. "Tweens 'R' Us." *New York Times*, November 28, 31.

Hull, Gordon. 2003. "Digital Copyright and the Possibility of Pure Law." *Qui Parle* 14 (1): 21–48.

Huyssen, Andreas. 1986. "Mass Culture as Woman: Modernism's Other." In *Studies in Entertainment: Critical Approaches to Mass Culture*, ed. Tania Modleski, 188–208. Bloomington: Indiana University Press.

"Identity Theft Fastest Growing White Collar Crime in Nation." 2003. *State Legislatures* 29 (4): 9.

Ignacio, Dino. 2001. "Good Bye Bert." www.fractalcow.com/bert/bert.

Jameson, Fredric. 1981. *The Political Unconscious: Narrative as a Social Symbolic Act*. Ithaca: Cornell University Press.

———. 1998. "Notes on Globalization as a Philosophical Issue." In *The Cultures of Globalization*, ed. Fredric Jameson and Masao Miyoshi, 54–77. Durham: Duke University Press.

Johns, Adrian. 1998. *The Nature of the Book: Print and Knowledge in the Making*. Chicago: University of Chicago Press.

Johnson, Deborah. 1994. *Computer Ethics*. Englewood Cliffs, N.J.: Prentice Hall.

Johnson, Steven. 2001. *Emergence: The Connected Lives of Ants, Brains, Cities, and Software*. New York: Scribner.

Jules-Rosette, Benetta. 1990. *Terminal Signs: Computers and Social Change in Africa*. New York: Mouton de Gruyter.

Kahn, Jennifer. 2001. "Let's Make Your Head Interactive." *Wired* 9:106–15.

Kalpagam, U. 2000. "Colonial Governmentality and the Economy." *Economy and Society* 29 (3): 418–38.

Kant, Immanuel. 1949. *Fundamental Principles of the Metaphysic of Morals*. New York: Bobbs-Merrill.

Kaplan, Bonnie, Ramesh Farzanfar, and Robert Freeman. 1999. "Research and Ethical Issues Arising from Ethnographic Interviews of Patients' Reactions to an Intelligent Interactive Telephone Health Behavior Advisor." In *New Information Technologies in Organizational Processes*, ed. Ojelanki Ngwenyama, Lucas Introna, Michael Myers, and Janice DeGross, 67–78. Boston: Kluwer Academic Publishers.

Kaplan, Nancy. 2000. "Literacy beyond Books." In *The World Wide Web and Contemporary Cultural Theory*, ed. Andrew Herman and Thomas Swiss, 207–34. New York: Routledge.

Katz, James, and Ronald Rice, eds. 2002. *Social Consequences of Internet Use: Access, Involvement, and Interaction*. Cambridge: MIT Press.

Keenan, Thomas. 1993. "Windows: Of Vulnerability." In *The Phantom Public Sphere*, ed. Bruce Robbins, 121–41. Minneapolis: University of Minnesota Press.

Kellner, Douglas. 2003. "Globalization, Technopolitics and Revolution." In *The Future of Revolutions: Rethinking Radical Change in the Age of Globalization*, ed. John Foran, 180–94. London: Zed Books.

Kelly, Kevin. 1994. *Out of Control: The New Biology of Machines, Social Systems and the Economic World*. Cambridge: Perseus Books.

Kinder, Marsha. 1991. *Playing with Power in Movies, Television and Video Games: From Muppet Babies to Teenage Mutant Ninja Turtles*. Berkeley: University of California Press.

Kittler, Friedrich A. 1986. *Grammophon, Film, Typewriter*. Berlin: Brinkmann and Bose.

———. 1990. *Discourse Networks: 1800/1900*. Stanford: Stanford University Press.

Kittler, Friedrich A., and John Johnston. 1997. *Essays: Literature, Media, Information Systems*. Amsterdam, G + B Arts International.

Klein, Melanie. 1964. *Contributions to Psycho-analysis: 1921–1945*. New York: McGraw-Hill.

Koyré, Alexander. 1958. *From the Closed World to the Infinite Universe*. New York: Harper and Row.

Lacan, Jacques. 1968. "The Mirror-Phase as Formative of the Function of the I." *New Left Review* 51:71–77.

Laclau, Ernesto. 1990. *New Reflections on the Revolution of Our Time*. New York: Verso.

Landow, George P. 1994. *Hypertext Theory*. Baltimore: Johns Hopkins University Press.

Lane, Christopher, ed. 1998. *The Psychoanalysis of Race*. New York: Columbia University Press.

Lanham, Richard. 1989. "The Electronic Word: Literary Study and the Digital Revolution." *New Literary History* 20 (2): 265–90.

Latham, Rob. 2002. *Consuming Youth: Vampires, Cyborgs, and the Culture of Consumption*. Chicago: University of Chicago Press.

Layton, Lynne. 1995. "Trauma, Gender Identity and Sexuality: Discourses of Fragmentation." *American Imago* 52 (1): 107–25.

Lee, Jennifer. 2003. "Identity Theft Victimizes Millions, Costs Billions." *New York Times*, September 4, A20.

Lee, Kwang-Suk. 2005. "The Momentum of Control and Autonomy: A Local Scene of Peer-to-Peer Music-Sharing Technology." *Media, Culture and Society* 27 (5): 799–809.

Lefebvre, Henri. 1966. *Le language et la société*. Paris: Gallimard.

———. 1969. *The Explosion: Marxism and the French Revolution*. New York: Monthly Review Press.

———. 1971a. *Au-delà du structuralisme*. Paris: Anthropos.

———. 1971b. *Everyday Life in the Modern World*. New York: Harper Torchbook.

———. 1987. "The Everyday and Everydayness." *Yale French Studies* 73:7–11.

———. 1991. *Critique of Everyday Life: Volume 1, Introduction*. London: Verso.

Lessig, Lawrence. 1999. *Code and Other Laws of Cyberspace*. New York: Basic Books.

———. 2001. *The Future of Ideas: The Fate of the Commons in a Connected World*. New York: Vintage.

Levack, Daniel. 1988. *PKD: A Philip K. Dick Bibliography*. London: Meckler.

Levinas, Emmanuel. 1985. *Ethics and Infinity: Conversations with Philippe Nemo*. Pittsburgh, Duquesne University Press.

Lévy, Pierre. 1995. "Toward Superlanguage." www.niah.fi.

———. 1997. *Collective Intelligence*. New York: Plenum Press.

Lindqvist, Nikke. 2001. "Mystery Solved?" www.lindqvist.com.

Linn, Susan E., and Alvin F. Poussaint. 1999. "The Trouble with Teletubbies." *American Prospect* 10 (44): 18.

Livingston, Brian. 2003. "Identity Theft Crisis." *eWeek*.

Livingstone, Sonia. 2002. *Young People and New Media: Childhood and the Changing Media Environment*. London: Sage.

Locke, John. 1937. *Treatise of Civil Government and A Letter concerning Toleration*. New York: Appleton-Century-Crofts.

————. 1959. *An Essay concerning Human Understanding.* New York: Dover.

Lowe, Lisa. 1996. *Immigrant Acts.* Durham: Duke University Press.

Lukacs, John. 1970. "The Bourgeois Interior." *American Scholar* 29 (4): 616–30.

Luke, Carmen. 1990. *Constructing the Child Viewer: A History of the American Discourse on Television and Children, 1950–1980.* New York: Praeger.

Lury, Celia. 1993. *Cultural Rights: Technology, Legality and Personality.* New York: Routledge.

————. 1998. *Prosthetic Culture: Photography, Memory and Identity.* New York: Routledge.

————. 1999. "Marking Time with Nike: The Illusion of the Durable." *Public Culture* 11 (3): 499–526.

Lyon, David. 2003. *Surveillance after September 11.* London: Polity.

Lyotard, Jean-François. 1984. *The Postmodern Condition.* Minneapolis: University of Minnesota Press.

————. 1985. *Les Immatériaux: Epreuves d'écriture.* Paris: Centre Georges Pompidou.

————. 1991. *The Inhuman: Reflections on Time.* London: Polity.

MacCannell, Juliet. 1986. *Figuring Lacan: Criticism and the Cultural Unconscious.* Lincoln: University of Nebraska Press.

MacPherson, C. B. 1962. *The Political Theory of Possessive Individualism.* New York: Oxford University Press.

Mann, Katrina. 2004. " 'You're Next!' Postwar Hegemony Besieged in *Invasion of the Body Snatchers.*" *Cinema Journal* 44 (1): 49–68.

Mannoni, Octave. 1990. *Prospero and Caliban: The Psychology of Colonization.* Ann Arbor: University of Michigan Press.

Manovich, Lev. 2001. *The Language of New Media.* Cambridge: MIT Press.

Marchand, Roland. 1985. *Advertising and the American Dream: Making Way for Modernity, 1920–1940.* Berkeley: University of California Press.

Marcuse, Herbert. 1964. *One-Dimensional Man.* Boston: Beacon.

Marshall, P. David. 2004. *New Media Cultures.* London: Arnold.

Marvin, Carolyn. 1988. *When Old Technologies Were New: Thinking about Electric Communication in the Late Nineteenth Century.* New York: Oxford.

Marx, Karl. 1967. "On the Jewish Question." In *Writings of the Young Marx on Philosophy and Society,* ed. Loyd Easton and Kurt Guddat, 216–48. New York: Anchor.

————. 1973. *Grundrisse: Introduction to the Critique of Political Economy.* New York: Random House.

Maturana, Humberto, and Francisco Varela. 1980. *Autopoiesis and Cognition: The Realization of the Living.* Boston: D. Reidel.

Mbembe, Achille. 2001. *On the Postcolony.* Berkeley: University of California Press.

McCarthy, Anna. 2001. *Ambient Television: Visual Culture and Public Space.* Durham: Duke University Press.

McCourt, Tom, and Patrick Burkart. 2003. "When Creators, Corporations and Consumers Collide: Napster and the Development of On-line Music Distribution." *Media, Culture and Society* 25 (3): 333–50.

McLeod, Kembrew. 2001. *Owning Culture: Authorship, Ownership, and Intellectual Property Law.* New York: Peter Lang.

McLuhan, Marshall. 1964. *Understanding Media: The Extensions of Man.* New York: McGraw-Hill.

McNamara, Paul. 2003. "Net Buzz: Identity Theft." *Network World*, 56.

Memmi, Albert. 1965. *The Colonizer and the Colonized.* New York: Orion Press.

Meyrowitz, Joshua. 1985. *No Sense of Place: The Impact of Electronic Media on Social Behavior.* New York: Oxford University Press.

Michael, Mike. 2000. *Reconnecting Culture, Technology and Nature: From Society to Heterogeneity.* New York: Routledge.

Mihm, Stephen. 2003. "Dumpster-Diving for Your Identity." *New York Times*, December 21, 42–47.

Mikkelson, Barbara, and David Mikkelson. 2001. "Bert Is Evil!" www.snopes.com, Urban Legends Reference Pages, December 10.

Miller, Daniel, and Don Slater. 2000. *The Internet: An Ethnographic Approach.* New York: Berg.

Miller, Greg. 1999a. "Former Internet Exec Says Online Pursuit of Girl Was Role-Playing." *Los Angeles Times*, December 10, C1, C8.

———. 1999b. "Online Chat Is Sting of Choice in Illicit-Sex Cases." *Los Angeles Times*, September 25, A1, A20, A21.

Miller, J. Hillis. 1995. "Narrative." In *Critical Terms for Literary Study*, ed. Frank Lentricchia and Thomas McLaughlin, 66–79. Chicago: University of Chicago Press.

Miller, J. Hillis, and Manuel Asensi. 1999. *Black Holes (Cultural Memory in the Present).* Stanford: Stanford University Press.

Miller, Paul. 2004. *Rhythm Science.* Cambridge: MIT Press.

Mingers, John. 1995. *Self-Producing Systems: Implications and Applications of Autopoiesis.* New York: Plenum Press.

Mirzoeff, Nicholas. 1999. *An Introduction to Visual Culture.* New York: Routledge.

Mitchell, Claudia, and Jacqueline Reid-Walsh. 2002. *Researching Children's Popular Culture: The Cultural Spaces of Childhood.* New York: Routledge.

Mitchell, William J. 2003. *ME++: The Cyborg Self and the Networked City.* Cambridge: MIT Press.

Montag, Warren. 1999. *Bodies, Masses, Power: Spinoza and His Contemporaries.* London: Verso.

Moore-Gilbert, Bart. 1997. *Postcolonial Theory: Contexts, Practices, Politics.* London: Verso.

Moravec, Hans. 1988. *Mind Children: The Future of Robot and Human Intelligence.* Cambridge: Harvard University Press.

Morely, David. 1986. *Family Television: Cultural Power and Domestic Leisure.* London: Routledge.

Moulthrop, Stuart. 1997. "No War Machine." In *Reading Matters: Narratives in the New Media Technology*, ed. Joseph Tabbi and Michael Wutz, 269–92. Ithaca: Cornell University Press.

Mowshowitz, Abbe. 1992. "Virtual Feudalism: A Vision of Political Organization in the Information Age." *Information and the Public Sector* 2:213–31.

Muñoz, Lorenza, and Jon Healey. 2001. "Pirated Movies Flourish Despite Security Measures." *Los Angeles Times*, December 4, A1, A28.

Mustapha, Abdul-Karim, and Bülent Eken. 2001. "Dossier on Empire." *Rethinking Marxism* 13 (3–4).

Nancy, Jean-Luc. 2002. *La création du monde ou la mondialisation*. Paris: Galilée.

———. 2003a. "The Confronted Community." *Postcolonial Studies* 6 (1): 23–36.

———. 2003b. "Deconstruction of Monotheism." *Postcolonial Studies* 6 (1): 37–46.

———. 2003c. "The War of Monotheism." *Postcolonial Studies* 6 (1): 51–53.

Negri, Antonio. 1997. "Reliquia Desiderantur: A Conjecture for a Definition of Democracy in the Final Spinoza." In *The New Spinoza*, ed. Warren Montag and Ted Stolze, 219–47. Minneapolis: University of Minnesota Press.

———. 2002. "Towards an Ontological Definition of the Multitude." *Approximations*.

Negus, Keith. 1999. *Music Genres and Corporate Cultures*. New York: Routledge.

Nelson, Alondra, and Thuy Linh N. Tu, eds. 2001. *Technicolor: Race, Technology, and Everyday Life*. New York: New York University Press.

Newman, Jane O. 1985. "The Word Made Print: Luther's 1522 New Testament in an Age of Mechanical Reproduction." *Representations* 11:95–133.

Nichols, Bill. 1988. "The Work of Culture in the Age of Cybernetic Systems." *Screen* (winter): 22–47.

Nietzsche, Friedrich. 1966. *Beyond Good and Evil: Prelude to a Philosophy of the Future*. New York: Vintage.

———. 1967. *On the Genealogy of Morals*. New York: Vintage.

———. n.d. *Thus Spake Zarathustra*. New York: Random House.

O'Brien, Timothy. 2004. "Identities Stolen in Seconds." *New York Times*, October 24.

Ong, Aihwa. 1999. *Flexible Citizenship: The Cultural Logics of Transnationality*. Durham: Duke University Press.

Ortigues, Marie Cécile, and Edmond Ortigues. 1966. *Oedipe africain*. Paris: Librarie Plon.

Passavant, Paul, and Jodi Dean. 2002. "Representation and the Event." *Theory and Event* 5 (4).

———, eds. 2004. *Empire's New Clothes: Reading Hardt and Negri*. New York: Routledge.

Paulson, William. 1997. "The Literary Canon in the Age of Its Technological Obsolescence." In *Reading Matters: Narratives in the New Media Ecology*, ed. Joseph Tabbi and Michael Wutz, 227–49. Ithaca: Cornell University Press.

Pavic, Milorad. 1988. *Dictionary of the Khazars: A Lexicon Novel*. New York: Vintage.

Pohl, Frederik, and Cyril Kornbluth. 1953. *The Space Merchants*. New York: Ballantine Books.

Poschardt, Ulf. 1998. *DJ-Culture*. London: Quartet Books.

Poster, Jamie M. 2002. "Trouble, Pleasure, and Tactics: Anonymity and Identity in a Lesbian Chat Room." In *Women and Everyday Uses of the Internet*, ed. Mia Consalvo and Susanna Paasonen, 230–52. New York: Peter Lang.

Poster, Mark. 1990. *The Mode of Information: Poststructuralism and Social Context*. Chicago: University of Chicago Press.

———. 1991. "Narcissism or Liberation? The Affluent Middle-Class Family." In *Postsuburban California: The Transformation of Orange County since World War II*, ed. Rob Kling, Spencer Olin, and Mark Poster, 190–222. Berkeley: University of California Press.

———. 2001. *What's the Matter with the Internet?* Minneapolis: University of Minnesota Press.

———. 2003. "Perfect Transmissions: Evil Bert Laden." *Television and New Media* 4 (3): 283–95.

Poster, Winifred. 2005. "Who's on the Line? Indian Call Center Agents Pose as Americans for U.S.-Outsourced Firms." *Industrial Relations*. Forthcoming.

Postma, Louise. 2001. "A Theoretical Argumentation and Evaluation of South African Learners' Orientation towards and Perceptions of the Empowering Use of Information." *New Media and Society* 3 (3): 313–26.

Pratt, Mary Louise. 1992. *Imperial Eyes: Travel Writing and Transculturation*. New York: Routledge.

Rajagopal, Arvind. 2001. *Politics after Television: Hindu Nationalism and the Reshaping of the Public in India*. New York: Cambridge University Press.

Ramonet, Ignacio. 2002. "L'empire des medias." *Le Monde diplomatique* (May–June): 63.

Resnick, Stephen, and Richard Wolff. 2001. "Empire and Class Analysis." *Rethinking Marxism* 13 (3–4): 61–69.

Rheingold, Howard. 1993. *The Virtual Community: Homesteading on the Electronic Frontier*. New York: Addison-Wesley.

Rideout, Victoria, Elizabeth Vandewater, and Ellen Wartella. 2003. "Zero to Six: Electronic Media in the Lives of Infants, Toddlers and Preschoolers." Kaiser Family Foundation.

Rose, Mark. 1993. *Authors and Owners: The Invention of Copyright*. Cambridge: Harvard University Press.

Rose, Nikolas. 1998. *Inventing Our Selves: Psychology, Power, and Personhood*. New York: Cambridge University Press.

———. 1999. *Powers of Freedom: Reframing Political Thought*. New York: Cambridge University Press.

Rosenzweig, Roy. 2003. "Scarcity or Abundance? Preserving the Past in a Digital Era." *American Historical Review* 108 (3): 735–62.

Ross, Kristin. 1996. "Streetwise: The French Invention of Everyday Life." *Parallax* 2:67–75.

Rowe, John Carlos. 1994. "Spin-Off: The Rhetoric of Television and Postmodern Memory." In *Narrative and Culture*, ed. Janice Carlisle and Daniel R. Schwarz, 97–120. Athens: University of Georgia Press.

———. 2003. "Nineteenth-Century United States Literary Culture and Transnationality." *PMLA* 118 (1): 78–89.

Ryan, Marie-Laure, ed. 1999. *Cyberspace Textuality: Computer Technology and Literary Theory*. Bloomington: Indiana University Press.

———. 2001. *Narrative as Virtual Reality: Immersion and Interactivity in Literature and Electronic Media*. Baltimore: Johns Hopkins University Press.

Saenger, Paul. 1989. "Books of Hours and the Reading Habits of the Later Middle Ages."

In *The Culture of Print: Power and the Uses of Print in Early Modern Europe*, ed. Roger Chartier, 141–73. London: Polity Press.

Said, Edward. 1982. "Traveling Theory." *Raritan* (winter): 41–67.

Sanjek, Russell. 1988. *American Popular Music and Its Business: The First Four Hundred Years*. New York: Oxford University Press.

Sassen, Saskia. 1998. *Globalization and Its Discontents*. New York: New Press.

———. 2000. "Digital Networks and the State." *Theory, Culture and Society* 17 (4): 19–33.

Sassower, Raphael. 1997. *Technoscientific Angst: Ethics + Responsibility*. Minneapolis: University of Minnesota Press.

Schwab, Gabriele. 1996. *The Mirror and the Killer Queen: Otherness in Literary Language*. Bloomington: Indiana University Press.

Schwartz, John. 2004. "A Heretical View of File Sharing." *New York Times*, April 5.

Schwartz, Vanessa. 2001. "Walter Benjamin for Historians." *American Historical Review* 106 (5): 1721–43.

Scott, David. 1995. "Colonial Governmentality." *Social Text* 43:191–220.

Segrave, Kerry. 1994. *Payola in the Music Industry*. London: McFarland.

Shannon, Claude, and Warren Weaver. 1949. *The Mathematical Theory of Communication*. Urbana: University of Illinois Press.

Shemel, Sidney, and William Krasilovsky. 1990. *This Business of Music*. New York: Watson-Guptill.

Shudson, Michael. 1978. *Discovering the News: A Social History of American Newspapers*. New York: Harper Torchbooks.

Sieyès, Emmanuel Joseph. 1789. *Qu'est-ce que le tiers-état?* Paris.

Silverstone, Roger. 1994. *Television and Everyday Life*. London: Routledge.

Siochru, Sean O. 2003. "Global Governance of Information and Communication Technologies: Implications for Transnational Civil Society Networking." Social Science Research Council.

Smith, Daniel. 1998. "The Place of Ethics in Deleuze's Philosophy: Three Questions of Immanence." In *Deleuze and Guattari: New Mappings in Politics, Philosophy, and Culture*, ed. Eleanor Kaufman and Kevin Heller, 251–69. Minneapolis: University of Minnesota Press.

Sobchack, Vivian. 1997. *Screening Space: The American Science Fiction Film*. New Brunswick, N.J.: Rutgers University Press.

Spigel, Lynn. 1992. *Make Room for TV: Television and the Family Ideal in Postwar America*. Chicago: University of Chicago Press.

Spillers, Hortense. 1996. "All the Things You Could Be by Now If Sigmund Freud's Wife Was Your Mother: Psychoanalysis and Race." *Critical Inquiry* 22:710–34.

Spinello, R. 1999. "Ethical Reflections on the Problem of Spam." *Ethics and Information Technology* 1 (3): 185–91.

Spitz, David, and Starling Hunter. 2005. "Contested Codes: The Social Construction of Napster." *Information Society* 21 (3): 169–80.

Spivak, Gayatri. 1988. "Can the Subaltern Speak?" In *Marxism and the Interpretation of Cul-*

ture, ed. Cary Nelson and Lawrence Grossberg, 271–313. Chicago: University of Illinois Press.

———. 1999. *A Critique of Postcolonial Reason: Toward a History of the Vanishing Present*. Cambridge: Harvard University Press.

———. 2003. "Righting Wrongs." In *Human Rights, Human Wrongs*, ed. Nicholas Owen, 164–227. New York: Oxford University Press.

Stephenson, Neal. 1999. *Cryptonomicon*. New York: Harper Collins.

Sterne, Jonathan. 2003. *The Audible Past: Cultural Origins of Sound Reproduction*. Durham: Duke University Press.

Stoler, Ann Laura. 1995. *Race and the Education of Desire: Foucault's History of Sexuality and the Colonial Order of Things*. Durham: Duke University Press.

Stone, Allucquere Rosanne. 1995. *The War of Desire and Technology at the Close of the Mechanical Age*. Cambridge: MIT Press.

"Stop Thieves from Stealing You." 2003. *Consumer Reports*, 12–17.

Strangelove, Michael. 2005. *The Empire of Mind: Digital Piracy and the Anti-Capitalist Movement*. Toronto: University of Toronto Press.

Strehovec, Janez. 2000. "Atmospheres of Extraordinary in Installation Art." A-R-C, no. 3 (November).

Stroehl, Andreas. 2002. *Vilém Flusser: Writings*. Minneapolis: University of Minnesota Press.

Sundaram, Ravi. 2000. "Beyond the Nationalist Panopticon: The Experience of Cyber-publics in India." In *Electronic Media and Technoculture*, ed. John Thornton Caldwell, 270–94. New York: Routledge.

Surman, Mark, and Katherine Reilly. 2003. "Appropriating the Internet for Social Change: Towards the Strategic Use of Networked Technologies by Transnational Civil Society Organizations." Social Science Research Council.

Swiboda, Marcel, and Kirt Hirtler. 2001. "A Multitude of Possibilities." *Parallax* 7 (4): 138–41.

Taussig, Michael. 1993. *Mimesis and Alterity: A Particular History of the Senses*. New York: Routledge.

Tavani, Herman. 1996. *Bibliography of Computing Ethics and Social Responsibility*. New York: CPSR Press.

Taylor, Mark. 2001. *The Moment of Complexity: Emerging Network Culture*. Chicago: University of Chicago Press.

Tebbel, John. 1975. *A History of Publishing*. New York: R. R. Bowker.

Tedeschi, Bob. 2003. "E-commerce Report: If You Liked the Web Page, You'll Love the Ad." *New York Times*, August 4.

Thornton, Sarah. 1996. *Club Cultures: Music, Media and Subcultural Capital*. Hanover, N.H.: Wesleyan University Press.

Turkle, Sherry. 1995. *Life on the Screen: Identity in the Age of the Internet*. New York: Simon and Schuster.

Ulmer, Gregory. 1994. *Heuretics: The Logic of Invention*. Baltimore: Johns Hopkins University Press.

Urry, John. 1990. *The Tourist Gaze: Leisure Travel in Contemporary Societies*. New York: Simon and Schuster.

Vaidhyanathan, Siva. 2001. *Copyrights and Copywrongs: The Rise of Intellectual Property and How It Threatens Creativity*. New York: New York University Press.

Van Gelder, Lindsy. 1996. "The Strange Case of an Electronic Lover." In *Computerization and Controversy: Value Conflicts and Social Choices*, ed. Rob Kling, 533–46. New York: Academic Press.

Vergès, Françoise. 1999. *Monsters and Revolutionaries: Colonial Family Romance and Métissage*. Durham: Duke University Press.

Vibe, Bo. 2004. "Go with the Flow." *CTheory* 27 (1–2).

Villalobos-Ruminott, Sergio. 2001. "Empire, a Picture of the World." *Rethinking Marxism* 13 (3–4): 31–42.

Virno, Paolo. 2004. *A Grammar of the Multitude: For an Analysis of Contemporary Forms of Life*. New York: Semiotext(e).

Warner, Michael, ed. 1993. *Fear of a Queer Planet: Queer Politics and Social Theory*. Minneapolis: University of Minnesota Press.

Watkins, Evan. 1993. *Throwaways: Work Culture and Consumer Education*. Stanford: Stanford University Press.

Weber, Max. 1978. *Economy and Society: An Outline of Interpretive Sociology*. Berkeley: University of California Press.

Weber, Samuel. 1995. *Mass Mediauras: Essays on Form, Technics and Media*. Stanford: Stanford University Press.

———. 2002. *Theatricality as Medium*. Stanford: Stanford University Press.

Weinstein, Henry, and Greg Miller. 1999. " 'Virtual' Child Porn Is Legal, Court Rules." *Los Angeles Times*, December 18, A1, A38, A39.

Weiser, Mark. 1991. "The Computer for the 21st Century." *Scientific American*, 94–100.

———. 1993a. "Some Computer Science Issues in Ubiquitous Computing." *Communications of the ACM* 36 (7): 74–85.

———. 1993b. "Ubiquitous Computing." *Computer* 26 (10): 71–72.

———. 1997. "Less Intrusion Is More Useful." *Computerworld* 31 (7): 81–82.

———. 1998. "The Future of Ubiquitous Computing on Campus." *Communications of the ACM* 41 (1): 41–42.

Wharton, Edith. 1975. *The Decoration of Houses*. New York: Arno Press.

Wheeler, Deborah. 1998. "Global Culture or Culture Clash: New Information Technologies in the Islamic World—a View from Kuwait." *Communication Research* 25 (4): 359–76.

———. 2001. "New Technologies, Old Culture: A Look at Women, Gender, and the Internet in Kuwait." In *Culture, Technology, Communication: Towards an Intercultural Global Village*, ed. Charles Ess, 187–212. Stony Brook: SUNY Press.

White, Hayden. 1981. "The Value of Narrativity in the Representation of Reality." In *On Narrative*, ed. W. J. T. Mitchell, 1–23. Chicago: University of Chicago Press.

Wiener, Norbert. 1950. *The Human Use of Human Beings: Cybernetics and Society*. New York: Doubleday.

Wilcox, James. 2003. "Where Have All the CDs Gone?" *Sound and Vision* 68:87–89.

Woodson, Stephani. 2000. "Exploring the Cultural Topography of Childhood: Television Performing the 'Child' to Children." *Bad Subjects* 47.

Wright, Will. 1975. *Sixguns and Society: A Structural Study of the Western.* Berkeley: University of California Press.

Young, Robert. 1995. *Colonial Desire: Hybridity in Theory, Culture, and Race.* New York: Routledge.

Yúdice, George. 1992. "We Are Not the World." *Social Text* 31–32 (1992): 202–16.

Zuboff, Shoshana. 1988. *In the Age of the Smart Machine: The Future of Work and Power.* New York: Basic Books.

INDEX

REPUBLICATION ACKNOWLEDGMENTS

Chapters of this book have appeared in earlier versions in the following journals and collections: chapter 1, *Television and New Media* 4, no. 3 (August 2003): 283–95; chapter 3, *Comparative Literature Studies* 41, no. 3 (2004): 317–34; chapter 4, PMLA 117, no. 1 (January 2002): 98–103; chapter 5, *Cultural Studies* (forthcoming); chapter 6, *Culture Machine* 4 (March 2002), http://culturemachine.tees.ac.uk/frm_f1.htm, and *Frame* 16, nos. 1–2 (March 2002): 4–18; chapter 7, Gunnar Liestøl, ed., *Digital Media Revisited* (Cambridge: MIT Press, 2003), 521–45, and Gerald McKenny and Edith Wyshogrod, eds., *The Ethical* (New York: Blackwell, 2003), 181–96; chapter 8, Robert Mitchell and Phillip Thurtle, eds., *Data Made Flesh: Embodying Information* (New York: Routledge, 2003), 87–101; chapter 9, *Fast Capitalism* 1, no. 2 (2005), www.uta.edu/huma/agger/fastcapitalism/home; chapter 10, *New Literary History* 33, no. 4 (autumn 2002): 743–60; chapter 11, *Cultural Studies* 18, nos. 2–3 (March–May 2004): 408–22; chapter 12, Randy Rutsky and Sande Cohen, eds., *Consumption in the Age of Information* (New York: Berg, 2005), 21–39.

Mark Poster is a professor of history and film and media studies at the University of California, Irvine. He is the author of several books, including *What's the Matter with the Internet?* (2001) and *The Mode of Information* (1990).

Library of Congress Cataloging-in-Publication Data
Poster, Mark.
Information please : culture and politics in the age of digital machines /
Mark Poster.
p. cm.
Includes bibliographical references and index.
ISBN-13: 978-0-8223-3801-7 (cloth : alk. paper)
ISBN-10: 0-8223-3801-7 (cloth : alk. paper)
ISBN-13: 978-0-8223-3839-0 (pbk. : alk. paper)
ISBN-10: 0-8223-3839-4 (pbk. : alk. paper)
1. Information society. 2. Digital media—Social aspects. I. Title
HM651.P67 2006
303.48'33—dc22   2006004595